H50 117 6

D1577407

28 Ar

Please renew/return this item by the last da

So that your telephone call is charged at loc
please call the numbers as set out below:

	From Area codes 01923 or 020:	From the res
Renewals:	01923 471373	01438 737
Enquiries:	01923 471333	01438 73
Textphone:	01923 471599	01438 73

L32   www.hertsdirect.org/librarycat

POETRY IN THE WARS

POETRY
— IN THE —
WARS

EDNA LONGLEY

BLOODAXE BOOKS

Copyright © Edna Longley 1986
All rights reserved

The acknowledgements on pages 259-60 constitute
a continuation of this copyright page.

ISBN: 0 906427 74 6 hardback
      0 906427 99 1 paperback

First published 1986 by
Bloodaxe Books Ltd,
P.O. Box 1SN,
Newcastle upon Tyne NE99 1SN.

Bloodaxe Books Ltd acknowledges the financial assistance
of the Arts Council of Northern Ireland
in the publication of this book.

Bloodaxe Books Ltd also acknowledges
the financial assistance of Northern Arts.

HERTFORDSHIRE
LIBRARY SERVICE

No.

H50 117 626 7

Class
821.912 09358

Supplier   Price   Date
DN   12.75   6/89

- 4 OCT 1989

Typesetting by True North, Newcastle upon Tyne.

Cover printing by
Tyneside Free Press Workshop Ltd, Newcastle upon Tyne.

Printed in Great Britain by
Robert Hartnoll Ltd, Bodmin, Cornwall.

Contents

'Poetry is and must always be apparently revolutionary if active, anarchic if passive.'

— EDWARD THOMAS, *Feminine Influence on the Poets.*

'Art, unlike life, has one mechanism built into it, one device, the notion of cliché. In real life you can tell the same maxim or the same joke all the time and raise a great deal of laughter or a great deal of support; in art repeating the same joke for the second or third time is called cliché. What art hates most of all is to repeat itself, to do something again . . . This is why an artist frequently finds himself in a position which is subsequently described as ahead of his time. It is not that he has been ahead of his time; it is simply that the material, the stuff, the sense of harmony, of aesthetics, refused to be repeated. If we were to translate political life into terms of art, a great deal of politicians . . . belong solely in the Middle Ages.'

— JOSEPH BRODSKY

Introduction

My title suggests that poetry is fought over, that in some sense it fights, and that these arenas overlap. As I wrote or rewrote the following essays, two themes converged: poetry's relation to public conflicts of the last seventy-five years; and the conflict between "traditionalism" and "Modernism" which has raged in its own backyard. The very term "Modernism" stakes a claim to the century. Military and political vocabulary pervades accounts of early twentieth-century poetry, such as Robert H. Ross's *The Georgian Revolt* and Michael H. Levenson's *A Genealogy of Modernism*. In one of Levenson's chapters, 'The War Among the Moderns', three consecutive sentences contain: 'defend . . . embattled . . . challenged . . . factionalised . . . polemical . . . violent disputes'.[1] Poetic faction-fights continue today. On a less mock-heroic front, the making of modern poetry from, say, 1910 to 1920, evidently coincided with troubled times in Europe, Britain, Ireland. Wilfred Owen's imaginative crash-course telescoped and epitomised other developments. W. B. Yeats and Edward Thomas forged their aesthetics amidst obvious historical change. Later, various transitions left varying marks on the work of poets discussed in this book: on Louis MacNeice in 1938 as world war suspended class war; on Keith Douglas in 1940; on Philip Larkin in post-war England; on Seamus Heaney, Derek Mahon and Paul Muldoon in Ulster's 'uncivil wars'.[2]

However, this is not just a case of simple cause and effect, nor of the sophisticated historical determinism embraced by Stan Smith in *Inviolable Voice: History and Twentieth-Century Poetry*:

> A poem is produced at the intersection of two histories: the history of the formal possibilities available to the poet – conventions, themes, language – and the history of the individual as a particular expressive "medium", a product of his own time and place.[3]

A poem may indeed be historically inscribed, though never pre-scribed or foreseen: the poet's wisdom before or during the event becomes the critic's long after it. Only a non-poem is written by its period or by Smith's processing assembly-belt. Unlike Marxist mechanism, Louis MacNeice's organic metaphor leaves room for artistic manoeuvre: 'poetry is . . . a separate self; in the same way a living animal is an individual although it is on the one hand conditioned by heredity and environment and the laws of nature in general and on the other hand has a function outside itself, is a link in a chain'.[4] Transcendence and historicity are not as mutually exclusive as structuralism makes out. Yeats's shuttling gyres, perceived from the still point of their vortex, stylise the ultimately unifying structure of any poet's imagination. And a poem's 'histories', perhaps many more than two, need encompass neither an agreed flow of great events nor their agreed destination within an ideological grand design. Smith's concern about poetry's seeming refusal to be raped by history may put history in the wrong place and poetry in a false position. We do not know, for instance, the available 'formal possibilities' until a poem has been accomplished. Form at once belongs to the unfolding history and secures permanence. It is a mysterious rather than mechanical phenomenon that real poems, en route from the particular to the universal, should carry historical inscriptions (contrast the dated stop-press of non-art). Poetry appears prophetic later because it is accurate, picks up psychic history not yet enacted or resolved. Hence, for instance, the imagery of darkness and rottenness in mid-sixties poems by Mahon and Heaney. Paul Muldoon says: 'one of my main duties as a writer is to write about what is immediately in front of me, or immediately over my shoulder'.[5] But contrary to the utilitarian view that literature must either be means to an end, or by default prove an end's inevitability, poetry is the opposite of built-in obsolescence. Even after visibly serving as a 'midwife to society' (like Yeats's work, up to a point) it does not disappear with its forceps but maintains a full presence. Critics who concentrate on poems as historical documents pay an unconscious tribute to the other reasons for their survival.

Perhaps "war", not "history" or "politics", covers the broadest imaginative contingencies; indicating that poetry engages – *as poetry* – on many battlegrounds. Less comprehensive political readings can be reductive. Smith's summary reduces Edward Thomas's 'Old Man': 'It embodies as myth the crisis of liberal humanism before the vastness and impenetrability of a world it can hardly begin to understand.'[6] Beyond what 1914 gives to the poem – not only the crisis of liberal humanism – the human imagination has often stood dismayed before 'an avenue, dark, nameless, without end'. (And if 'Old Man' is to be read on that level, why should it not exemplify the courage and stamina of liberal humanism?) As MacNeice says, rebuking a critic who 'is always talking about poets asking questions and finding answers to them': 'poets through the ages have often concerned themselves, like certain modern playwrights such as Beckett and like ordinary people in their inner moments, with the old chronic unanswerables, such as "Why – or even how – are we

10

here?"[7] MacNeice took issue with an earlier wave of Marxist literary critics:

> Like other doctrinaires, e.g. psychologists, they absurdly oversimplify, confusing condition and cause. That a writer is conditioned by his social background is undeniable: so is a mathematician; but the theorem of Pythagoras is neither proved nor disproved by Pythagoras's bank balance. As literary *historians* Marxists are some use along broad lines, but broad lines, alas, in both history and literature are far less than half the battle; it is the brush strokes that count.[8]

Perhaps scenting an antagonist, Smith disparages Northern Irish poetry 'that looks back to the sceptical Protestant tradition of Louis MacNeice [and] takes up a worried, disapproving but finally uncomprehending stance towards an experience with which it feels no sense of affinity'.[9] Smith implies that MacNeice, like Thomas, would have comprehended all if political light had dawned. In fact his poetic scepticism, never that of the 'elegant . . . out-and-out rejecters'[10] whom he rejected, lost its innocence to Irish fanaticisms:

> My diehard countrymen like drayhorses
> Drag their ruin behind them.
> Shooting straight in the cause of crooked thinking . . .
> From all which I am an exile.
>
> ('Eclogue from Iceland')

MacNeice's inoculation against the political naivety of some English literary contemporaries still applies to his successors. And if his poetry or Yeats's or Thomas's stems from classes superfluous to history's purposes, surely the point is that all kinds of margins and alienations foster art – such as a lonely childhood, which MacNeice had too. Poetry itself is always an outsider, always instead of Utopia. In a different sense from Sir Philip Sidney's, most poets still try to deliver a golden world. The positive side of twentieth-century poetry abounds in communal models: Yeats's and MacNeice's friends, Thomas's fleeting 'homes', Owen's 'eternal reciprocity of tears', Larkin's 'Whitsun Weddings', Heaney's Mossbawn *pietas*. Thomas's 'Lob', spirit of poetry as well as of English culture, will abandon the struggle not just after radical revolution, but when the *impossible* demands of the imagination have been met by society:

> · He never will admit he is dead
> Till millers cease to grind men's bones for bread,
> Not till our weathercock crows once again
> And I remove my house out of the lane
> On to the road.

"War poetry" in the more confined sense (to which it should not be confined) has been neglected by Modernist-based or -biased criticism. On the one hand, poets rather than critics absorbed Owen's formal significance and Rosenberg's redirection of Imagism. On the other, war seems too vulgar a version of history to count with structuralists and other Modernists. Art for art's sake and totalitarianism fraternise round the back. This may have helped to divorce literary criticism from the rest of the human race. Is it not dandyish, even dangerous, of Hugh Kenner and Charles Tomlinson to salute Pound's *Cathay* as 'among the most durable of all poetic responses to World War I'?[11] In *The Great War and Modern Memory* Paul Fussell, an American critic more alert than Kenner to British culture, persuasively traces the war's shockwaves still rippling through. British poetry, if not American, redefined its literary and social languages during the First World War. Rosenberg's ambiguous lark above the battlefields has come a long way from Shelley and Wordsworth.

Not only Owen, Rosenberg, Sorley and Sassoon, but Thomas, Lawrence and Graves are part of that redefinition and its continuing dynamic. To liberate war poetry from its ghetto is not to advocate a conservative realism, though *Cathay* seems unduly remote. No genuine poetry falls into the subject-matter fallacy, classically demolished by Thomas before the war: 'Anything, however small, may make a poem; nothing, however great, is certain to.'[12] Poets, in Muldoon's metaphorical sense, do write about what is immediately in front of them or immediately over their shoulder. They finely judge their imaginative whereabouts, their ethical bearings. Thomas did not pretend to write from the trenches, though his poetry divined them; Owen, facing an imperative subject-matter, did not pretend he had been nowhere else. Just as Thomas's poems, in one symbolic dimension, are roads to France; so Owen's road does not end there. His whole oeuvre, as well as individually inclusive poems like 'Exposure' or 'Spring Offensive', straddles pre-war and post-war experience, symbolises what war distilled (not only pity): 'All their eyes are ice,/ But nothing happens'; 'Halted against the shade of a last hill'. Owen's 'warning' is a tragic revelation about human nature and circumstances. If Rosenberg prefigured Douglas in his (Jewish?) grasp of persecutions, Owen's poetry dramatises arrival at the same bleak crux, a loss of (Christian?) innocence. One contemporary corollary of all this might be Northern Irish poets searching for balance – on a shifting front line – between close-up and perspective, documentation and symbol, presumption and responsibility. Muldoon defines the Catch-22: 'the trouble with this place is that if you don't engage in it, you're an ostrich (whatever "engage in it" means). If you do engage in it, you're using the situation as a kind of . . . you're on the make, almost, cashing in.'[13]

Since criticism was built into the walls of the Modernist enterprise, it is not surprising that critical schools should be its last redoubt. Levenson analyses *The Waste Land* as 'consolidating the work of two decades', as 'itself a doctrinal act, the poem as a critical gesture'.[14] Irrespective of Eliot's own poetic achievements, in my view Modernism has promoted narrow, abstract readings of twentieth-century poetry, with structuralism merely a further twist. For instance, the formalist emphases of Modernism are largely redundant in the presence of a mode where form has always been the *sine qua non*. Joyce was a much more revolutionary artist than Eliot or Pound. Again, the parasitic literariness in Modernism (whereby some academics now take their own sterilities as covering the landscape of creative possibility) has hit poetry hard. At the turn of the century Edward Thomas disputed the pretensions of that period's "objective" and "scientific" critical avant-garde (see page 29) and already feared an academic takeover-bid for literature: 'Every book that Arnold seriously considered left an essential addition to his house of thought. Mr Brownell merely adds to his museum.'[15] He also appreciated the trend of the aesthetic criticism which fathered Modernism: 'These critics pretend to explain their authors; but Ruskin, in criticism of Dante or Homer, and Pater, in criticism of Rossetti or Du Bellay, simply borrow or steal a thought and speculate with it, until it produces 100 per cent.'[16] Charles Tomlinson inherits a tradition of literary and academic inbreeding and interbreeding when he states:

> And once one has mentally translated the Italian ['Sorella, mia sorella'] one realises that Pound's maddening habit of quite arbitrarily making the going difficult for his reader had hidden from one, within the Italian phrase, a fragment from Swinburne's poem, *Itylus*: 'Swallow, my sister, O sister swallow'. These are the words of the tongue-bereft Philomela to Procne, Pound travelling back to the poet who, as he said, kept alive a measure of paganism 'in a papier-mâché age', whereas Eliot with *his* 'O swallow swallow' in *The Waste Land* travels back to Tennyson, the poet of impaired Christian belief.[17]

The scholarly trappings of Modernism often allow old pedantries to masquerade as new criticism. Paul Muldoon's long poem, 'The More a Man Has the More a Man Wants' (see p.208), also partly depends on literary cross-reference; but in a spirit that comically deflates it.

Inter-genre and international, Modernism dissolves boundaries between modes and cultures, boundaries which criticism might still profitably observe. Further, its philosophical tendency (and philosophy is poetry's traditional enemy) dissolves criticism itself into exegesis or metaphysics. All of which relegates evaluation to the sidelines as either frivolity or irrelevance. Geoffrey Thurley argues in the excellent *Counter-Modernism in Current Critical Theory:*

> the problem is not merely that of choosing between a value-judgement criticism, with all its aura of subjectivism and impressionism, on the one hand, and a purely objective criticism, concerned only to describe the text, on the other; the problem is rather that of recognising and experiencing the text as *literature in the first place.*[18]

Of course the latter 'problem' has also been finally dissolved by the pseudo-democracy of "text" and "discourse". It is a ludicrous equation of art with society to assume that if we distinguish a poem on merit, it will instantly seize power. Some critics are ungrateful to the value-judgements which have been instrumental in serving them Yeats's head on a platter, instead of the words of forgotten versifiers. Or perhaps structuralism, like monetarism, masks philistine hostilities. The hard task of judging between poetry and non-poetry does not only provide a waste-disposal system for the ninety-nine per cent rubbish published. To recognise poetry as soon as possible, and to go on recognising it, is a social as well as aesthetic act. Owen said 'the true Poets must be truthful'. We will not experience this truth unless we discover the true poets.

Modernism, which tends to collapse history or anticipate the millennium, has been allowed to write too much literary history. Pound and Eliot as Americans, Joyce as an Irishman, inevitably took a less evolutionary view of literature than Thomas and Owen. Nevertheless the course of twentieth-century poetry in the British Isles exhibits many evolutions (which need not preclude cosmopolitan horizons). Indeed, poets themselves carry out the task of "deconstruction" more rapidly and radically than critics. MacNeice and Auden, in practice and theory, deconstructed Yeats and Eliot. The later Yeats deconstructed the earlier. Such positive "interrogation" neither replaces nor invalidates the fruits of a prior aesthetic. Literary history, like history in literature, can also be a complex graph of wider history. Since poetry is particularly incapable of cliché, in Joseph Brodsky's words 'hates . . . to repeat itself', it spots cliché elsewhere. Here social and literary criticism fuse within a larger whole. Thus from 1914 the poetry of Thomas, Sorley, Rosenberg and Owen dismantled the 'old Lie' and 'the word Imperialism'; in 1942 Patrick Kavanagh's *The Great Hunger* smashed both the Yeatsian and the Irish Nationalist icon of the peasant; today, Paul Muldoon's poetry implicitly subverts the rhetorics of Irish and British Nationalism. These different clocks (all three still ahead of the societies in question) point to a further accuracy on the part of poetic history. It does not prematurely homogenise different kinds and rates of cultural evolution in different places. If poetry's idealism foreshadows progress, its realism records stagnation.

Even the history of forms comments on social conditions, and its pace cannot be forced. For instance, the idea in the 1930s and 1940s that there "ought" to be a Modernist Irish poetry led to an over-estimation of such poets as Denis Devlin and Brian Coffey. Meanwhile Kavanagh's indigenous technical revolution – which involved digestion but not imitation of *The Waste Land* – remained under-appreciated. (Similarly, Lawrence was the *English* free-verse revolutionary.) Some of the best contemporary Southern Irish poetry, the work of Paul Durcan and Brendan Kennelly's *Cromwell*, is now able to capitalise on freedoms won by *The Great Hunger*. The formal differences between *Cromwell* and Muldoon's *Quoof* are striking, and must reflect disjunctions between South and North. Both collections are mainly written in sonnet-form and probe historical trauma. But whereas *Cromwell* is explosive, expansive, prolific, explicit; *Quoof* is implosive, intensive, concentrated, oblique. They differ as utterly as convex and concave, even if within Ireland and within poetry they ultimately share the same contour. There might be many explanations, including the obvious factor of individual talents, why Northern Irish poetry displays such notable formal concentration – sometimes attacked (like Larkin's) as anachronistic. Even if art moved in a straight line from constraint to liberty, by a simplistic analogy with how society supposes itself to progress, anachronism depends on where the real clock stands. Seventeenth-century religious strains may indeed encourage methods akin to those of Donne and Herbert. However, the fact that Ulster is a "province" in two contexts counts too. Northern Irish poetry of the sixties in certain respects assimilated and transmuted the Movement's formality. Political biases, as well as unnoticed cultural time-warps, throw conventional literary history out of kilter. The special hybridisations of Northern Irish poetry can escape both the Southern Irish Europeanism which ignores England and the English Atlanticism which ignores Ireland. Irish poetry often refuses to recognise its English dimension; while English poetry overlooks its Irish debts, such as the centrality of Yeats. Thus Louis MacNeice has long languished on the margin of 'the Auden generation' on the one hand, and of the Clarke-Kavanagh generation on the other. MacNeice's reputation, as Derek Mahon says, has significantly 'come to rest'[19] in Ulster; where Mahon, starting to write, found him 'a familiar voice whispering in my ear'.[20] The broader political parallels to literary misunderstandings and exclusions need not be laboured. In any case, a number of histories and literary histories uniquely intersect in Northern Ireland, though poetic diversity is a frail silver lining of communal division.

Northern Irish poets may also follow MacNeice in following Yeats's compulsion towards shape, his acceptance of 'those traditional metres that have developed with the language'.[21] Nominating Yeats as closer in spirit than Eliot to the thirties generation, MacNeice implies a connection between formal intensity and a rage – or need – for social order: 'it is the poet's job to make sense of the world, to simplify it, to put shape on it . . . [These younger poets] stood with Yeats for system against chaos, for a positive art against a passive impressionism'.[22] The thirties formal counter-revolution also finds expression under 'F' in MacNeice's 'Alphabet of Literary Prejudices':

> *Free Verse* had to be tried but now – with rare exceptions – ought to be dropped . . . In the arts bars can be cross-bars and limitations an asset. Verse is a precision instrument and owes its precision very largely to the many and subtle differences which an ordinary word can acquire from its place in a rhythmical scheme.[23]

Similarly, Randall Jarrell calls Modernism 'a sort of canvas whale from which Jonah after Jonah, throughout the late 20s and early 30s, made a penitent return, back to rhyme and metre and plain broad Statement'.[24] Contemporary poets can range between tight stanzas and free verse on the perimeter, discover infinite variations on a formal base (including the evergreen iambic pentameter), so long as 'precision' stays in view. But, as I have indicated, choosing forms or being chosen by them falls somewhere between invisible local historical forces and raiding the shelves of an internationally stocked supermarket. And overall, the more traditional team makes a formidable bunch. Headed by Yeats, so often inaccurately co-opted for Modernism despite his clear protestations, it contains Hardy, Frost, Thomas, Owen, Graves, Auden, MacNeice, Douglas, Larkin, Heaney, Mahon. Again, what these poets say about poetry should be central to academic syllabuses, displace a few Modernist pundits.

Yeats said: 'all that is personal soon rots; it must be packed in ice or salt'.[25] By this he meant other structural techniques besides traditional metres. Primary among these was what can be termed 'the dramatic lyric'. In 1912 Yeats devoured Grierson's edition of Donne. Surely it was he, rather than Eliot, who learned from Donne's deep structures: specifically, how to develop 'a powerful and passionate syntax, and a complete coincidence between period and stanza'.[26] Although criticism now sensibly talks of "personae" and "speakers", there is still much confusion over the subjectivity/ objectivity of the lyric poem. Eliot did not patent or even reinvent "impersonality". A lyric has always had an objective status whether its author's theory was a matter of Elizabethan convention, Romantic overflow, or Modernist "classicism". Edward Thomas wrote in *Maurice Maeterlinck* (1911):

> Whatever be the subject, the poem must not depend for its main effect upon anything outside itself except the humanity of the reader. It may please for the moment by the aid of some irrelevant and transitory interest – political interest, for example; but, sooner or later, it will be left naked and solitary, and will so be judged, and if it does not create about itself a world of its own it is condemned to endure the death which is its element. These worlds of living poems may be of many different kinds.[27]

Nor does the 'I' of a lyric poem egocentrically claim any "privilege" as structuralists would have it. Strategically individualist but truly collective, a poem suppresses self in being for and about everyone's 'humanity'. When structuralism denies imagination, it misses drama. Haunted by Shakespeare, Yeats defined his lyrical procedures as a distillation of poetic drama:

> A poet writes always of his personal life . . . he never speaks directly as to someone at the breakfast table, there is always a phantasmagoria . . . he is more type than man, more passion than type. He is Lear, Romeo, Oedipus, Tiresias; he has stepped out of a play . . .[28]

Louis MacNeice wrote twelve years later:

> The word "lyric" has always been a terrible red herring. It is taken to connote not only comparative brevity but a sort of emotional parthenogenesis which results in a one-track attitude labelled "spontaneous" but verging on the imbecile. In fact all lyric poems, though in varying degrees, are *dramatic* . . . there may be only one actor on the stage but the Opposition are on their toes in the wings – and crowding the auditorium; your lyric in fact is a monodrama.[29]

MacNeice then describes poems as containing 'an internal conflict, cross-talk, backwash, come-back or pay-off';[30] just as Frost extolled 'making the sentences talk to each other as two or more speakers do in drama'.[31] In the 1890s the poetic cosmos had shrunk,

17

or been purified, to 'life at its intense moments'.[32] This extreme of Romanticism polarised mood and essence against the outer world. But it also marked the point where poetry would begin to reclaim the world: by fully dramatising the isolated psyche, by giving the lonely centre a cosmic circumference. In 1901 Edward Thomas remarkably prophesied how the dramatic lyric would come into its own during the twentieth century:

> the lyric will prosper, at least so long as individualism makes way in literature. Increasing complexity of thought and emotion will find no such outlet as the myriad-minded lyric, with its intricacies of form as numerous and as exquisite as those of a birch-tree in the wind.[33]

Yeats's dramatic-lyrical sequence, 'Nineteen Hundred and Nineteen', was at least as epoch-making and epoch-defining as *The Waste Land*; and it may have proved more paradigmatic of poetry in this century. Written at roughly the same time (1921 was the key year), the poems have certain common factors: pessimism about contemporary conditions; a grand historical perspective on such pessimism; a sense that western civilisation, as an imaginative and spiritual construct, has been 'broken in bits'. In each case poetry confronts all its enemies, its own ruin. But Yeats's elegy for fallen civilisation is also a war-poem. That 'Many ingenious lovely things are gone' can be attributed to specific causes:

> That country round
> None dared admit, if such a thought were his,
> Incendiary or bigot could be found
> To burn that stump on the Acropolis,
> Or break in bits the famous ivories . . .

'Incendiary or bigot' intertwines the sack of Athens with Irish political agents. The poem's more immediate historical setting expands from local episodes of the Anglo-Irish war, to the prospect of that war becoming civil war, to the First World War, to the Russian Revolution, to Yeats's global apprehension of 'the growing murderousness of the world'.[34] Thus 'some horrors at Gort' reverberate within the scope suggested by the original title ('Thoughts upon the Present State of the World') and Yeats's résumé in a letter: 'a lamentation over lost peace and lost hope'.[35] The 'horrors at Gort' were atrocities committed by the Black and Tans, particularly the shooting of Mrs Ellen Quinn with a baby in her arms (1 November 1920):

Now days are dragon-ridden, the nightmare
Rides upon sleep: a drunken soldiery
Can leave the mother, murdered at her door,
To crawl in her own blood, and go scot-free;
The night can sweat with terror as before
We pieced our thoughts into philosophy,
And planned to bring the world under a rule,
Who are but weasels fighting in a hole.

This murder seals the transition from a pre-1914 belief in progress to an enforced recognition of endemic barbarism. The mainly first-person-plural speaker acts as scapegoat for a comprehensive list of no longer tenable corporate illusions, although general guilt does not amnesty particular war crimes. The poem's ironies savage false consciousness in a manner characteristic of war poetry. Yeats subsumes his political and cultural idealism into mockery (but 'Mock mockers after that') of all 'lost hopes' and failed ideals:

O but we dreamed to mend
Whatever mischief seemed
To afflict mankind, but now
That winds of winter blow
Learn that we were crack-pated when we dreamed.

Shakespearean echoes there, and the sequence's ultimate scope gives the dramatic lyric the substance of tragic drama. The scenario resembles civil-war Scotland in *Macbeth*, 'Almost afraid to know itself', and spawns similar images of anarchy: animal ferocity, blood, 'foul storm', night, nightmare. Like *Macbeth*, 'Nineteen Hundred and Nineteen' broods on the violation of inner shrines (motherhood, sleep, the 'ancient image made of olive wood'), and embodies the violating evil as an irresistible momentum: 'a dragon of air . . . on its own furious path'. The storm blows itself out in the apocalyptic final section, where witchcraft and a sinister vacuity add to the parallels with *Macbeth*:

                    evil gathers head:
Herodias' daughters have returned again,
A sudden blast of dusty wind and after
Thunder of feet, tumult of images,
Their purpose in the labyrinth of the wind . . .
But now wind drops, dust settles; thereupon
There lurches past, his great eyes without thought
Under the shadow of stupid straw-pale locks,
That insolent fiend Robert Artisson
To whom the love-lorn Lady Kyteler brought
Bronzed peacock feathers, red combs of her cocks.

This vision could be Macbeth's 'tale/ Told by an idiot, full of sound and fury,/ Signifying nothing'. Like Herodias' daughters, Lady Kyteler was a witch (in fourteenth-century Kilkenny). Her subservience to the 'insolent fiend' echoes the theme of Macbeth's damnation, and sums up civilisation perverted. The debasement of 'Bronzed peacock feathers', by travestying 'ornamental bronze and stone' mentioned in the first stanza, symbolically condenses all transitions.

'Nineteen Hundred and Nineteen' engages more actively with a 'tumult of images' than does *The Waste Land* with its 'heap of broken images'. Yeats's lyrical self-dramatisation reaches an apotheosis in generating a tragic hero. The plural chorus-scapegoat becomes singular as the 'solitary soul' who takes on a universal burden:

> But is there any comfort to be found?
> Man is in love and loves what vanishes,
> What more is there to say?

More Hamlet than Macbeth, the solitary soul soliloquises about the problem of action in dragon-ridden days, fusing questions of personal and artistic responsibility. At lowest ebb he conceives suicide, creative abdication: 'a rage/ To end all things, to end/ What my laborious life imagined, even/ The half-imagined, the half-written page'. But although 'Nineteen Hundred and Nineteen' finds no comfort, it does find more to say. It thus reproduces Hamlet's 'the readiness is all'. Yeats's discharging of linguistic and formal obligations supports the protagonist's role in the tragic encounter with anarchy. His version of 'two languages' (variously at war in other poetry of the period) discriminates, by progressive redefinitions, between civilisation and barbarism – as sides of the same human coinage:

> We, who seven years ago
> Talked of honour and of truth,
> Shriek with pleasure if we show
> The weasel's twist, the weasel's tooth.

Each section is formally different, yet also participates in the dynamic of definition which pivots on the plain statement of that quintessential quatrain. (So much for the necessary "difficulty" of modern poetry.) All the structural resources of 'Nineteen Hundred and Nineteen' reclaim significant ground for the lyric poem, when it might seem most challenged.

Whether or not MacNeice is right to classify *The Waste Land* as 'passive impressionism' (it does have something in common with the religious supplications of nineties poetry), 'Nineteen Hundred and Nineteen' certainly qualifies as 'positive art'. Yeatsian "heroics" come under fire as "valorising" art. But in championing the imagination his poetry only asserts what all poetry must assume. In 'Nineteen Hundred and Nineteen' and the related later sequences ('Meditations in Time of Civil War', 'The Tower'), he dramatises a twentieth-century crisis of faith: for humanity and poetry. That his strategy is not really to 'lament' but to engage, exposes the spirit of resistance latent in poetry. The dialectic between poet and man of action in 'Meditations in Time of Civil War' enacts a more explicit recovery of artistic nerve. By identifying with a besieged man-at-arms, former tenant of the tower, Yeats establishes poetry as at least a marginal stronghold 'through long wars and sudden night alarms'.

Edward Thomas and Robert Frost

'It speaks, and it is poetry' – Thomas on *North of Boston*

1.

In October 1917, six months after Edward Thomas's death at Arras, Robert Frost wrote to Amy Lowell:

> the closest I ever came in friendship to anyone in England or anywhere else in the world I think was with Edward Thomas . . . He more than anyone else was accessory to what I have done and was doing. We were together to the exclusion of every other person and interest all through 1914 – 1914 was our year. I never had, I never shall have another such year of friendship.[1]

In my view the importance of this friendship to twentieth-century poetry has been as underestimated as the Pound-Eliot alliance has been aggrandised. Stephen Spender says: 'It is perhaps idle to ask whether if Frost had remained in England and if Thomas had not been killed, English poetry might have had a different development.'[2] But poets, less erratic guides than academics, have remained continuously interested in Frost and Thomas.[3] A lot can happen in a year, including events as yet unfolded. To pick up Frost's word 'accessory': Thomas was the major critical accessory after the fact of Frost's poetry; Frost the major creative accessory before the fact of Thomas's. Their poetry has never ceased to be accessory. The achievement of one reinforces that of the other, and their joint strength wrenches conventional perspectives on the 'new poetic' of the early twentieth century. Divide them, and important qualities of poetry fall.

When they met in October 1913, Frost was thirty-nine, Thomas thirty-five. Frost had written most of the poems in his first three books, but published only one collection: *A Boy's Will* (1913). Thomas, a 'hurried & harried prose man',[4] had written no poetry other than suppressed juvenilia. His vast literary output since leaving Oxford in 1900 included books about the countryside, personal essays, critical studies, and over a million words of reviewing.[5] He reviewed other people's books about the countryside, editions of earlier poetry (then multiplying), and a mass of contemporary verse at a period when 'An imbecile with ten pounds in his pocket can easily add one to the number of the volumes from which the lover of poetry has to choose'.[6] Although Thomas mocked himself as 'a doomed hack',[7] blanket dismissals of his prose as hackwork are now discredited. Apart from the mysterious processes whereby most of his poems evolved from earlier prose species, and his prose-style's increasing 'leanness',[8] Thomas's critical activity also prepared him for poetry. A good case can be made for calling him the most influential poetry reviewer in England before the First World War. His judgments not only stand the test of time, they prepared him for Frost. Thomas's three reviews of *North of Boston* in 1914[9] spearheaded the English reputation which subsequently launched Frost's American success. He saw and said that *North of Boston* was as 'revolutionary' as *Lyrical Ballads*. Thomas's recognition of Frost's poetry, and of its call to his own potential, was matched by Frost's 'admiration for the poet in him before he had written a line of poetry'.[10] They had much else in common: histories of psychological illness to the point of suicidal depression; imaginative affiliations with the landscapes of Hampshire and New Hampshire; and new ideas about 'speech & literature'.[11] As Frost wrote in 1921: 'The most our congeniality could do was confirm us both in what we were.'[12]

The cross-fertilisation of 1914, paradoxically accelerated by the war, led to Thomas writing his first poems in December. But during 1915, to quote from a poem which Frost actually conceived as a joke against Thomas, 'Two roads diverged in a yellow wood'.[13] In February Frost returned to America. In July Thomas enlisted. He too could have taken the American route, since Frost wanted them eventually to farm together in New Hampshire. Thomas's letters from the Front, as well as his poetry, lie behind this expression (to Helen Thomas) of Frost's grief: 'People have been praised for self-possession in danger. I have heard Edward doubt if he was as brave as the bravest. But who was ever so completely himself right up to the verge of destruction, so sure of his thought, so sure of his word?'[14] One of the tenderest epitaphs by one poet for another, its uniqueness among Frost's letters bears out his later avowal: 'Edward Thomas was the only brother I ever had.'[15] Perhaps the notoriously unbrotherly Frost, with all his carapaces and caprices, should be understood in this light. And if Frost's true or best self lingers near Thomas, why do most studies of the former never mention the latter? Frost's *Paris Review* interviewer representatively inquires into his contention with Pound rather than his 'congeniality' with Thomas.

Thomas's poem 'The Sun Used to Shine' complements Frost's elegiac letters and the short poem 'To E.T.'. A prophetic valediction written in May 1916, it looks back to the 'year of friendship' from Thomas's participation in a war now less 'remote'. The ironically golden August of 1914, spent together at Ledington near Ledbury on the Gloucestershire-Herefordshire border, epitomises the year. 'Slow' balanced phrases – two by two – dramatise both a suspended moment and the equilibrium of the relationship:

> The sun used to shine while we two walked
> Slowly together, paused and started
> Again, and sometimes mused, sometimes talked
> As either pleased, and cheerfully parted
>
> Each night. We never disagreed
> Which gate to rest on. The to be
> And the late past we gave small heed.

Into this Edenic harmony between man and man, man and Nature, Thomas infiltrates history, war, death:

> We turned from men or poetry
>
> To rumours of the war remote
> Only till both stood disinclined
> For aught but the yellow flavorous coat
> Of an apple wasps had undermined . . .

Darker hues, deepening to 'sunless', undermine 'the yellow flavorous coat' of the poem itself:

> Or a sentry of dark betonies,
> The stateliest of small flowers on earth,
> At the forest verge; or crocuses
> Pale purple as if they had their birth
>
> In sunless Hades fields. The war
> Came back-to mind with the moonrise
> Which soldiers in the east afar
> Beheld then. Nevertheless, our eyes
>
> Could as well imagine the Crusades
> Or Caesar's battles.

Remembered sunlit landscape haunts and taunts all First World War poetry. But 'The Sun Used to Shine' is a richly ambiguous instance since the landscape may be a ghost from the past, or the war a ghost from the future. And Thomas sets not only peace but the whole meaning of his friendship with Frost, the whole shared cosmos of their poetry, against the fall which retrospectively shadows innocence. Yet the poem's overall thrust affirms and transmits the validity of what has been. 'Moonlight', suggestive of the imagination, presides over an ultimate poise between conflicting time zones, light and dark, relish and relinquishment, that rescues the experience from historical oblivion ('memory's sand'):

> Everything
> To faintness like those rumours fades –
> Like the brook's water glittering
>
> Under the moonlight – like those walks
> Now – like us two that took them, and
> The fallen apples, all the talks
> And silences – like memory's sand
>
> When the tide covers it late or soon,
> And other men through other flowers
> In those fields under the same moon
> Go talking and have easy hours.

The war's immediacy, by an implied reversal, now causes everything else to fade; yet these summarising impressions seem far from 'faint' as the ghosts of past and future meet. Although a progressive movement overcomes equilibrium, or sand runs faster through the poem's hour-glass, pattern still controls. The repetitions of the final quatrain turn the serial into the affirmative; while the last line's present tense is more habitual than the past of the first. Uncomplaining gratitude, in conjunction with a perspective beyond war and death, creates a tone of bequest or benediction.

2.

Thomas hands on the experience not only to 'other men' but to other poets, who 'under the same moon/ Go talking'. The bequest is technical as well as spiritual. 'The Sun Used to Shine' concentrates, indeed celebrates, the gains of the revolution Frost initiated:

> Summoning [sentence tones] is not all. They are only lovely when thrown and drawn and displayed across spaces of the footed line. Everyone knows that except a free-verster.[16]

Thomas almost exaggerates such display, running clause and sentence over the bounds fixed by line and quatrain, letting stress over-ride regular iambics as in the first line's alliterative metre:

> The sun used to shine while we two walked . . .

Here is the heart of the Frost-Thomas revolution, or evolution. Like Yeats, they transformed traditional metres by feeding them the roughage of speech. But they pitch the transformation at a different level (Yeats refers to 'passionate, normal speech'),[17] with blank verse rather than rhymed pentameter as the bottom-line. 'Talk', more completely subsumed by Yeats, is as important a word in 'The Sun Used to Shine' as it is in the theory of Frost and Thomas. Rhymed twice with 'walk', which ratifies Thomas's rhythmic fusion of these mental and physical processes, it implies one of his special contributions to the theory. Before he wrote poetry himself, his instinctive search for vital speech had led him to prose-writers like William Cobbett:

> He comes to us offering . . . the pleasure of watching a fighter whose brain and voice are, as it were, part of his physical and muscular development. The movement of his prose is a bodily thing. His sentences do not precisely suggest the swing of an arm or a leg, but they have something in common with it. His style is perhaps the nearest to speech that has really survived.[18]

The swinging speech-rhythms of 'The Sun Used to Shine' carry over into poetry this stylistic unity of being, this bodily movement. As a model, it is a less heroic version of Yeats's regret six years earlier in *Discoveries* that: 'In literature, partly from the lack of that spoken word which knits us to normal man, we have lost in personality, in our delight in the whole man – blood, imagination, intellect, running together.'[19]

But 'The Sun Used to Shine' lies in the shadow cast both by the under-estimation of Thomas and by what Richard Poirier terms 'condescensions directed at Frost by many admirers of the classical texts in English of twentieth-century modernism'.[20] Adverse discussions of Frost's poetry often paint a more revealing portrait of the critic than of the artist. Indeed what critics miss in Frost negatively illuminates what he and Thomas have to offer. John A. Meixner's censure, for instance, exemplifies a kind of school-report, must-try-harder attitude: 'If Frost is a lesser figure than Eliot or Yeats . . . part of the reason is that he was not active and important also as a dramatist or a critic or a cultural philosopher or an intricate systematiser of historical visions.'[21] Frost may have been 'lazy' as Meixner and others suggest. Or, wisely passive given the nature of his talent, he may have steered clear of 'talk round poetry',[22] of 'poems . . . actually done in the language of evaluation . . . too critical in spirit to admit of further criticism'.[23] Perhaps Frost's letters, prefaces and the records of his talk say more than many spun-out pages. Perhaps 'The Sun Used to Shine' enshrines a mystery on which we can only eavesdrop: 'We turned from men or poetry . . .' On the other hand, Thomas's voluminous criticism before the poetic event – and after the event he no longer cared about criticism – remained buried and ignored for years.

Frost's refusal of the extra-curricular literary activity made compulsory by Pound and Eliot is also seen as typifying his poetry's refusal of certain intellectual and spiritual efforts. Yvor Winters, whom Poirier calls a 'tone-deaf rationalist',[24] takes umbrage at Frost in 'The Bear' 'satirising the intelligent man from the point of view of the unintelligent'.[25] He complains: 'The uncaged bear, or the unreflective cave-man, is inferior to Thomas Aquinas and to Richard Hooker, to Dante and to Ben Jonson, and to assert the contrary is merely irresponsible foolishness'.[26] The insulted intelligent critic misses the point, and the mode, of a satire on human self-division ('His mood rejecting all his mind suggests') not the intellect alone. Winters's essay is subtitled 'The Spiritual Drifter as Poet': 'a spiritual drifter is unlikely to have either the intelligence or the energy to become a major poet'.[27] He thus gives Frost low marks for Religious Education too, having made the unsurprising discovery that Frost's relativism 'derives from no intense religious conviction'.[28] Winters takes Arnold much too literally on poetry as a substitute for religion: like Frost's man-as-caged-bear, poetry 'almost looks religious but [it's] not'. Raging for theological order he falls into the subject-matter fallacy: 'a poem which merely describes a stone may be excellent, but will certainly be minor; whereas a poem which deals with man's contemplation of death and eternity, or with a formative decision of some kind, may be great'.[29] No sermons in stones? Thomas's epigram in *Maurice Maeterlinck* remains definitive: 'Anything, however small, may make a poem; nothing, however great, is certain to.'[30] Denis Donoghue too finds Frost 'weak on ultimates',[31] whereas Eliot like a good student 'has spent a lifetime trying to get things straight and concentrating all his *mental* powers to that end'[32] (my italics). Neither does Frost serenade Donoghue with any of 'the great hymns to the human intelligence'[33] sung in Pound's *Cantos*. Even if the 'systematic repudiation of systematic thought'[34] sometimes becomes a shallow mannerism in late Frost, such criticism essentially looks for flattery of qualities which should more properly belong to the critic than to the poet. Excellent critics – Randall Jarrell, Reuben Brower, Richard Poirier – have come to Frost's rescue, but their arguments should prevail in a wider context.

Jarrell sums up the difference between intelligence and poetic intelligence when he says of 'Provide, Provide': 'if we murmur something about its crudities and provincialism, History will smile tenderly at us and lay us in the corner beside those cultivated people from Oxford and Cambridge who thought Shakespeare a Hollywood scenario-writer'.[35]

As for Thomas, Donald Davie, that mid-Atlantic Poundian, condescends as follows:

> Thomas was not alone in his generation in . . . [thinking] that the oceanic feelings aroused by a prospect of the Kentish Weald or Salisbury Plain somehow bypassed the whole tradition of European *thinking* about the supernatural; from Plato and Aristotle through Aquinas and Berkeley to F.H. Bradley . . . Thomas's vocabulary lacks nearly all the English words that stand for *disciplined conceptual thinking* about the things that preoccupied him most. (My italics)[36]

Grading Thomas low, Davie knows nothing about the extent of his reading and thinking; even if poetry without any obvious bibliography were necessarily simple-minded. Nor does he know his remark (in 1907) about the intellectually progressive poet John Davidson: 'We ought to guess the philosophy from the poetry no more than we guess the athlete's meals from the length of his leap.'[37] The conclusion of the review might apply to Pound's shop-window erudition: 'You cannot make yourself into a giant by bolting two or even three oxen and a complement of potatoes.'[38]

Despite Frost's popular and critical success, he always felt that the Modernists – 'the Pound-Eliot-Richards gang'[39] – had got the inside track, carried the intellectual constituency by remaking poetry in their own image. The prejudice of 1936 had its roots in the principles of 1915, when he wrote to Sidney Cox from England:

> nothing literary can come from the present ways of the professionally literary in American universities . . . I like the good old English way of muddling along in these things that we can't reduce to a science anyway such as literature love religion and friendship. People make their great strides in understanding literature at most unexpected times. I never caught another man's emotion in it more than when someone drew his finger over some seven lines of blank verse . . . saying simply 'From there to – there'. He knew and I knew. We said no more. I don't see how you are going to teach the stuff except with some such light touch. And you cant afford to treat it all alike, I mean with equal German thoroughness and reverence if thoroughness is reverence.[40]

The man was probably Edward Thomas. As a humble reviewer,

Thomas early in the century had also sniffed out the prospective convergence of literature, criticism and the university. Reviewing a critical work in 1902, he says: 'such intelligence . . . would become rather an evil than a good, if it should spread and cause . . . an increase in the tonnage of the British Museum'.[41] In 1905 the Germanic inclinations of the American critic Paul Elmer More prompted a defence of impressionism: 'reasonable judgments have caused more waste of paper and more of that tedium which is sapping the vitality of the old races, than all the irresponsible impressionism. Reasonable judgments are so often related to obesity of mind, to unconscious hypocrisy and a retarding respect for authority, that we are disposed to pass them over eagerly in search of the voice of a human being'.[42] Thomas's consistent attitude anticipates Jarrell's decades later. In 'The Age of Criticism' Jarrell attacks 'an astonishingly graceless, joyless, humourless, long-winded, niggling, blinkered, methodical, self-important, cliché-ridden, prestige-obsessed, almost-autonomous criticism'.[43] And that was *before* structuralism, though Jarrell spots the trend: 'And critics are already like conductors, and give you *their* "Lear", *their* "Confidence Man", *their* "Turn of the Screw".'[44]

In fact an Age of Criticism, unconsciously reciprocating Thomas's feelings, has neglected him in England much more than Frost in America. Or, like Frost's advocates, excellent individual books[45] on Thomas barely dent Modernist orthodoxy. For instance, the Open University Twentieth-Century Poetry course strongly features Pound, Eliot, Eliot's criticism, 'Modernism and its Origins', Leavis, Empson. It mentions only two poems by Thomas: 'Old Man' sympathetically, but also as an instance of 'the objective correlative';[46] and 'October', patronised for old-fashioned 'derivativeness' (see page 70 below). Davie ultimately champions Thomas, though with a shade of Modernist reservation ('we gave a great poet to the world, or at least to the English-speaking world'[47]). But he praises 'Cock-Crow' by subsuming it to Imagism:

> This has all the 'hardness' and 'dryness' that T.E. Hulme had asked for . . . It is a great pity, and cause for wonder, that neither Pound nor any one else apparently should have recognised that, if Imagism means anything, it surely means a small impersonal masterpiece like this.[48]

Thomas, who exclaimed in a letter to Gordon Bottomley 'What imbeciles the Imagistes are',[49] would not have been complimented. D.J. Enright observes in his introduction to *The Oxford Book of Contemporary Verse*: 'It is a tribute to Eliot's poetry and to Pound's that, so long afterwards, obscurity should be regarded in some circles as a wellnigh infallible sign of seriousness'.[50] He notes 'the embarrassment caused by poetry unamenable to high-level exegesis: try, for example, to give a lecture course on the work of Edward Thomas'.[51] However, weighing the nuances, always *linguistic*, of a Thomas or Frost poem can exercise more muscles than construing Eliot.

Besides sharing a position about criticism, Frost and Thomas also of course shared a critical position. Here Pound himself, rather than a Poundian future, constitutes the enemy. It is well-known that for Frost Pound rapidly declined from 'my dazzling friend'[52] into 'an incredible ass'.[53] Less well-known is Thomas's similar *volte-face*. In 1909 he saluted *Personae* as 'a revolt against the crepuscular spirit in modern poetry' and as 'the old miracle . . . nothing more than a subtle entanglement of words, so that they rise out of their graves and sing'.[54] A few days later he wrote to Bottomley: 'Oh I do humble myself over Ezra Pound. He is not & cannot ever be very good. Certainly he is not what I mesmerised myself – out of pure love of praising the new poetry! – into saying he was.'[55] Even in that first enthusiastic review Thomas had found Pound's 'pride in revolt' excessive: an 'abruptness as of a swift beetle that suddenly strikes your cheek and falls stunned with its own force.'[56] Reviewing *The Spirit of Romance* in 1910, he detected the same qualities in Pound the critic: '[The book] is restlessly opinionated. He has, or desires to have, an opinion upon everything; and if he has not then his eccentric speech makes it appear that he has . . . His personality is negative, and rises to the appearance of being positive only by contradiction.'[57] If Pound's criticism mixes 'dryasdust' with showbiz – 'At one moment he is a scholar writing in a way which is over the heads of the unlearned, and at another he is the free, courageous man wearing his learning lightly like a daisy'[58] – his poetry exhibits similar confusion and 'eccentric speech': 'Mr Ezra Pound's verses look so extraordinary, dappled with French, Provencal, Spanish, Italian, Latin, and old English, . . . with crudity, violence and obscurity, with stiff rhythms and no rhythms at all . . .'[59] This review (of *Exultations*) ends:

> he is, as a rule, so pestered with possible ways of saying a thing that at present we must be content to pronounce his condition still interesting – perhaps promising – certainly distressing. If he is not careful he will take to meaning what he says instead of saying what he means.[60]

These are no mere reactionary outbursts. Thomas's 'pure love of praising the new poetry' had made him a pioneering advocate of

Hardy, Yeats, and Lawrence as well as Frost. His doubts about Pound's poetry issue from a long critical and creative effort to distinguish between dead literary language and the language of life. Thomas praises Frost's metre because it 'avoids not only the old-fashioned pomp and sweetness, but the later fashion also of discord and fuss'.[61] He had attacked the 'old-fashioned pomp and sweetness' of English poetry in many reviews long before Pound came on the scene to savage the same target. But to him Pound's revolt or 'discord and fuss' ultimately seemed a new strain of the old virus of late-Romantic literariness. The latter he had already diagnosed in Pater's aesthetic criticism and the 'exquisite unnaturalness'[62] of his prose style, and in Swinburne's 'jargon': 'For it may be said of most poets that they love men and Nature more than words; of Swinburne that he loved them equally.'[63] If Pater and Swinburne represented a literariness and wordiness of which Thomas wished to purge himself, Arthur Symons's criticism represented a related, though more advanced position. Symons (as critic and poet) is a comparatively neglected link between aestheticism and the Modernist versions of Symbolism. While respecting Symons's abilities, Thomas took issue with him on his critical aspiration to fragment long poems into lyrical nuggets (see page 70 below): a French Symbolist doctrine behind those Imagist long poems, *The Waste Land* and *The Cantos*. Thomas felt that Symbolism detached language both from its own history and from human experience; which, in a progressive fission, reduced larger formal units to the isolated word. (Frost too condemned 'an age of mere diction and word-hunting'.)[64] Thomas's view of Pater's influence as 'encouraging meticulosity in detail and single words, rather than a regard for form in its largest sense',[65] chimes with his critique of Maeterlinck's Symbolist poem 'Serres Chaudes':

> the piece is hardly more than a catalogue of symbols that have no more literary value than words in a dictionary. It ignores the fact that no word, outside works of information, has any value beyond its surface value except what it receives from its neighbours and its position among them. Each man makes his own language in the main unconsciously and inexplicably, unless he is still at an age when he is an admiring but purely aesthetic collector of words; certain words – he knows not why – he will never use; and there are a hundred peculiarities in his rhythms and groupings to be discovered. In the mainly instinctive use of his language the words will all support one another, and, if the writing is good, the result of this support is that each word is living its intensest life. The first few words of a work of art teach us, though we do not know it at the time, exactly how much value we are to give to all the rest, whether they are to be words only, or images, or spirits. They admit us, or teach us that we cannot be

admitted, to the author's world. Any writer whose words have this power may make a poem of anything – a story, a dream, a thought, a picture, an ejaculation, a conversation.[66]

We cannot tell whether *The Waste Land* would have passed Thomas's tests for organic form. But he does remark of 'Serres Chaudes' that 'To give such a poem significance it would be necessary to make a key to it, like St Melito's key to the Bible'.[67]

Modernism as an international style – 'dappled verses' cosmopolitan in time or space – of course partly originated in American and Irish rebellion against the English literary tradition which claimed Thomas's main allegiance. (Not that his reading was in the least insular.) Pound and Joyce, and critics who take their cue from them, emphasise the provincialism of twentieth-century English literary culture, thus reversing historic slights. But whereas Pound was eventually to call the English 'shaggy and uncouth marginalians',[68] Frost homed to the tradition of Wordsworth and Hardy. This must have helped Thomas to love his poetry at first sight. Samuel Hynes, in a lecture mischievously entitled 'Frost as an English Poet', places him among the Georgians, alongside Thomas, and in 'the Hardy tradition':

> If you read through the whole of *A Boy's Will* and *North of Boston*, you will find the manners and the materials of the later work, but with a couple of exceptions you will not find the sensibility fully expressed . . . One must conclude that he found something in England that was lacking in New Hampshire, something that enriched and completed his talent. What he found, I think, was the Hardy tradition, alive and working in the poetry of men he came to know and admire. He could have read Hardy's poems without leaving home; but he could not have met the tradition-in-action in America. He had to come to England to find his natural allies.[69]

In fact *A Boy's Will* bears the imprint of Hardy's sensibility and vocabulary; while Thomas had been a pioneer in valuing Hardy's poetry above his fiction (see page 114 below).[70] Hynes's motive (as an American) in 'taking Frost out of New England' is not to tie him down elsewhere, but to universalise his role in 'a tradition that is not bound by nationality, or by national power or influence, but by the time in which we all live'.

Yet, paradoxically, whereas Pound and Eliot now bestride the Atlantic, it divides Frost and Thomas. And this is *because* their myth, unlike Eliot's 'mind of Europe', is not cosmopolitan but the parochial cosmos. Yeats is perhaps the only poet of the period who fused 'home and abroad, hence his ambiguous status between modern and Modernist: 'While seeing all in the light of European literature [I] found my symbols of expression in Ireland' (1907).[71] Of Eliot, Frost once said slyly: '[He] has left us and you know he's never really found them.'[72] A concept of "Englishness", as I argue in the next essay, goes deep in Thomas's poetry. One of his many prose definitions of a native literature corresponds to one of Frost's. Thomas wrote in 1904, years before Eliot's essay 'Tradition and the Individual Talent':

> Poetry is a natural growth, having more than a superficial relation to roses and trees and hills. However airy and graceful it may be in foliage and flower, it has roots deep in a substantial past. It springs apparently from an occupation of the land, from long, busy, and quiet tracts of time, wherein a man or a nation may find its own soul. To have a future, it must have had a past.[73]

Thomas and Frost often use natural and organic metaphors for poetry. Frost wrote in 1918:

> I am as sure that the colloquial is the root of every good poem as I am that the national is the root of all thought and art. It may shoot up as high as you please and flourish as widely abroad in the air, if only the roots are what and where they should be.[74]

Thomas and Frost, in practice as well as theory, assume (though not as a foregone conclusion) possibilities of continuity, rather than the discontinuity which Modernism seeks to remedy by transplantation.

Anglo-American divisions may also have prevented Thomas's poetry from travelling to America, as Frost's has to England. David Bromwich recently commented: 'In America Thomas is of course mentioned now and then in connection with Frost; but his poems are not read.'[75] Could Frost, years ago, have done more for his friend's poetry? Certainly both before and after Thomas's death he boosted his work as he never did that of any other contemporary. He arranged for the American publication of Thomas's *Poems* (1917); for George F. Whicher to write an essay on them; and for Harriet Monroe to publish poems by Thomas in *Poetry*. But Frost in the years after his return to America was always anxious to play down his 'British-made reputation',[76] English connections that might offend patriotic poetry-lovers. In 1921 he warned Grace Walcott Conkling who had 'linked Edward Thomas's name with mine in one of your lectures': 'You will be careful, I know, not to say anything to exalt either of us at the expense of the other. There's a story going round that might lead you to exaggerate our debt to each other.'[77] This seems faintly prudential, not just a wish to assert each poet's individuality, or that there was 'never a moment's thought about who may have been influencing whom'.[78] If the issue is seen as one of American literature appropriating an English poet, or vice-versa, the whole significance of the 'special relationship' collapses. Donald J. Greiner, in a survey of Frost criticism (1974), takes a contrary view to Hynes's: 'John Freeman's essay in the *London Mercury* (December 1925) . . . begins with the questionable statement that Frost seems to have a firmer grasp on English tradition than any other contemporary American poet.'[79] In 1963 another American, Radcliffe Squires, observed: 'While it is true that there is no school of Frost, he has had some effect on some poets. One glances at them not for what they reveal about modern poetry but for what they reveal about Frost's poetry . . . One can feel that had Thomas lived his poetry might have asserted its individuality.'[80] In retaliation some English critics rush to rescue Thomas from foreign clutches. William Cooke, one of Thomas's best advocates, argues that 'Frost's advice was no more than what he claimed it was – the appreciation and encouragement of a friend. The decisive influence came from elsewhere.'[81] Cooke means the First World War. But perhaps 'The Sun Used to Shine' holds the true balance between all Thomas's 'influences': Nature, Frost, literature, war.

3.

As a basis for assessing the creative interaction between Frost and Thomas, and its reverberation today, we might cling to two statements: Frost's 'The most our congeniality could do was confirm us both in what we were'; and Thomas's affidavit in a letter to Frost shortly after the poems started to come: 'I will put it down now that you are the only begetter right enough.'[82] The first testifies to a profound bond though appearing to deny one, while the second need not make Thomas a Frost clone. A 'begetter' does not own his child. Thomas himself had enough confidence in his own 'individuality' to write to John Freeman in March 1915: 'since the first take off they haven't been Frosty very much or so I imagine'.[83] There was, too, Cooke's 'decisive influence'. The war not only urgently released Thomas's imaginative sense of England; it also launched his poetry on a swifter trajectory than Frost's. In two years Thomas wrote a lifetime's poems: poems that scooped up all his past, poems that fought off the darkness that might silence him. In 'March', the third poem he wrote (5 December 1914), thrushes at twilight symbolise an abbreviated creative time-span:

34

What did the thrushes know? Rain, snow, sleet, hail,
Had kept them quiet as the primroses.
They had but an hour to sing. On boughs they sang,
On gates, on ground; they sang while they changed perches
And while they fought, if they remembered to fight:
So earnest were they to pack into that hour
Their unwilling hoard of song before the moon
Grew brighter than the clouds.

These different clocks mean that some of Thomas's poems either
influenced, or have affinities with, poetry Frost wrote later on.
'March' itself, for instance, is related to 'Our Singing Strength', and
twenty years separate two poems compared below: Thomas's 'Rain'
written in a 'bleak [army] hut' and Frost's 'Desert Places'.

The Frost-Thomas revolution was fought on behalf of the ear
against the eye. Whereas their own poetry's self-images are rhythmic
and organic, they employ hard-edged metaphors from the visual,
plastic arts, or from the manipulation of mineral objects, when
criticising alien methods. The following suggests that Frost would
have considered 'The Poet as Sculptor', the subtitle of Davie's book
on Pound, a logical impossibility:

> I can hear Edward Thomas saying in defense of In the Home Stretch
> that it would cut just as it is into a dozen or more of your Chinese
> impressionistic poems and perhaps gain something by the cutting for
> the reader whose taste had been formed on the kiln-dried tabule
> poetry of your Pounds and Masterses. I look on theirs as synthetical
> chemical products put together after a formula.[84]

Thomas's *Walter Pater* chips away at Pater's 'hard and stationary
refinement';[85] his use of 'words as bricks, as tin soldiers, instead of
flesh and blood and genius';[86] his style's 'inhuman . . . marble'.[87]
Thomas similarly calls the Imagist anthology a 'tall marble
monument',[88] and he told Edward Garnett when he failed to *hear*
'Lob': 'you read too much with the eye perhaps'.[89] Before he met
Frost, Thomas's criticism had uncannily worked towards Frost's
credo: 'We must write with the ear on the speaking voice. We must
imagine the speaking voice.'[90] As he told Frost: 'my "Pater" would
show you I had got on to the scent already'.[91] In fact a central
statement in *Walter Pater* suggests that Thomas already connected
'the speaking voice' and human revelation more inwardly than Frost:

> Literature is . . . divided in outward seeming from speech by what
> helps to make it in fact more than ever an equivalent of speech. It has to
> make words of such a spirit, and arrange them in such a manner, that
> they will do all a speaker can do by innumerable gestures and their

innumerable shades, by tone and pitch of voice, by speed, by pauses, by all that he is and all that he will become.[92]

Thomas's 'myriad-minded lyric', the Yeatsian 'soliloquy', covers poetry of immense range and variety. But all such poems, in mediating between a speaker and the world, enact rather than (like Hardy) state a case. They open out from the individual psyche into wider metaphysical or spiritual areas: a *reculer pour mieux sauter* on the part of Romanticism, perhaps. Thomas again illuminates the special intricacy of his own 'inner theatre'[93] in the following important defence of Frost's principles:

> All [Frost] insists on is what he believes he finds in all poets — absolute fidelity to the postures which the voice assumes in the most expressive intimate speech. So long as these tones & postures are there he has not the least objection to any vocabulary whatever or any inversion or variation from the customary grammatical forms of talk. In fact I think he would agree that if these tones & postures survive in a complicated & learned or subtle vocabulary & structure the result is likely to be better than if they survive in the easiest form, that is in the very words & structures of common speech . . .[94]

To compare short poems by Frost and Thomas, in illustration of their complementary qualities, is itself to locate a ground of difference. After his very first poem, 'Up in the Wind' (which resembles Frost's 'A Servant to Servants'), Thomas gave his main allegiance to the lyric and avoided narrative-dramatic pieces, the Frostian eclogue. He told Frost in March 1916: 'Your talking of epic & play rather stirred me. I shall be careful not to *indulge* in a spring run of lyrics. I had better try again to make other people speak.'[95] But he did go on indulging himself lyrically, and throughout his poetry 'other people speak' much less frequently and more briefly than in Frost. Almost always they speak either in relation to a poet-figure or as alternative voices of the poet. However, lyrics which keep 'the universe alone' throw the difference, as well as the affinity, between Frost and Thomas into sharper relief. Jarrell in his great essay on Frost, poses rhetorical questions which beg the answer 'Edward Thomas': 'what poet since Arnold has written so much about isolation, and said so much more about it than even Arnold? What other poet, long before we had begun to perfect the means of altogether doing away with humanity, had taken as an obsessive subject the wiping-out of man, his replacement by the nature out of which he arose?'[96] But whereas for Frost 'the wiping-out of man' generally figures as a spatial fear, derived from his sense of North

American wilderness and climate ('There Are Roughly Zones'), for Thomas it figures as a historical, evolutionary fear intensified by the war: 'When gods were young/This wind was old' ('The Mountain Chapel'). Similarly, 'The past hovering as it revisits the light' ('It Rains')lies behind Thomas's personal poems. Frost's plea-bargaining with life takes place within a more constricted time-zone. Both poets symbolise human existence as a man in a house in a wood or forest. But Thomas's old countrymen become notably obsolescent, disappear up lanes into the past. The keeper in 'Under the Woods' (an oppressive title) leaves behind only a dead stoat 'shrivelled and green,/And with no scent at all'. The man in 'House and Man' fades away in the memory:

> half
> Ghost-like, half like a beggar's rag, clean wrung
> And useless on the briar where it has hung
> Long years a-washing by sun and wind and rain.

Frost's protagonists in a similar situation, even in 'An Old Man's Winter Night', undergo less erosion. They await the issue rather than succumb to historical necessity:

> He consigned to the moon – such as she was,
> So late-arising – to the broken moon,
> As better than the sun in any case
> For such a charge, his snow upon the roof,
> His icicles along the wall to keep;
> And slept.

Just as Frost found 'the Hardy tradition' alive and stimulating in England (where Pound and Eliot found mostly a museum), so Thomas may have been roused by Frost's Americanness, as well as by the war, to some contrasting imaginative structures and definitions.

This broad distinction, between being terrified in time and terrified in space, applies to the metaphysical issues raised by Thomas in 'Old Man' and by Frost in 'The Most of It', and to the more directly psychological scenarios of Thomas's 'Rain' and Frost's 'Desert Places'. Thomas's poems speak from historical locations 'between death and birth' ('The Signpost'), with obliteration on both horizons, whereas Frost's take off from 'empty spaces' in the present. In 'Old Man' language, poetry, faces a historical darkness:

> Old Man, or Lad's-love, – in the name there's nothing
> To one that knows not Lad's-love, or Old Man,
> The hoar-green feathery herb, almost a tree,

Growing with rosemary and lavender.
Even to one that knows it well, the names
Half decorate, half perplex, the thing it is:
At least, what that is clings not to the names
In spite of time. And yet I like the names.

Thomas's most fundamental artistic objectives were to fit word exactly to 'thing', and to 'name' what oblivion would otherwise claim. 'Women He Liked' registers the latter process as an irony. Although the trees planted by 'shovel-bearded Bob' eventually turn a lane 'to slough/ And gloom', it at last 'earns' the name it somehow lacked during his lifetime: 'the name alone survives, Bob's Lane'. The victories of art in Thomas's poetry tend to be more Pyrrhic than in Yeats's. 'Old Man' pursues 'the thing it is' (not just a plant) through ambivalent names ('Old Man, or Lad's-love'), *genera* (herb? tree? bush?), feelings ('The herb itself I like not, but for certain/ I love it'), only to be challenged by further dimensions of definition:

I have mislaid the key. I sniff the spray
And think of nothing; I see and I hear nothing;
Yet seem, too, to be listening, lying in wait
For what I should, yet never can, remember:
No garden appears, no path, no hoar-green bush
Of Lad's-love, or Old Man, no child beside,
Neither father nor mother, nor any playmate;
Only an avenue, dark, nameless, without end.

The poem has gradually separated the word 'nothing' into its component parts: a separation which emphasises the paradox involved in 'thinking of nothing', and thus revitalises a cliché. Thomas's final version of non-being or anti-matter, cancelling with negatives all that represents life, is redeemed only by being uttered, by being itself not a 'nameless' avenue.

Frost's linguistic philosophy stresses the complex relation between seeing and saying, rather than between word and thing. The long poems in *North of Boston* angle language according to contrary perceptions. They thus cast intersecting rays of light on emotional or moral misunderstandings. 'The Most of It' comments on this essentially epistemological procedure, Poirier's *Work of Knowing*. A representative man or poet seeks 'response' from a more immediate void than Thomas's. And Frost's seekers rarely remain 'listening, lying in wait', they more often go out and holler:

He thought he kept the universe alone;
For all the voice in answer he could wake
Was but the mocking echo of his own

From some tree-hidden cliff across the lake.
Some morning from the boulder-broken beach
He would cry out on life, that what it wants
Is not its own love back in copy-speech,
But counter-love, original response.
And nothing ever came of what he cried
Unless it was the embodiment that crashed
In the cliff's talus on the other side,
And then in the far-distant water splashed,
But after a time allowed for it to swim,
Instead of proving human when it neared
And someone else additional to him,
As a great buck it powerfully appeared,
Pushing the crumpled water up ahead,
And landed pouring like a waterfall,
And stumbled through the rocks with horny tread,
And forced the underbrush – and that was all.

Poirier calls the 'cry' a 'naive version' of the Romantic attitude.[97]
Frost, like Thomas (see page 68), continually tests Romantic
demands and promises, the poet's own *folie de grandeur*. However,
his protagonist here may be poised between dissatisfaction with
Romantic subjectivity and solipsism, and unreadiness for the
"other", for objective 'embodiment'. In fact the poem interprets the
whole aesthetic of the dramatic lyric. The 'buck' is both a dusty
answer, materialising as disturbingly out of space as Thomas's
avenue dematerialises into time, and an indication that nobody
asked the right question. And yet Frost's own poem 'powerfully'
represents Nature's poem (as opposed to a Nature poem) even if his
stand-in cannot cope. The conclusion is also one of those where Frost
quantifies a result against some elusive mathematical base. As he
computes the ambiguous artithmetic of 'Our Hold on the Planet', his
poems sometimes announce the discovery of 'something', a 'most' or
'all', which might be maximal or minimal. And 'The Most of It', like
'Old Man', plays around with positives and negatives, with plus and
minus signs: 'And nothing ever came . . . / Unless it was'. However,
the apparition's power bids up the final understatement. What
Poirier terms 'a vision of some fabulousness beyond domestication'[98]
resembles the intrinsic mysteries Thomas too elicits beyond
Romanticism. In any case 'Old Man' and 'The Most of It', by wholly
different methods, dramatise the modern problem of rescuing or
securing meaning from the phenomenal world, from oblivion and
wilderness.

The techniques of Thomas's 'Rain' and Frost's 'Desert Places'
assume more settled demarcations between the universe and man.

The one both defines its own separateness, and embodies the other's cry. How the poems relate 'outer' and 'inner weather' also reflects on the ways in which Thomas and Frost reconcile mimesis with self-dramatisation, detail with symbol:

> Rain, midnight rain, nothing but the wild rain
> On this bleak hut, and solitude, and me
> Remembering again that I shall die
> And neither hear the rain nor give it thanks
> For washing me cleaner than I have been
> Since I was born into this solitude.
> Blessed are the dead that the rain rains upon:
> But here I pray that none whom once I loved
> Is dying tonight or lying still awake
> Solitary, listening to the rain,
> Either in pain or thus in sympathy
> Helpless among the living and the dead,
> Like a cold water among broken reeds,
> Myriads of broken reeds all still and stiff,
> Like me who have no love which this wild rain
> Has not dissolved except the love of death,
> If love it be for what is perfect and
> Cannot, the tempest tells me, disappoint.

What distinguishes this from the more monotonous and moralised monologues of Hardy's imagination 'In Tenebris', is the fluid dynamic that makes 'Rain' and 'disappoint' members of a single action in the Donnean sense ('but the last clause is as the impression of the stamp, and that is it that makes it currant'). The repeated monosyllable 'rain', in conjunction with cold, liquid, hissing sounds renders tangible the downpour levelling all consciousness towards death. But the mimetic properties of the rhythm merge into the cadences of the poet's voice, thus fusing the downpour with despair, mental with physical coldness, the pressure of Nature on man with his interior pressures. Thomas further achieves his goal of arranging words to reproduce 'innumerable gestures and their innumerable shades', by redefining them in new contexts: the triple 'rain' in the first line; 'solitude' / 'this solitude' / 'Solitary'; the explicit gloss on 'the love of death'. ('Old Man' too explores by redefinition, from the point where the plant's names diverge.) The ultimate dynamising agent in 'Rain' is form, charging the sensual and emotional current. Metre provides its own emphasis: for instance, in the unobtrusive irregularities of the first and last lines; in the dramatically appropriate end-pausing on 'dead' and 'reeds' (the poem's closest off-rhyme), 'stiff' and 'death'; and in the line-break 'and/ Cannot' – a routine effect nowadays, but rarely so purposeful. 'Rain' is also an example of the fine accommodation which Thomas, more than Frost, achieved between blank verse and stanzaic metre: a verse-freeing revolution which has not received its due. 'Rain' and 'Old Man' introduce sentence-sounds into a tauter structure than 'Mending Wall' and 'The Wood-Pile' in *North of Boston*. A most delicate balance between off-rhyme and assonance contributes to the poem's backbone and tune. Thomas also strengthens his structures by means of internal rhyme ('thing'/'clings', 'snipping the tips', 'dying'/'lying', 'rain'/'pain') and by end-rhyming on a repeated key-word: 'names' and 'rain' three times each. 'Rain' is a seamless garment which satisfies the profound Yeatsian, rather than shallow Maeterlinckean, requirements for Symbolism. It 'evokes an emotion which cannot be evoked by any other arrangement of colours and sounds and forms'.[99]

Frost in 'Desert Places' harps on 'snow' and 'loneliness' as does Thomas in 'Rain' on 'rain' and 'solitude' (obvious and subtle Anglo-American distinctions?):

> Snow falling and night falling fast, oh, fast
> In a field I looked into going past,
> And the ground almost covered smooth in snow,
> But a few weeds and stubble showing last.
>
> The woods around it have it — it is theirs.
> All animals are smothered in their lairs.
> I am too absent-spirited to count;
> The loneliness includes me unawares.
>
> And lonely as it is, that loneliness
> Will be more lonely ere it will be less –
> A blanker whiteness of benighted snow
> With no expression, nothing to express.
>
> They cannot scare me with their empty spaces
> Between stars – on stars where no human race is.
> I have it in me so much nearer home
> To scare myself with my own desert places.

Frost has often been criticised by literalists not only for spiritual drifting but for emotional evasiveness. Meixner considers that 'in his work pain was not explored, was not made to be felt, was only gone at by abstract statement and by hint'.[100] In fact the sound and movement of 'Desert Places', punctuated like 'Rain' by repetition, dramatise mimetically and tonally what is not fully declared until the final quatrain. Frost's redefinitions convey both relentlessly falling snow and a progressive 'smothering' of the spirit (the poet in a spiritual snow-drift?): 'And lonely as it is, that loneliness/Will be more lonely ere it will be less'. Like 'Rain', 'Desert Places' conceives an alarming annihilation: all humanity 'dissolved', or lost in a white-out. But the poems also differ in theme as in form. Thomas's historical deathwatch (which includes dead soldiers in 'Myriads of broken reeds all still and stiff') contrasts with the Frostian fear of man being unable to impose on Nature, of his failing to keep house or the universe, of being imposed on himself and collapsing into an inward vacuum. Thomas's poetry, with its assimilation of English rural writing since Gilbert White, bears the mark of longer-term negotiations between man and landscape, man and history. For better and worse, some issues which agitate Frost's imagination have been resolved. Both poems, however, identify the loss of human with the loss of artistic confidence. 'Rain' presents the poet as 'Helpless among the living and the dead' in 1916; 'Desert Places' presents him as unable to impose the imagination too on 'A blanker whiteness of benighted snow', a *tabula* that remains *rasa*.

As for formal differences: perhaps because for Thomas the terms are ultimately clearer on which the natural can stand for the human, his 'I' blends more readily into the rain. 'Desert Places' proceeds more by statement (after the Thomas-like initial omission of the main verb), which interrupts the absolute fusion of inner and outer. Thomas's poems hardly ever draw such explicit conclusions: in this respect Frost sometimes stays closer to Hardy. Again, 'Desert Places' and 'The Most of It' (disguised quatrains) representatively take off from a more prefabricated form than 'Rain'. 'Rain', among its other metrical audacities, also summons the ghost of sonnet-structure. It 'turns' on the slow line-unit 'Blessed are the dead that the rain rains upon', braced against blocks of six and eleven lines. Although Frost does vary his metres, if less than his tones of voice, 'After Apple-Picking' remains a curiously unpursued experiment among blank verse, sonnets, quatrains and couplets. Frost also uses fuller rhyme when he rhymes. And in his later poetry ready-made forms can yield ready-made answers alien to his true findings:

> It is but a trick poem and no poem at all if the best of it was thought of first and saved for the last. It finds its own name as it goes . . . [101]

On the other hand, Frost's blank verse rarely composes such a sustained lyrical dynamic as the thirty-nine line 'Old Man'.

Syntax, so often seen as unpoetic or anti-poetic, is fundamental to any poetry born of sentence-sounds. Yeats too gave it priority: 'As I altered my syntax I altered my intellect.'[102] Louis MacNeice, baptised into syntax by the classics, says in a review of Brower's book on Frost: 'I have often been surprised that reviewers of verse pay so little attention to syntax. A sentence in prose is struck forward like a golfball; a sentence in verse can be treated like a ball in a squash court. Frost . . . is a master of angles.'[103] To continue the squash metaphor: Thomas has perfected the back-wall bounce, whereas Frost whacks the ball more *toward* the front from off the sides of his forms. Inversion is a particularly marked feature of Thomas's syntax. By no means a reflex archaism, it serves both his back-and-forth trawls for meaning, and his historically bridging role. A syntactical as well as verbal chiasmus, the first two lines of 'Old Man' move forward into mysteries by moving back. Thomas's syntax also moves through the complicating resistance of clauses that begin 'Even', 'At least', 'And yet'; and of phrases like 'Half decorate, half perplex' – which sums up the effect. Frost's syntax lacks some of Thomas's half-tones. 'Rain' and 'Desert Places' end on very different sentence-sounds. Engaging more in the quarrel with others, or with the world, Frost enlists the syntactical modes of argument and speculation. 'The Most of It' not only 'embodies' but also emphatically points alternatives: 'For all . . . Was but . . . Unless . . . But . . . Instead of'. Thomas's perplexed syntax, whatever its ramifications, never quite leaves the stage of interior drama, of the quarrel with oneself. While playing off his angles, Frost yet thrusts towards 'Truth? A pebble of quartz?' Part of his epistemological strategy is to ask questions, half-rhetorical, half-unrhetorical: 'What but design of darkness to appall?' Thomas's poems sometimes begin with a question: 'Beauty' with 'What does it mean?', 'Digging' with 'What matter makes my spade for tears or mirth . . .?' However these initiate (as do other rhetorical tactics) a process that approximates less to Socratic dialogue than to a progressive archaeological probe. In 'The Glory' self-questioning represents an effort to 'bite the day to the core'. When two poems end with questions ('The Signpost', 'It Was Upon') they are prefaced by 'wondering'. It may just be the difference between extroverted and introverted forms of the same technique. In any case this is how Thomas can fail to ask a simple question:

> How at once should I know,
> When stretched in the harvest blue
> I saw the swift's black bow,
> That I would not have that view
> Another day
> Until next May
> Again it is due?

Again, as compared with Thomas's periodic networks, some of Frost's most striking effects build up one-sentence lines, or an intense accumulation like the end of 'The Most of It'. But if 'The Most of It' packs a force unusual in Thomas, the crescendo of negatives at the end of 'Old Man' unleashes the full rhetorical power implicit in the poem's syntactical subtlety.

As Frost has been called 'an American pragmatist' so Thomas may be called an English empiricist. Their imaginations agree in working on the given earth. They might also be contrasted as sceptic and agnostic: the one interrogating the universe, the other more quietly investigating. Like all such poetry – Louis MacNeice's for example – their endeavours assume the overall symbolic pattern of a journey: amid changing light, topography, weather and season. Whether conditioned by temperament, or English climate or culture, Thomas's journey follows his syntax into more numerous by-ways, and into such fine shadings as 'And Spring's here, Winter's not gone'. However, from mid-1916, the date of 'The Sun Used to Shine', the shades darken and the options close. With the trenches now on his near-horizon, Thomas's poetry more and more confirms Frost's insight that 'It ought to be called Roads to France'.[104] Thomas's three criss-crossing paths increasingly converge: the inner quest, the trek of all human life towards death, and his recognition that 'Now all roads lead to France' ('Roads'). The later poems both say goodbye to actual places and people – with characteristic ambivalence rather than sentimental regret – and take more symbolic leave:

> I have come to the borders of sleep,
> The unfathomable deep
> Forest where all must lose
> Their way, however straight,
> Or winding, soon or late;
> They cannot choose.
>
> ('Lights Out')

Images of roads ending in the 'forest' (whose implications include the 'unknown', the unconscious, extinction) interact with those of a darkening or disintegrating house. Such images intensify earlier usages: the allegorical journey in 'The Other' had wound between forest and 'the sum/Of what's not forest'. If the forest represents what is being entered, the house represents what is being left. The persona speaks from outside the house, outside the body, outside life. He stays 'Out in the dark' with the fallow fawns on a winter night. He looks back – from where? – in 'The Long Small Room':

When I look back I am like moon, sparrow, and mouse
That witnessed what they could never understand
Or alter or prevent in the dark house.

Frost's poetic journey, not being run against the clock, had no such concentrated finale. But 'Directive' sums up his route as 'The Other' anticipates Thomas's. Also, both poems celebrate poetry's staying-power against confusion. The middle stanzas of 'The Other', set like all Thomas's poems between problematic past and problematic future, suggest the integration he achieved both through poetry and in poetry: 'one star, one lamp, one peace/Held on an everlasting lease'. 'Directive' ends with a similarly healing vision:

I have kept hidden in the instep arch
Of an old cedar at the waterside
A broken drinking goblet like the Grail
Under a spell so the wrong ones can't find it,
So can't get saved, as Saint Mark says they mustn't.
(I stole the goblet from the children's playhouse.)
Here are your waters and your watering place.
Drink and be whole again beyond confusion.

Poirier criticises Frost's multiple allusions to earlier poems ('instep arch' from 'After Apple-Picking' etc.), as 'claustrophic self-reference'.[105] In fact this self-quotation signals that 'Directive' is both, as Jarrell says, Frost's last word about 'isolation . . . extinction . . . and the final limitations of man',[106] and a retrospect on how his own words have covered these matters. But as Frost pursues a 'backward motion toward the source' of his poetry, to its 'lofty and original' · well-springs, I would like to think that he also alludes to and quotes from Edward Thomas: the 'getting lost' as in 'Lights Out', perhaps 'the brook's water' ('A brook that was the water of the house') from 'The Sun Used to Shine' and Ledington. The 'destination' scheduled by this Reader's Guide may take some colour from the Frost family's circumstances in summer 1914: 'a house that is no more a house/Upon a farm that is no more a farm', a field 'no bigger than a harness gall', 'the children's playhouse'. Thomas's 'What Shall I Give?' portrays his younger daughter Myfanwy as 'Wanting a thousand little things'; 'Directive' commands of the children's 'playthings': 'Weep for what little things could make them glad'.

To Helen Bacon the following lines signify 'the twin cults of Apollo and Dionysus':[107]

The height of the adventure is the height
Of country where two village cultures faded
Into each other. Both of them are lost.

I would prefer to interpret them as symbolising the Anglo-American interchange between Thomas and Frost on a county border. 'Directive' rolls Frost's career historically back to its inspirations. Secretive and teasing, why should he not have woven Edward Thomas, 'the only brother I ever had', and their shared poetic landscape into the intricate fabric of his aesthetic *summa*? He certainly either quotes from, or unconsciously parallels, Thomas at the precise point where 'Directive' initiates us into craft-mysteries: 'I have kept hidden . . . Under a spell so the wrong ones can't find it'. This echoes Thomas's 'I Never Saw that Land Before':

> some goal
> I touched then; and if I could sing
> What would not even whisper my soul
> As I went on my journeying,
>
> I should use, as the trees and birds did,
> A language not to be betrayed;
> And what was hid should still be hid
> Excepting from those like me made
> Who answer when such whispers bid.

The common heart of Frost's and Thomas's mysteries, their joint 'goal' and 'Grail' is the high value they set on poetry. Unfortunately this, like the value of their poetic brotherhood, sometimes remains too well-hidden.

'Worn New': Edward Thomas and English Tradition

1.

Apart from his transatlantic connections, Edward Thomas is important to the history of twentieth-century poetry in English because he developed specific qualities of English poetry itself. He stands 'On a strange bridge alone' ('The Bridge') between Romantics and Moderns. This bridge, some of whose critical girders I discussed in the previous essay, should not be consigned to the indiscriminate demolition-yard of the term "Georgian". Thomas's long poem 'Lob' focuses his role as a radical continuator. It celebrates a spirit that has historically informed and interconnected the countryside, character, folklore, language and literature of England:

> He is English as this gate, these flowers, this mire.
> And when at eight years old Lob-lie-by-the-fire
> Came in my books, this was the man I saw . . .

Updating the start of the *Canterbury Tales* prologue, the poet represents himself as setting out on a part deliberate, part unconsciously guided quest for this spirit, which the face of an old countryman prefigures:

> At hawthorn-time in Wiltshire travelling
> In search of something chance would never bring,
> An old man's face, by life and weather cut
> And coloured, – rough, brown, sweet as any nut, –
> A land face, sea-blue-eyed, – hung in my mind . . .

But besides including a portrait of the artist in search of Lob, and portraits of Lob as artist – 'Calling the wild cherry tree the merry tree . . . On sleepless nights he made up weather rhymes/ Which others spoilt' – the poem indirectly establishes Thomas's own qualifications for becoming as well as eliciting what is 'English as this gate, these flowers, this mire'; for redefining Lob's responsibilities at a time (1915) when they seemed usurped, threatened and obsolescent.

A poet senses the fine currents that run between general cultural conditions and the state of the art he practises. Thus Lob may be at once objective and subjective: Thomas's material and his metaphor for himself as poet (like Yeats's Fisherman in 'grey Connemara clothes'); 'the giant coming to destroy/Shrewsbury by flood' can stand for the Kaiser or Ezra Pound. The affinities between creator and creation (Thomas may of course have made Lob in his own image or, more mysteriously, Lob made Thomas in his) begin where the poem does, with Lob's very elusiveness. Just as Lob 'disappears' up the winding lanes of Wiltshire and memory, so Thomas's poetry is strangely difficult of access, infinitely complex beneath its surface transparency, understated, often underrated, easily overlooked, similarly lying in wait for the right discoverer. Just as Lob 'never could spare time for school/ To unteach what the fox so well expressed, /On biting the cock's head off, – Quietness is best –', yet 'can talk quite as well as anyone/After his thinking is forgot and done', so Thomas wished his poetry (which also took its time rising to the surface) to speak a 'language not to be betrayed'. His discoveries and recoveries, like Lob's ancient and instinctive wisdom, are hedged by a reserve that conceals reservoirs.

More broadly, the archetypal old man described by the 'squire's son' who takes over from the poet as narrator 'was wild/And wandered. His home was where he was free'. Thomas himself wandered actually and imaginatively down the roads of England and life, finding 'home' or 'liberty' in unexpected harmonies of man and Nature:

Often I had gone this way before:
But now it seemed I never could be
And never had been anywhere else;
'Twas home; one nationality
We had, I and the birds that sang,
One memory.

('Home')

Such a sense of nationality with the animate and inanimate features of the English countryside is less accessible to Thomas, one of 'those modern people who belong nowhere',[1] than to Lob. But his whole effort to overcome the restrictions incurred by the self-conscious spiritual immigrant means that his poetry too is 'by life and weather cut/And coloured', etching and etched by the 'copses, ponds, roads, and ruts' of England, reproducing the land's face with occasional glimpses of the sea. Thomas also shares with Lob, if again less sure of his birthright, the ultimate nationality of being 'An old inhabitant of earth' ('The Other'). The 'squire's son', who is finally revealed as an incarnation of Lob, 'loved wild bird and beast, and dog and gun/For killing them. He had loved them from his birth,/One with another, as he loved the earth'. Thomas's own more complicated love of the earth certainly goes beyond easy love of Nature, and involves equally paradoxical commitments which bespeak acclimatisation and naturalisation: 'And yet I still am half in love with pain . . . With things that have an end, with life and earth . . .' ('Liberty'). One index of shared nationality is a common language. The squire's son remarks of Lob: 'Our blackbirds sang no English till his ear/Told him they called his Jan Toy "Pretty Dear"', and Thomas metaphorically interprets the 'language' of 'birds and trees', attunes his ear to 'the small brown birds/ Wisely reiterating endlessly/ What no man learnt yet, in or out of school' ('Sedge-Warblers'). His poetry in the largest sense absorbs the communications of the natural world, which seems nearly as well adapted to his psychological as to Lob's bodily shape (and even Lob's relationship with the earth is a two-way traffic). Most of the poems are 'weather rhymes' of one sort or another, from the straightforward opening of 'November': 'November's days are thirty:/November's earth is dirty', to 'Rain', undoubtedly made up on a sleepless night.

All this exposure to 'life and weather' that both Lob and Thomas's imagination have undergone should in itself guarantee that neither poem nor poet simply offers a passport to a golden or lost world. Raymond Williams feels, however, that 'Lob' falls, if from greater height than usual, into Georgian conventions:

> All countrymen, of all conditions and periods, are merged into a singular legendary figure. The varied idioms of specific country communities – the flowers, for example, have many local names – are reduced not only to one "country" idiom but to a legendary, timeless inventor, who is more readily seen than any actual people. And this is the point at which the Georgian imagination broke down: the respect of authentic observation overcome by a sub-intellectual fantasy: a working man becoming "my ancient" . . .[2]

It is surely the business of poetry to generalise, synthesise, symbolise: to construct, given reasonably concrete lineaments, an archetype. What Williams appears to demand from Thomas is not a glancingly inventive poem but a heavily documentary regional novel – or perhaps George Bourne's *Bettesworth Book*.[3] This was probably one of Thomas's sources for 'Lob' but the poem is a delta. As for the charge which Williams also levels at the Georgians in general, of remoteness from an 'actual and working rural community',[4] I don't suppose he would accept Thomas's allusion to 'poor Jack of every trade' as covering this aspect. But in an earlier, more limited encounter with Lob ('Man and Dog') he does prove his ability to evoke rural and semi-urban labour, to enter into the experience of 'a working man', to place him in history:

Then he went on against the north-east wind –
Straight but lame, leaning on a staff new-skinned,
Carrying a brolly, flag-basket, and old coat, –
Towards Alton, ten miles off. And he had not
Done less from Chilgrove where he pulled up docks.
'Twere best, if he had had 'a money box',
To have waited there till the sheep cleared a field
For what a half-week's flint-picking would yield.
His mind was running on the work he had done
Since he left Christchurch in the New Forest, one
Spring in the 'seventies, – navvying on dock and line
From Southampton to Newcastle-on-Tyne, –
In 'seventy-four a year of soldiering
With the Berkshires, – hoeing and harvesting
In half the shires where corn and couch will grow . . .

This reported speech translates the living record of *The Bettesworth Book* into literature without intrusive patronage or interpretation, or approximation to the Georgian 'elegiac, neo-pastoral mode' of which Williams complains.[5] But in 'Lob' the professional features of the old countryman (apart from his proverbial childhood employment 'scaring sparrows'), as well as the personal, are deliberately minimised or non-specific, so that his symbolic transmigrations into place and flower names, proverb, folk-hero, 'tall Tom that bore/The logs in', may be smoothly achieved. And Lob is forceful even at his most fantastic:

He kept the hog that thought the butcher came
To bring his breakfast. 'You thought wrong', said Hob . . .

                    He too ground up the miller,
The Yorkshireman who ground men's bones for flour.

The hinted violence in these images also introduces a very contemporary awareness of the war, which becomes more explicit towards the end of the poem:

The man you saw . . .
Although he was seen dying at Waterloo,
Hastings, Agincourt, and Sedgemoor too, –
Lives yet. He never will admit he is dead
Till millers cease to grind men's bones for bread . . .

Although Thomas 'was seen dying' at Arras, having become 'One of the lords of No Man's Land', the parallels with Lob's career may indicate that his poetry 'lives yet' in a special sense: that it is a gesture not of despairing nostalgia, but of human and cultural assertion, made against the odds and in the nick of time, a Noah's ark transmitting essentials over the flood. If Owen warns, Thomas salvages.

Since I believe that the marshalling of English tradition in 'Lob' epitomises Thomas's position as a crucial missing link (missing because inadequately acknowledged) in the particular tradition of English poetry, I would like to suggest how it symbolises the very nature of a historical culture – indeed anticipates Williams's own investigations. Like Noah's ark, the poem is a cultural survival-kit, crystallising the aims of Thomas's anthology *This England*: 'I wished to make a book as full of English character and country as an egg is of meat.'[6] A number of his chosen poems and prose extracts furnished Thomas with sources and allusions for 'Lob', and a comment in his essay 'England' on *The Compleat Angler* (well represented) further illustrates its spirit:

> Since the war began I have not met so English a book, a book that filled me so with a sense of England, as this, though I have handled scores of deliberately patriotic works ... In Walton's book I touched the antiquity and sweetness of England – English fields, English people, English poetry, all together.[7]

The various threads of 'Lob' similarly interweave 'English fields, English people, English poetry' into a significant pattern. The first part of the poem lays down the primal connection between the old man and the earth, and thus the origin of all culture with man ('Old Adam Walker') in his environment, each beginning to leave an imprint on the other: 'A girl proposed Walker of Walker's Hill,/ "Old Adam Walker. Adam's Point you'll see/Marked on the maps"'. Lob is the genius of those flower, bird, and place names which at once humanise nature and naturalise man: 'Milkmaids', 'the Traveller's-joy', 'Jenny Pooter', 'Mother Dunch's Buttocks'. He is the flavour of proverb and idiom, that folk-poetry which combines the instincts of a people with the genius of their language: 'He first of all told someone else's wife,/For a farthing she'd skin a flint and spoil a knife/Worth sixpence skinning it'. Then Lob inhabits culture at its first stage of articulation, in folklore: 'While still/So young, our Jack was chief of Gotham's sages'. The squire's son recounts briefly the tales of 'The Princess of Canterbury', 'Lazy Jack', 'Jack the Giant-Killer', as well as that of the Shropshire cobbler's boy and the giant, which feeds back into landscape:

> The giant let fall from his spade
> The earth for damming Severn, and thus made
> The Wrekin hill; and little Ercall hill
> Rose where the giant scraped his boots.

Nor is the highest articulation of culture forgotten, while at the same time neither are its origins:

> This is tall Tom that bore
> The logs in, and with Shakespeare in the hall
> Once talked, when icicles hung by the wall.

'Lob' ends on a rhetorical flourish of naming which concentrates and accelerates all previous levels of allusion:

> Lob-lie-by-the-fire, Jack Cade,
> Jack Smith, Jack Moon, poor Jack of every trade,
> Young Jack, or old Jack, or Jack What-d'ye-call,
> Jack-in-the-hedge, or Robin-run-by-the-wall,
> Robin Hood, Ragged Robin, lazy Bob,
> One of the lords of No Man's Land, good Lob . . .

The speed of these transitions dramatises the flickering of Lob from history into literature (Jack Cade), from ordinary life into common linguistic usage ('Young Jack, or old Jack, or Jack What-d'ye-call', 'poor Jack of every trade'), from the countryside to its names ('Jack-in-the-hedge, or Robin-run-by-the-wall'). 'Robin Hood' too is a flower-name as well as the legendary outlaw, and 'One of the lords of No Man's Land' brings an English folk concept chillingly up to date. Williams characterises this passage and what follows as 'the casual figure of a dream of England, in which rural labour and rural revolt, foreign wars and internal dynastic wars, history, legend, and literature, are indiscriminately enfolded into a single emotional gesture. Lob or Lud, immemorial peasant or yeoman or labourer: the figure was now fixed and its name was Old England.'[8] Apart from the continued anti-poetic bias in favour of documentary, properly 'historical' approaches, if 'casual', 'indiscriminately' and 'emotional' are taken out, Williams has economically saluted Thomas's synthesis. Again, the figure is not 'fixed' but fluid (metamorphosis is the poem's message as well as its method), and its changing names brace 'Old England' for an unknown future and a long haul: 'Till millers cease . . .' 'Lob' defines and models, in a universal rather than vaguely 'timeless' sense, in a precisely inclusive rather than 'emotional' or 'dreaming' spirit, the cellular tissue of mutually reinforcing relationships that makes up any culture, supplies the foundations of any tradition.

In this definition of an organic culture Thomas approaches and exemplifies Yeats's belief that 'all art should be a Centaur finding in the popular lore its back and its strong legs'[9] (I shall return later to a technical aspect of this correspondence). For both, this was not so much a matter of going back to folk-art and lore, and confining their aesthetic within such limits, as going forward from them. Thomas, like Yeats, did not only see the modern poet as needing to get in touch with such sources, but the sophisticated artist in any age as completing and reflecting that process which springs 'Antaeus-like' from 'contact with the soil'. Thomas was always interested in the special intermediate, intermediary position of such writers as Clare, Burns, Jefferies, Cobbett and Davies on the road that leads to 'intricacies of form', to what Yeats called 'gradual Time's last gift':

> This country and its people was the subject of half [Jefferies's] work, and the background, the source, or the inspiration, of all but all the rest. He, in his turn, was the genius, the human expression, of this country, emerging from it, not to be detached from it any more than the curves of some statues from their maternal stone.[10]

> William Cobbett is the only Cobbett in the *Dictionary of National Biography*, but through him speak a thousand Cobbetts, too horny-handed to hold a pen, hairy, weather-stained, deep-chested yeomen and peasants . . .[11]

If the old man in 'Lob' is based on Thomas's Wiltshire friend, David Uzzell, the squire's son resembles that other Wiltshireman and formative influence, Richard Jefferies. Not only does Thomas credit Jefferies with similar robust ambiguities – 'sharing the sportsman's tenuous emotion of loving the hare that he has killed',[12] '[Jefferies] arose out of the earth, and he had its cruelty' –[13] but in his role as Lob's interpreter the squire's son 'expresses' to the poet, as Thomas felt Jefferies had done, 'part of [the] silence of uncounted generations'.[14] The poet-figure in the poem constitutes the final stage of the process so dramatically telescoped in the confrontation and communication between 'tall Tom' and Shakespeare. In *The Country* too Thomas collapses – collectivises? – the cultural span:

> When a poet writes, I believe he is often only putting into words what such another old man puzzled out among the sheep in a long lifetime.[15]

More personally, he writes of the ancestry that his own poetry was to distil, of the Welsh horizons complicating 'Englishness':

> the West calls, out of Wiltshire and out of Cornwall and Devon beyond, out of Monmouth and Glamorgan and Gower and Caermarthen, with a voice of dead Townsends, Eastaways, Thomases, Phillipses, Treharnes, Marendaz, sea men and mountain men.[16]

In 'Are You Content?' Yeats similarly rehearses *his* lineage (asking 'Have I that put it into words/Spoilt what old loins have sent?'):

> He that in Sligo at Drumcliff
> Set up the old stone Cross,
> That red-haired rector in County Down,
> A good man on a horse,
> Sandymount Corbets, that notable man
> Old William Pollexfen,
> The smuggler Middleton, Butlers far back,
> Half legendary men.

Such a view of the writer's inheritance, of tradition, essentially differs from that of T.S. Eliot in starting with people rather than with books, in taking in folk-museums on its way to the Louvre, in having as its basis and framework a regional or national rather than cosmopolitan context: 'I can never get out of my head that no man, even though he be Shakespeare, can write perfectly when his web is woven of threads that have been spun in many lands'.[17] '[Wordsworth] said . . . that this earth is "where we have our happiness or not at all". For most of those who speak his language he might have said that this England is where we have our happiness or not at all. He meant to say that we are limited creatures, not angels, and that our immediate surroundings are enough to exercise all our faculties of mind and body . . . Only the bad workman complains of his tools'.[18]

Nearer home, Thomas's efforts to harvest meaning from the English past, as provision for the uncertain future, associate him with an almost exact contemporary, E.M. Forster. It is easy to see the general coincidence between their preoccupations and symbols. *The Longest Journey*, like 'Lob' and the first chapter of *Richard Jefferies*, locates 'The Heart of England' (the title of a Thomas prose-work) in Wiltshire:

> Here is the heart of our island: the Chilterns, the North Downs, the South Downs radiate hence. The fibres of England unite in Wiltshire, and did we condescend to worship her, here we should erect our national shrine.[19]

The opening of Forster's next paragraph expresses a characteristic view of Thomas's, one that classically separates a Georgian from a Victorian or Edwardian sensibility:

> People at that time were trying to think imperially. Rickie wondered how they did it, for he could not imagine a place larger than England.[20]

I wonder how many others feel the same, that we have been robbed . . . of the small intelligible England of Elizabeth and given the word Imperialism instead. [Thomas][21]

Howards End, the 'converted farm', and its wych-elm are a symbolic stone's throw from Thomas's 'old Manor Farm':

> . . . But 'twas not Winter –
> Rather a season of bliss unchangeable
> Awakened from farm and church where it had lain
> Safe under tile and thatch for ages since
> This England, Old already, was called Merry.

Forster's Stephen Wonham, conceived as racy of the soil, is a Lob figure close to the squire's son level of incarnation (and significantly 'related' to Rickie):

> Though he could not phrase it, he believed that he guided the future of our race, and that, century after century, his thoughts and his passions would triumph in England. The dead who had evoked him, the unborn whom he would evoke – he governed the paths between them.[22]

Forster's 'phrasing', less discreetly foisted on to his creation, resembles Thomas's 'Does he keep clear old paths that no-one uses/ But once a lifetime when he loves or muses?', and in 'Words': 'Strange as the races/Of dead and unborn'.

What Thomas gains over Forster, or poetry over the novel, in suggestiveness, he does not necessarily lose in realistic assimilation of facts. His images of personal and social upheaval form a war poetry of the Home Front, complementing that of Wilfred Owen, which pits change against traditional patterns. 'As the Team's Head-Brass' dismembers literal and literary pastoral:

> 'Have you been out?' 'No.' 'And don't want to, perhaps?'
> 'If I could only come back again, I should.
> I could spare an arm. I shouldn't want to lose
> A leg. If I should lose my head, why, so,
> I should want nothing more . . . Have many gone
> From here?' 'Yes.' 'Many lost?' 'Yes, a good few.
> Only two teams work on the farm this year.
> One of my mates is dead. The second day
> In France they killed him. It was back in March,
> The very night of the blizzard, too. Now if
> He had stayed here we should have moved the tree.'
> 'And I should not have sat here. Everything
> Would have been different. For it would have been
> Another world.' 'Ay, and a better, though
> If we could see all all might seem good.'

Metrical patterns are upset here too. Thomas was indeed briefly commissioned by *The English Review* as a kind of Home Front correspondent, and in August 1914 'travelled through England, from Swindon to Newcastle-on-Tyne, listening to people, in railway carriages, trams, taverns, and public places, talking about the war and the effects of it'.[23] On the documentary ground-work of the resulting essays he gradually built up the newly urgent meaning of England to himself, finally blending the personal, the local, the national and the universal in a way that looks forward to the structural procedures of poems such as 'Adlestrop':

> I believe . . . that all ideas of England are developed, spun out, from such a centre into something large or infinite, solid or aery, according to each man's nature and capacity; that England is a system of vast circumferences circling round the minute neighbouring points of home.[24]

Real people – true poets – inhabit microcosmic parishes, not 'the word Imperialism'. Compare Patrick Kavanagh's essay, 'The Parish and the Universe':

> The parochial mentality . . . is never in any doubt about the social and artistic validity of his parish. All great civilisations are based on parochialism – Greek, Israelite, English.[25]

Thomas's concept of 'Home', 'one nationality', substitutes internal self-realisation for external self-assertion:

> Beside my hate for one fat patriot
> My hatred of the Kaiser is love true . . .

Similarly, 'One memory' gives natural, local, cultural history precedence over the political record. He enlisted to fight 'literally' for English earth.[26] His favourite 'war poem' was Coleridge's 'Fears in Solitude' which 'no newspaper or magazine, then or now [December 1914], would print . . . since a large part of it is humble'.[27] Symbolically ahead not only of Forster, but of English society today, Thomas's vision owes something to his profound understanding of Yeats and the Irish Literary Revival: '[Irish poets] sing of Ireland herself with an intimate reality, often missing from English poetry, where Britannia is a frigid personification.'[28] All Thomas's poetry exudes 'intimate reality', inverts the popular recipe of the day:

> The worst of the poetry being written today is that it is too deliberately, and not inevitably English. It is for an audience: there is more in it of the shouting of rhetorician, reciter, or politician than of the talk of friends and lovers.[29]

'The talk of friends and lovers' has foundations in true memory rather than in propagandised history. 'Does he keep clear old paths . . .?' Thomas's pursuit of Lob typifies a whole poetry of path-clearing and excavation into the personal and historical past, of penetration through 'bramble, thorn, and briar', 'hazel and thorn tangled with old-man's-beard', into overgrown lanes, combes, chalk pits, hollows, woods, forests and ruins, which convey perennial mysteries and terrors:

> Only the sound remains
> Of the old mill;
> Gone is the wheel;
> On the prone roof and walls the nettle reigns.
>
> Water that toils no more
> Dangles white locks
> And, falling, mocks
> The music of the mill-wheel's busy roar . . .
>
> Sometimes a thought is drowned
> By it, sometimes
> Out of it climbs;
> All thoughts begin or end upon this sound,
>
> Only the idle foam
> Of water falling
> Changelessly calling,
> Where once men had a work-place and a home.

In contrast with the emblematic 'safety' of 'The Manor Farm', presumably still 'a work-place and a home', 'The Mill-Water' concentrates Thomas's perception, reinforced by war, of how natural forces conspire with those of time to level human landmarks: 'prone . . . reigns'. The repeated 'Only' offers no escape from this recognition, while the freed water 'mocks' man's futile activity by parodying his attributes. 'Changelessly' reverses 'Unchangeable' in 'The Manor Farm'. (The contrast between the poems resembles that between *Howards End* and *A Passage to India*.) But Thomas's imaginative archaeology into the English countryside is in any case finally a metaphor and a myth for processes by which, in understanding our origins and dark avenues, we might discover ourselves. A chapter in *The South Country*, 'History and the Parish', illuminates his belief in a rounded, ultimately poetic approach to history-through-geography, and his pioneering ecological philosophy:

The peculiar combination of soil and woodland and water determines the direction and position and importance of the ancient trackways; it will determine also the position and size of the human settlements. The early marks of these – the old flint and metal implements, the tombs, the signs of agriculture, the encampments, the dwellings – will have to be clearly described and interpreted. Folk-lore, legend, place-names must be learnedly, but bravely and humanly used, so that the historian who has not the extensive sympathy and imagination of a great novelist will have no chance of success . . . In some places history has wrought like an earthquake, in others like an ant or mole; everywhere, permanently; so that if we but knew or cared, every swelling of the grass, every wavering line of hedge or path or road were an inscription, brief as an epitaph, in many languages and characters.[30]

Thomas was himself exceptionally equipped to read the language of landmarks, decipher 'inscriptions' and palimpsests, reconstruct lives from relics like nettle-covered roofs and walls, a clay pipe, 'fragments of blue plates': to expose in an exploded view the layers of human settlement and sediment we stand on, psychologically as well as physically.

2.

If landscape is a language, language may signify a landscape, and Thomas's approach to his medium is also based on an uncovering of historical foundations. A neglected observation in Yeats's introduction to his *Oxford Book of Modern Verse* runs: 'Folk-song, unknown to the Victorians as their attempts to imitate it show, must, because never declamatory or eloquent, fill the scene. If anybody will turn these pages attending to poets born in the 'fifties, 'sixties, and 'seventies, he will find how successful are their folk-songs and their imitations.'[31] Yeats and Thomas shared the belief that folk-song, in accordance with the Centaur view of culture, could provide powerful hindquarters for a complex literary art. Thomas, who preferred '"All round my hat" . . . to Beethoven',[32] affirms in *The Heart of England* that 'of all music, the old ballads and folk songs and their airs are richest in the plain, immortal symbols . . . They are in themselves epitomes of whole generations, of a whole countryside. They are the quintessence of many lives and passions made into a sweet cup for posterity.'[33] (Thus they represent literary distillation at a stage before Jefferies.) He also speculated: 'Can [the recovery of old ballads] possibly give a vigorous impulse to a new school of poetry that shall treat the life of our time and what in past times has most meaning for us as freshly as those ballads did the life of their time?'[34] This sense of again going forward rather than back, of how the energies of folk-poetry might be *harnessed* like hydro-electricity, corresponds to Yeats's attitude in correcting Katharine Tynan: 'I do not mean that we should not go to old ballads and poems for inspiration, but we should search them for new methods of expressing ourselves.'[35] Just as Yeats's rhythms quickened with 'Down by the Salley Gardens' and 'The Stolen Child', so among the earliest poems Thomas wrote, when he was at last finding the true method of 'expressing himself', are two given the same title, 'An Old Song'. More empirically than essays on 'Tradition and the Individual Talent', these poems uncover the traditional roots of personal utterance. Thomas's brand-new song takes off 'delightedly' from some very well-worn cadences:

> For if I am contented, at home or anywhere,
> Or if I sigh for I know not what, or my heart beats with some fear,
> It is a strange kind of delight to sing or whistle just:
> 'Oh, 'tis my delight of a shiny night in the season of the year'.

Writing to Eleanor Farjeon about this poem, Thomas spells out the 'vigorous impulse': 'I don't think "to whistle and to sing" which is formally correct is as good. If I am consciously doing anything I am trying to get rid of the last rags of rhetoric and formality which left my prose so often with a dead rhythm only.'[36] Written the next day (26 December 1914), Thomas's second 'Old Song' dramatises the discovery of poetic vocation, the writing of a poem, as happening on a 'bridge' between celestial summons and cultural hinterland, between the light of inspiration and a haunting air:

> A light divided the swollen clouds
> And lay most perfectly
> Like a straight narrow footbridge bright
> That crossed over the sea to me;
> And no one else in the whole world
> Saw that same sight.
>
> I walked elate, my bridge always
> Just one step from my feet:
> A robin sang, a shade in shade:
> And all I did was to repeat:
> 'I'll go no more a-roving
> With you, fair maid.'

Remarkably, Thomas first set down that symbol of lyrical self-expression in the 1901 review which prophesied the prosperity of the lyric: 'Everyone must have noticed, standing on the shore, when the sun or the moon is over the sea, how the highway of light on the water comes right to his feet, and how those on the right and on the left seem not to be sharing his pleasure, but to be in darkness.'[37] In 'An Old Song' art's substance, as well as its summons, is once again inseparable from Nature:

> The sailors' song of merry loving
> With dusk and sea-gull's mewing
> Mixed sweet . . .

'The Gallows', written later in Thomas's poetic career and closer to his departure for the trenches, signals – as does Yeats's *Words for Music Perhaps* – the continuing need for the Antaeus of style to recharge its batteries by contact with a mode only one step away from the spoken word in origin and transmission:

> There was a weasel lived in the sun
> With all his family,
> Till a keeper shot him with his gun
> And hung him up on a tree,
> Where he swings in the wind and rain,
> In the sun and in the snow,
> Without pleasure, without pain,
> On the dead oak tree bough.

This gallows-humour, like 'One of the lords of No Man's Land', starkly renews folk-idiom to characterise the war. A month before enlisting, Thomas wrote to Frost about Rupert Brooke: 'those sonnets about him enlisting are probably not very personal but a nervous attempt to connect with himself the very widespread idea that self-sacrifice is the highest self indulgence . . . I daren't say so, not having enlisted or fought the keeper.'[38] (Frost, when living in Gloucestershire at 'The Gallows', had been harassed by 'a bad gamekeeper'.) Whereas the first 'Old Song' includes the line 'Since then I've thrown away a chance to fight a gamekeeper', 'The Gallows' un-selfindulgently confronts the 'keeper' (ironic abbreviation) whose habits suggest the grim reaper in France:

> And many other beasts
> And birds, skin, bone, and feather,
> Have been taken from their feasts
> And hung up there together,
> To swing and have endless leisure . . .

Thomas's interest in folk-song and other rhymes is only part of a whole stylistic principle and practice based on going 'back . . .

60

through the paraphernalia of poetry into poetry again'[39] to a state of linguistic innocence in which word and idiom would be as fresh as when Lob first coined his proverbs, and as physically involved with human life as Cobbett's prose: 'a bodily thing . . . perhaps the nearest to speech that has really survived'.[40] And an ear for sentence-sounds begins (but does not end) with attention to the phrasing and cadence of rural speech, or speech at its least self-conscious. Thomas told his brother that he wished to make his later prose 'as near akin as possible to the talk of a Surrey peasant'; on which Julian Thomas comments: 'He was thinking, no doubt, of George Sturt's Bettesworth'.[41] The talk of the old countryman early in 'Lob' provides a ground-bass for the poem:

> All he said was: 'Nobody can't stop 'ee. It's
> A footpath, right enough. You see those bits
> Of mounds – that's where they opened up the barrows
> Sixty years since, while I was scaring sparrows.
> They thought as there was something to find there,
> But couldn't find it, by digging, anywhere.'

Such idiomatic force, overriding and revivifying metre, mocking conventional notions of rhyme (It's, bits), passes without a jar into the more elaborate utterance of the poet and the squire's son. In 'Man and Dog' conversational and other interchange between 'peasant' and poet, the poet listening, is located more precisely in history:

> 'No rabbit, never fear, she ever got,
> Yet always hunts. Today she nearly had one:
> She would and she wouldn't. 'Twas like that. The bad one!
> She's not much use, but still she's company,
> Though I'm not. She goes everywhere with me.
> So Alton I must reach tonight somehow:
> I'll get no shakedown with that bedfellow
> From farmers. Many a man sleeps worse tonight
> Than I shall.' 'In the trenches.' 'Yes, that's right . . .'

By interweaving three kinds of speech – countryman's, poet's, poet reporting the countryman – the poem as a whole lays bare the linguistic layers under complex soliloquies like 'Rain'. In accordance with their different aims, talk roughs up the couplets of 'Man and Dog' more thoroughly than those of 'Lob', as if the former poem specifically makes room for experience and language Williams would see English pastoral as excluding. The blank verse of 'As the Team's Head-Brass', another dialogue with a spokesman for the receding past, bears similar stretch-marks. By the end of 'Man and Dog' Thomas has placed different orders of language as well as Nature (man-robin-leaves) within a vision still tinged by change and war ('the twilight of the wood'). The poem remains faithful to the authenticities of the man's speech, and to the history it narrates and manifests, in completing a powerful symbol:

> Stiffly he plodded;
> And at his heels the crisp leaves scurried fast,
> And the leaf-coloured robin watched. They passed,
> The robin till next day, the man for good,
> Together in the twilight of the wood.

What local speech is to total self-articulation — origin and epitome — traditional idioms and proverbs are to the diction and imagery of poetry. Using the similes 'sweet as any nut', 'welcome as the nightingale', as if he had invented them, Thomas calls attention to the freshness of his own inventions:

> The swift with wings and tail as sharp and narrow
> As if the bow had flown off with the arrow.
>
> ('Haymaking')

Or again, his naming of birds, flowers, and places confirms, through sensitive orchestration of sound, the rightness of Lob's original baptism:

> Thrush, blackbird, all that sing in May,
> And songless plover
> Hawk, heron, owl, and woodpecker
>
> Harebell and scabious and tormentil
>
> If I should ever by chance grow rich
> I'll buy Codham, Cockridden, and Childerditch,
> Roses, Pyrgo, and Lapwater . . .

Sometimes Thomas ponders the 'reasons of his own' that lie behind Lob's choice: 'Old Man, or Lad's-love . . .', sometimes he invents a mythic etymology ('Bob's Lane') or gives his own reasons for investing a name with a nimbus of associations: 'Yes. I remember Adlestrop —/ The name, because . . .' Indeed, Thomas has effectively 'named' Adlestrop, because no one who has read the poem can ever separate the place from it.

The power of 'Words', the primary units of utterance, is determined by still more mysterious pedigrees:

I know you:
You are light as dreams,
Tough as oak,
Precious as gold,
As poppies and corn,
Or an old cloak:
Sweet as our birds
To the ear,
As the burnet rose
In the heat
Of Midsummer . . .
And familiar,
To the eye,
As the dearest faces
That a man knows,
And as lost homes are . . .

Thomas's relishing of words' lightness, toughness, preciousness and sweetness not only asserts but enacts their blood-relationship with the physical environment, and consequent capacity to reproduce every kind of sensuous response to it. That aural and other associations link 'Sweet . . . birds . . burnet . . . heat . . . Midsummer' guarantees the more intangible interactions also implied. Later, he calls words 'as dear/ As the earth which you prove/ That we love'. Thomas mimics birdsong, from 'the cooing in the alder/ Isles of the pool' to 'The speculating rooks at their nests cawed'; paints 'a picture of an old grange' ('Haymaking'); and (most difficult of all) makes us hear smell and touch: 'Odours that rise/ When the spade wounds the root of tree,/ Rose, currant, raspberry, or goutweed,/ Rhubarb or celery' ('Digging'). These sounds marry the thrusting of the spade to the sudden pungency of the released scents. His poetry typically 'gathers sight and sound' ('The Brook'), 'tastes deep the hour' ('Sowing'), and scrambles or fuses the senses: 'feel the light', 'tasted sunlight' ('The Other'). It emphasises how the life of the senses pervades all our life: 'Today I think/ Only with scents' ('Digging'), 'the wild rose scent that is like memory' ('The Word'). Thomas's respect for the physical life of words, as well as helping him to restore their metaphysical life, enabled him to reintroduce into English poetry perhaps the most complete sensuous texture since Keats:

'Twas the first day that the midges bit;
But though they bit me, I was glad of it:
Of the dust in my face, too, I was glad.
Spring could do nothing to make me sad.
Bluebells hid all the ruts in the copse,
The elm seeds lay in the road like hops . . .

('May the Twenty-third')

In *George Borrow* Thomas observes: 'Life itself is fleeting, but words remain and are put to our account. Every action, it is true, is as old as man and never perishes without an heir. But so are words as old as man, and they are conservative and stern in their treatment of transitory life . . . A new form of literature cannot be invented to match the most grand or most lovely life. And fortunately; for if it could, one more proof of the ancient lineage of our life would have been lost.'[42] The poem's plea 'Choose me,/ You English words' similarly salutes words as repositories of an inherent or inherited meaning which joins 'dead and unborn'. It is the poet's task – again perhaps urgent as never before – to unlock and replenish this treasury by finding the right combinations:

> But though older far
> Than oldest yew, –
> As our hills are, old, –
> Worn new
> Again and again:
> Young as our streams
> After rain . . .

Poetry thus becomes not an 'intolerable wrestle/ With words and meanings', but rather a form of judicious judo whereby a slight pressure in the right place can release enormous energies. The paradox 'Worn new' itself brilliantly revitalises a cliché. The English language indeed seems unusually 'at home' in Edward Thomas's poetry, which argues a special understanding between the poet and its historical genius. Praising 'Lob', Frost told Thomas: 'I never saw anything like you for English.'[43] 'Words' itself, like much of Thomas's poetry, does not range far beyond the Anglo-Saxon or Anglo-Norman, minimises the Latinate and abstract. Like Herbert, he can load with resonance the simplest value-terms: 'dear', 'sweet', 'strange', 'familiar'. He can make the most familiar words strange, whether by repeating 'rain', by moving through the degrees of the adjective 'old', by reminding us what 'nothing' consists of, by completing the weave of prophecy and retrospect in 'The New House' with an exact shuttle of tenses and moods (which also functions as internal rhyme):

> All was foretold me; naught
>   Could I foresee;
> But I learned how the wind would sound
>   After these things should be.

Here divinatory sound runs ahead of events. Between ruined mill and new house, words too are 'lost homes' to be excavated and reinhabited. Then, 'Worn new', the landscape of language may become 'Young as our streams/ After rain'. The freshened streams of Thomas's own poetry, defying contemporary and subsequent prophets of cultural and linguistic breakdown, everywhere demonstrate that, through continuous fertilisation by 'life and weather', and by the living and spoken word, language and tradition can indeed be 'Worn new/ Again and again'. As caretaker of the English language (that ultimate responsibility of and for Lob) Thomas kept clear its historical paths and cut away the Victorian dead wood and overgrowth that obscured the way forward. He undoubtedly injected a transfusion of 'old Jack's blood' into the hardening arteries of Edwardian/Georgian poetry.

The transfusion was rhythmic as well as verbal. The movement of Thomas's poetry helps to give his sentence-sounds an English ring, as compared with Frost's American accents or Yeats's rhetorical beat. Thomas's distinctive revitalisation of traditional forms has roots both in folk-song and in his historical sense of English metres. This enabled him, as early as 1902, to call the old 'system of prosody . . . ridiculous' and blank verse 'an infinitely varied line usually of ten syllables'.[44] Once again spanning first principles and ultimates, his poetry moves from 'to sing or whistle just' to 'intricacies of form as numerous and as exquisite as those of a birch-tree in the wind'.[45] I suggest in the previous essay that Thomas goes still further than Frost in reconciling the flexibilities of blank verse with lyrical concentration. This opens up a wide range of metrical possibilities, multiplied by his gradations between rhyme, off-rhyme and assonance. 'October' (discussed below) can postpone a rhyme for eight lines – 'gold'/'scold' frames the arrested scene – or relax into a resolving final couplet. Like 'Rain', it's almost a sonnet, writ large and new. Thomas's couplets deserve a study in themselves: their appropriately Chaucerian timbre in 'Lob' ('And in a tender mood he, as I guess,/ Christened one flower Love-in-idleness'); their conversational disturbance in 'Man and Dog'; their texture in 'May the Twenty-third' or 'Haymaking' ('The smooth white empty road was lightly strewn/ With leaves – the holly's Autumn falls in June'); their epigrammatic point in 'Liberty' ('There's none less free than who/ Does nothing and has nothing else to do'). But Thomas's formal 'intricacy' leaps most rapidly to the eye from a survey of his stanzaic poems, where his power to realise the character of line and stanza again invites comparison with Herbert. He employs stanzas varying from four to ten lines with regular or irregular line-lengths and rhyme-schemes; experiments with internal and consonantal rhyme; rhymes a poem or stanza on one sound; shrinks the line of 'Words' from six to two syllables; swells towards fourteeners, allied to folk-song, in 'The Gipsy':

> While his mouth-organ changed to a rascally Bacchanal dance
> 'Over the hills and far away.' This and his glance
> Outlasted all the fair, farmer, and auctioneer,
> Cheap-jack, balloon-man, drover with crooked stick, and steer . . .

The virtuosity of Thomas's quatrains particularly outlasts the fair. Unlike Hardy, he never prefabricates a form or rhythmically repeats himself. The last two stanzas of 'The Mill-Water' vary an already original form, while also implying the mimetic dimension of Thomas's formal, as of his other, inspiration:

> Sometimes a thought is drowned
> By it, sometimes
> Out of it climbs;
> All thoughts begin or end upon this sound,
>
> Only the idle foam
> Of water falling
> Changelessly calling,
> Where once men had a work-place and a home.

The repetition of 'sometimes' on a rhyming word emphasises a contrary upward movement, out of oblivion, until the quatrain 'ends' as it 'began' with the length and rhyme of the last line reasserting the sound's supremacy. The feminine rhyme 'falling'/'calling' continues the rhythm by echoing the sound. It stresses the indifference of Nature no longer harnessed by man, until the final line no longer harnesses the sound of water. The poet bleakly liberates his ear and imagination from subjection to an ominous 'call'.

At times Thomas pares his quatrains down to the absolute minimum, as in 'Interval' and 'Gone, Gone Again', which commence in a deceptively similar fashion:

> Gone the wild day:
> A wilder night
> Coming makes way
> For brief twilight.
>
> Where the firm soaked road
> Mounts and is lost
> In the high beech-wood
> It shines almost.

> Gone, gone again,
> May, June, July,
> And August gone,
> Again gone by,
>
> Not memorable
> Save that I saw them go,
> As past the empty quays
> The rivers flow.

In the first stanza of 'Interval' syntax and rhythm clear a space for the lull between 'wild day' and 'wilder night'. The chiasmus 'Gone . . . wild . . . wilder . . . Coming', with its threatening shift in the form of verb and adjective, seems complete until 'makes way' gives rise to a different balancing movement. The second stanza follows up this harmony by swinging its major stresses from the end of one line to the beginning of another and by maintaining a fluent self-contained syntax. This swaying balance, appropriate to the 'stormy rest' recorded in 'Interval', is replaced in 'Gone, Gone Again' by a monotonously serial progress. Thomas crams the maximum dull repetition of word and sound into the first stanza. 'Not memorable' paradoxically jolts with its polysyllabic and rhythmical exoticism before inert depression is sealed by an image that fixes the character of the poem's 'flow'.

The action of water is differently heard in the movement of 'Gone, Gone Again', 'Interval', 'The Mill-Water', 'Rain', and many other poems. Innumerable natural phenomena and processes leave similar sound-tracks, from the directly onomatopoeic to unobtrusive trace-elements. Identifying Thomas's sensibility with a tree, 'Aspens' both practises mimesis and interprets its role in his aesthetic:

> Over all sorts of weather, men, and times,
> Aspens must shake their leaves and men may hear
> But need not listen, more than to my rhymes.
>
> Whatever wind blows, while they and I have leaves
> We cannot other than an aspen be
> That ceaselessly, unreasonably grieves,
> Or so men think who like a different tree.

Form is crucial to this redefinition of the Romantic poet's Aeolian lyre, in which Thomas once more uncannily fulfils his 1901 prophecy. Exploring relations between the lyric imagination and 'all sorts of weather, men, and times', he evokes an aspen 'in the wind' to dramatise the poet's sensitive receivers and transmitters. The metre, veering between iambic and trisyllabic stress patterns, interacts with the syntactical pull between statement and qualification to create a demeanour of active receptivity, a tone of quiet confidence. It is the rhythms, not the surface content, of poetry which determine whether it will survive 'all sorts of weather, men, and times'. 'Aspens' may say this too. Just as 'The whisper of the aspens is not drowned' in the poem itself, its music persisting in 'ceaselessly, unreasonably', so Thomas's formal assurance prevails over his doubts about an audience. By combining the strengths of speech, song and Nature, his rhythms reanimated English metre.

3.

Thomas's clinching qualification for the position of 'missing link' is that no *English* poet so completely worked his way through and out of the moribund modes of the nineteenth century. His prose exhibits the same kind of stylistic development as Yeats's poetry. His criticism, culminating in the studies of Swinburne (1912) and Pater (1913), continued and redirected Yeats's quarrel with the Victorians. (Earlier than Yeats, he quarrelled with the nineties too.) Swinburne, in every respect Thomas's anti-self, bore the brunt of his assault on the poetic left-overs of Romanticism. Thomas dismisses 'A Channel Passage' as 'a man being poetical on a steamer',[46] notes that 'Swinburne's style touches actual detail only at its peril',[47] and that 'rhyme certainly acted upon Swinburne as a pill to purge ordinary responsibilities'.[48] He is most fundamentally infuriated by Swinburne's separation of sound from meaning: 'Other poets tend towards a grace and glory of words as of human speech perfected and made divine, Swinburne towards a musical jargon that includes human snatches, but is not and never could be speech.'[49] Thomas detected the opposite dissociation in *verse* of the Kipling-Watson-Newbolt school.

Thomas's own poetry reunited music and speech. But even after he had wrung the neck of his Romanticism, first in prose, then in poetry, he gave it occasional exorcisms. 'Sedge-Warblers' and 'The Chalk Pit' affirm the same aesthetic conversion, or conversion from aestheticism, as Yeats's 'A Coat', written three years previously. In 'Sedge-Warblers' the 'poison' of an early Keatsian reverie or 'dream', invoking a 'time/ Long past and irrecoverable' and 'a nymph whose soul unstained/ Could love all day, and never hate or tire', receives its antidote in the poet's decision to keep his eye on the object: 'So that I only looked into the water,/ Clearer than any goddess or man's daughter.' One speaker in the second poem is a man being poetical in a chalk pit: 'I prefer to make a tale,/ Or better leave it like the end of a play . . .' The more realistic voice, closer to Thomas's real voice, rejects the 'fancies' spawned by this vocabulary of art. The poem ends with his counter-preference for 'truth' and 'fact':

> 'I should prefer the truth
> Or nothing. Here in fact is nothing at all
> Except a silent place that once rang loud,
> And trees and us – imperfect friends, we men
> And trees since time began; and nevertheless
> Between us still we breed a mystery.'

In contrast with Swinburne's mere 'appearance of precision',[50] both poems emphasise the necessity to *see* clearly, without the haze of Romantic dream or fancy. The speaker to whose viewpoint and voice 'The Chalk Pit' gives that last word, allies the pit with a perceiver (akin to Thomas himself) able to return the gaze of Nature as it is: 'The wren's hole was an eye that looked at him/ For recognition'. 'Sedge-Warblers', in keeping with its subject, purifies the ear as well as the eye. Singing 'longer than the lark', that Romantic bird, the birds' unmusical music supplies yet another model of how poetry should adjust its sounds to the qualities of Nature:

> Quick, shrill, or grating, a song to match the heat
> Of the strong sun, nor less the water's cool,
> Gushing through narrows, swirling in the pool.
> Their song that lacks all words, all melody,
> All sweetness almost . . .

Thomas does use without irony words like 'vain' (useless), 'fast-pent', 'naught', 'vale'; phrases like 'the loveliness of prime', 'Wrought magic' – risky, even if a poem goes on to subvert them. But while these words may not always live as do his others, their half-life in his poetry again exemplifies its contact and continuity with Wordsworth, Keats and later nineteenth-century poets.

Even in correcting their Romanticism, 'Sedge-Warblers' and 'The Chalk Pit', constructed as inner dialogues, recognise that what had been an imaginative phase for Thomas, remains an imaginative dimension. The plain-speaker in 'The Chalk Pit' slyly moves from 'truth' to 'mystery' by playing on 'nothing' as does 'Old Man'. Like Yeats, Thomas preserved some attributes of earlier Romantic poetry, while discarding the mannerisms of decadence. Or rather, the dialectic of both poets continuously tests Romantic aspirations in the light of modern experience (whereas Hardy wrote elegies for them). Yeats principally tests the claims of Imagination, Thomas those of visionary Nature. 'The Other' sets a pattern for Thomas's poetry in that Romantic 'Desire of desire' is chastened to an agnostic, empirical quest, yet remains latent within it ('I dare not follow after/Too close'). Similarly, the residual 'And yet' at the end of 'Liberty' indicates a reluctance to break the last links with Romanticism. The luxurious extremism of 'Ode to a Nightingale' lingers in the rhythm, tone, and not quite matter-of-fact acceptance of the world as it is:

And yet I still am half in love with pain,
With what is imperfect, with both tears and mirth,
With things that have an end, with life and earth,
And this moon that leaves me dark within the door.

As a critic Thomas never let contemporary fashions cloud his devotion to Blake and Shelley, as well as Wordsworth and Keats. Thus he argues against Arthur Symons's view of the 'Romantic Movement', a view governed by the fact 'that in this critic's composition the literary aesthete is too predominant still, as at one time it was supreme'.[51] Thomas deplores Symons's eagerness to scissor 'Tintern Abbey' ('we have to unravel the splendours and if we can forget the rest'),[52] his 'revival and extension of Poe's opinion that there could be no such thing as a long poem'.[53]

Thomas's own absorption of the Romantic Movement, as opposed to a taste for edited highlights, is travestied by P.N. Furbank's description of 'October' as poetry which is 'derivative in a bad way – that is to say the poet does not know how derivative he is being':[54]

The green elm with the one great bough of gold
Lets leaves into the grass slip, one by one, –
The short hill grass, the mushrooms small, milk-white,
Harebell and scabious and tormentil,
That blackberry and gorse, in dew and sun,
Bow down to; and the wind travels too light
To shake the fallen birch leaves from the fern;
The gossamers wander at their own will.
At heavier steps than birds' the squirrels scold.
The rich scene has grown fresh again and new
As Spring and to the touch is not more cool
Than it is warm to the gaze; and now I might
As happy be as earth is beautiful,
Were I some other or with earth could turn
In alternation of violet and rose,
Harebell and snowdrop, at their season due,
And gorse that has no time not to be gay.
But if this be not happiness, – who knows?
Some day I shall think this a happy day,
And this mood by the name of melancholy
Shall no more blackened and obscured be.

Furbank, records his 'impression . . . that there are several well-known passages from Wordsworth and Keats lurking behind ['October']': Keats's evocation of stillness in 'Hyperion': 'No stir of air was there,/ Not so much life as on a summer's day/ Robs not one light seed from the feather'd grass,/ But where the dead leaf fell, there did it rest', Wordsworth's line in the 'Westminster Bridge' sonnet: 'The river glideth at his own sweet will', the last stanza of 'A slumber did my spirit seal': 'Rolled round in earth's diurnal course,/ With rocks, and stones, and trees'.[55] Steeped in English poetry, whose living trail can be glimpsed in unobtrusive allusions throughout his work, Thomas certainly knew (as much as T.S. Eliot) just 'how derivative he was being'. How then do the Keatsian and Wordsworthian echoes – the retrospect this time on the 'Ode to Autumn' as well as 'Ode to a Nightingale' – justify themselves?

The images of the wind and the gossamers are first of all not random sense-impressions but play their part in a skilfully paced and orchestrated movement. Perceived and perceiver blend, without either losing identity, in an autumnal landscape more integrated, more intimate, and more minutely psychological than that of Keats. It is as if Keats's generalised 'mellow fruitfulness' has been pruned and pressed to particularise a sensibility. Thomas's first line, in contrast to Keats's, prepares for an insistence on the individual components of the scene. 'One by one' picks up 'one great bough of gold' and narrows our sights from tree to leaf, while helping to emphasise that this splendour is a bonus of decay. Thomas goes on to give full weight to the kind of insignificant feature he habitually rescues from obscurity: 'The short hill grass, the mushrooms small, milk-white'. Not an adjective is wasted here, and the next line dispenses with them entirely: 'Harebell and scabious and tormentil'. In his short book on Keats, where he regards the Odes as a *summa*, a model for the future lyric ('the poet made for himself a form in which the essence of all his thought, feeling, and observation, could be stored without overflowing or disorder'),[56] Thomas points out:

> [The ode 'To a Nightingale'] and the ode 'On a Grecian Urn' are of a texture so consummate and consistent that the simple line, 'The grass, the thicket, and the fruit-tree wild', in one of them, and an equally simple line in the other, 'With forest branches, and the trodden weed' both gain from their environment an astonishing beauty, profound and touching.[57]

Thomas's own apparently simple naming achieves the same effect. The impact of the flower names, whose richness adds to the wealth implied by 'bough of gold', depends on the finest gradations of sound, the mutation of the broad 'a' between 'harebell' and 'scabious', the repeated 'b', the luscious 's's of 'scabious', and the off-rhyming of the first and last syllables of 'harebell' and 'tormentil' (the 'l' sounds connecting somehow with the touch of 'coolness' in

71

the scene) as they frame the central self-alliterating name. The next three lines, again with no excess baggage, introduce further precisely recorded vegetation: blackberry, gorse, birch, fern; and three kinds of weather: dew, sun, wind. The gossamers more emphatically maintain their individuality, assisted both by the syntactical independence of the line, and by the way our ear is cheated of the expected Wordsworthian unstressed syllable. Thomas's altogether more irregular and mimetic pentameter fits this waywardness. The wind 'travelling . . . light', with its disguised pun, suggests free movement as well as a Keatsian stillness.

All this autonomy of course takes place within a harmony: not just a succinctly complete evocation of flora, fauna, weather and season, but a co-operative system of natural relations in which it seems that some tacit conspiracy is preserving each component, preventing the 'fall' from being too sudden, and holding together a temporary truce between summer and winter ('Lets . . . slip', 'Bow down', 'travels too light'). Relevance to the human element, before the 'first person' appears separately in the poem, becomes clearer in the one-sentence line: 'At heavier steps than birds' the squirrels scold.' Three kinds of sound, three orders of existence are related and differentiated, as the noise of the squirrels paradoxically disturbs the stillness whose disruption they attack. The structural break here too reflects the special difficulty of continuously integrating man's or poet's consciousness (now exposed as intrusive) into a natural union, which will only break down as part of a larger harmony ('alternation of violet and rose'). This problem is further dramatised by some striking features in the syntax of the second part of the poem. The symmetrical comparison, 'and to the touch is not more cool/ Than it is warm to the gaze', which epitomises the poise of the scene and the seasons, is parodied by the partially failed symmetry and simile of 'and now I might/ As happy be as earth is beautiful'. The poem's most concentrated summary of the organic cycle of the year: 'or with earth could turn/ In alternation of violet and rose,/ Harebell and snowdrop, at their season due' is a further symmetry of structure and rhythm (emphasised by the 'turning' of one line on the hinge of internal rhyme and the chiasmus in the placing of the flower-names), towards which the surrounding subjunctives and rhetorical question wistfully aspire. Thomas's final provisional sketch of an alteration in perspective, which might constitute a complex equivalent of seasonal 'alternation', gains in confidence as it modulates from future tense to a virtually imperative mood and into a couplet whose rhythm hints at spring.

'October' should be read not as pastiche, but as Thomas's fullest inspection of the Romantic poets' legacy. Indeed the elm itself might symbolise that tradition and the poems that 'slip' from it. Like Frost's 'The Most of It', the poem may also hint at successive poetic periods: the Chaucerian poet who 'with earth could turn', the successful Romantic ('some other') and Thomas's own negotiations for a new imaginative contract with Nature. Accordingly, 'October' explores some of the untapped implications of 'earth's diurnal course': the role of man within but distinct from Nature, which still offers beauty, as it did to Wordsworth, but can no longer substitute for religion. Thomas's poetry agnostically stiffens his favourite quotation from Wordsworth (in the 1804 poem on the French Revolution): 'the very world', 'earth' in Thomas's versions, is 'the place where in the end/ We find our happiness, or not at all'. Romanticism can go no further than the intrinsic 'mystery' of 'men/ And trees' or 'things that have an end'. And if Thomas refines Wordsworth philosophically, he also redefines Keats psychologically. Hence his capacity to shift the meaning of the mood Keats made his own, or to complicate his categories of melancholy and happiness. He did write one very Keatsian poem called 'Melancholy': 'The rain and wind, the rain and wind, raved endlessly'. But its Romantic self-indulgence, of which Thomas shows his awareness by ironic references to a 'cuckoo' and 'dulcimers', throws into relief the subtler depression or despair in 'Rain' and 'Gone, Gone Again':

> I am something like that;
> Only I am not dead,
> Still breathing and interested
> In the house that is not dark: –
>
> I am something like that:
> Not one pane to reflect the sun,
> For the schoolboys to throw at –
> They have broken every one.

Furbank's disparagement of 'October' as 'less a spontaneous response to the natural scene than a comfortable "literary" reverie'[58] (whereas it astonishingly fuses 'response' with some uncomfortable literary criticism) appears all the more surprising when compared with his admiration of Pound and Eliot for 'raiding the past without compunction, appropriating whatever appealed to them'.[59] He appreciates smash-and-grab tactics, but not legitimate inheritance and redeployment. Modernism, in poetry mainly an American phenomenon, should not be taken as covering, even if it took over, the British Isles. Modernism of the Pound-Eliot variety was in a sense *impossible* to Yeats, Thomas, or Owen for the reasons Stephen Spender adduces:

> No European ever treated the traditional in quite [Eliot's] way, as though the dead stood up like spirit-statues with arms folded and looked down on the living, putting them in their places and reminding them of their inferiority . . . To him the past is the dead pressing down on the consciousness of the living; and every past, in being realised through that consciousness, is contemporaneous with every other past. But to the European the traditional is like memory, a continuous chain of events of which the most recent is the nearest to the person who remembers . . . If the European (viewing the tradition as emerging in a continuous line out of the past and himself as at the end of it) feels that the point of the line on which he finds himself is exhausted, then he travels back, as it were, along the line and finds a place on it where he feels a still energising current.[60]

Robert Frost was an external 'energising current'. But Thomas's poetry also represents a culmination of travels back and forwards along the line of English country writing from Jefferies to White; back and forwards along the line of English poetry from 'hawthorn-time' to Hardy. 'Lob', which quotes from Hardy as well as from Chaucer and Shakespeare, implies all this, together with Thomas's consequent power to symbolise historical transition.

Just before he wrote his first poems, Thomas ended a dismissive survey of recent war poetry ('the courage to write for oblivion') by praising Hardy's

> impersonal song [presumably 'Men Who March Away'] which seems to me the best of the time, as it is the least particular and occasional. He may write even better yet. I should also expect the work of other real poets to improve as the war advances, perhaps after it is over, as they understand it and themselves more completely.[61]

Thomas was to pre-empt this process, perhaps because the Muse, like fortune, favours the prepared. When Frost said that his friend's poems 'ought to be called Roads to France'[62] he recognised a literature of unusually deep preparation. Thomas's preparation went beyond his share in Blake's 'settled mystic patriotism, which wars could not disturb',[63] or in Coleridge's 'inevitably English' sensibility:

> There lives nor form nor feeling in my soul
> Unborrowed from my country!

The dark side of his vision foreknew the trenches, as he knew a changing England and English literature. After arriving in France he wrote to Julian: 'War, of course, is not altogether different from peace, except that one may be blown to bits and have to blow others to bits . . . Death looms, but however it comes it is unexpected, whether from appendicitis or bullet. An alternation of comfort and discomfort is always a man's lot . . . I have suffered more from January to March in other years than in this.'[64] More apocalyptically, something in his imagination was called or 'bemused' (pun?) 'by the roar and hiss/ And by the mighty motion of the abyss' ('A Dream'). This symbol for war and death, related to that of 'The Mill-Water', dominates a sonnet based on an actual dream when Thomas was deciding to enlist.[65] Like 'The Sun Used to Shine', 'A Dream' sets 'known fields' (life, sunshine, benign Nature, Frost's friendship) against 'strange' powers of darkness. Throughout Thomas's poetry specific cultural change ('the twilight of the wood') interacts with 'man's [universal] lot': 'The unfathomable deep/ Forest where all must lose/ Their way . . .'

'Two Houses' stylises the extremes of his imagination, 'Manor Farm' and 'Mill-Water':

> Between a sunny bank and the sun
> The farmhouse smiles
> On the riverside plat:
> No other one
> So pleasant to look at
> And remember, for many miles,
> So velvet hushed and cool under the warm tiles.
>
> Not far from the road it lies, yet caught
> Far out of reach
> Of the road's dust
> And the dusty thought
> Of passers-by, though each
> Stops, and turns, and must
> Look down at it like a wasp at the muslined peach.
>
> But another house stood there long before:
> And as if above graves
> Still the turf heaves
> Above its stones:
> Dark hangs the sycamore,
> Shadowing kennel and bones
> And the black dog that shakes his chain and moans.

And when he barks, over the river
Flashing fast,
Dark echoes reply,
And the hollow past
Half yields the dead that never
More than half hidden lie:
And out they creep and back again for ever.

'The muslined peach' encapsulates lost satisfactions of peace: forbidden fruit tantalising memory, 'caught/ Far out of reach'. The farmhouse – possibly timeless, possibly obsolete, possibly illusory – can only be passively 'looked at', in contrast with the disturbingly active other house:

Still the turf heaves . . .

And out they creep and back again forever.

These 'Two Houses' also speak two languages. Whereas 'The farmhouse smiles', 'the black dog . . . moans.// And when he barks . . . Dark echoes reply'. Paul Fussell has demonstrated how the trope of 'two languages' permeates First World War literature.[66] Thomas, in other contexts than Sassoon and Owen, specifically corrects false vocabularies. 'Fears in Solitude' is again the prototype, in castigating 'all our dainty terms for fratricide/ As if the soldier died without a wound'. William Cooke uncovers a rebuke to Rupert Brooke in 'No One Cares Less than I', where a Brookean bugle calls ambiguously, perhaps to destiny 'Under a foreign clod'. In any case 'Only the bugles' – not poets – 'know/ What the bugles say in the morning,/ And they do not care, when they blow . . .' But Thomas's two languages signify more than peace and war, or romantic and realistic attitudes to the latter. They engage on the comprehensive front signalled by the aesthetic and linguistic debates of 'The Chalk Pit' and 'Sedge-Warblers'. Thomas's *stylistic* preparedness extends to his all-consuming drive towards an exact emotional and moral *locus*, a single 'language not to be betrayed'. His obsession since 1900 with the proper alignment of 'word' and 'thing' suggests that poets scent trouble ahead of time. Similarly in 1912 Charles Sorley, a prodigy like Keith Douglas, not a slow developer like Thomas, diagnosed the unpreparedness of English poetry for any reality, let alone war.

> The voice of our poets and men of letters is finely trained and sweet to hear; it teems with sharp saws and rich sentiment: it is a marvel of delicate technique: it pleases, it flatters, it charms, it soothes: it is a living lie.[68]

Later, Sorley and Thomas thought alike on Brooke: 'He has clothed his attitude in fine words; but he has taken the sentimental attitude' (Sorley);[69] 'He was a rhetorician dressing things up better than they needed' (Thomas).[70] Whereas Brooke in a sense sold out poetry, Thomas rescued it from slavery to various rhetorics, including his own. His comments on Brooke (made in October 1916) continued: 'And I suspect he knew too well both what he was after & what he achieved. I think perhaps a man ought to be capable of always being surprised on being confronted with what he really is – as I am nowadays.'[71]

Poets rarely underestimate Edward Thomas,[72] perhaps because they divine his Lob-like role in 'keeping clear' essentials of the English poetic tradition. He metaphorically achieved the war-aim once proposed by Owen: to 'perpetuate the language in which Keats and the rest of them wrote'[73] – though protecting it chiefly against other speakers and writers of that language. The war helped to clarify and intensify for Thomas the meaning of life, death, poetry. Frost's tribute (see page 23) honours a brave poetry as much as a brave man: 'so sure of his thought, so sure of his word'.[74] Like the thrushes in 'March' who 'had but an hour to sing' between storm and night, he left behind a 'silence/ Stained with all that hour's songs' – a powerful afterglow. And any English poet travelling back to native and creative sources must have encountered Thomas at the crossroads, where 'one glimpse of his back, as there he stood,/ Choosing his way, proved him of old Jack's blood'.

Louis MacNeice: *Autumn Journal*

'Tonight we sleep / On the banks of Rubicon' (XXIV)

The European crisis of autumn 1938 concentrated nobody's mind more wonderfully than that of Louis MacNeice. 'Accountancy' is a running metaphor in *Autumn Journal*, and MacNeice's comprehensive audit weighs the life of the previous decade in the scale of its cataclysmic close. That 'Time is a country, the present moment/ A spotlight roving round the scene' (XXIV) provides both a theme and an artistic strategy, which make the poem a delta of MacNeice's imaginative concerns during the 1930s, a synthesis of all his modes and moods. Further, by exploring his particular consciousness at a 'moment' when 'the stream of history' (XIV) has accelerated, he captures in a universal sense 'the rhythm which the intercrossing/ Coloured waters permanently give' (XVII).

Samuel Hynes, in *The Auden Generation*, pays one of the most substantial tributes to MacNeice's achievement: '*Autumn Journal* is the best personal expression of the end-of-the-'thirties mood.'[1] He finely summarises the foundations of the poem's success: MacNeice's capacity 'to interweave the constituent parts of his life, and to show how those parts acted upon each other: how the past affected his responses to the present, and how the present forced him to judge the past; how the public world invaded private life, and how private losses coloured his attitude towards public crises. It is a poignant last example of that insistent thirties theme, the interpenetration of public and private worlds.'[2] Four lines in Section V put this 'interpenetration' in a nutshell:

> The cylinders are racing in the presses,
>> The mines are laid,
> The ribbon plumbs the fallen fathoms of Wall Street,
>> And you and I are afraid.

The shifting pronouns of *Autumn Journal*, I – we – you, enact MacNeice's conviction that 'a monologue/Is the death of language' (XVII) – a death which implies or implicates others. Yet it is the first person singular who controls that 'spotlight roving round the scene'. And in my view Hynes underestimates the resources of MacNeice's 'I', by characterising his attitude (not only in *Autumn Journal*) as 'nostalgia',[3] 'habitual sentimental melancholy',[4] 'the tone of the professional lachrymose Irishman'.[5] I will argue, as MacNeice argued on behalf of his generation, that 'the gloom is tragic rather than defeatist';[6] and that the poem's critical thrust (which begins at home) punctures both 'the delights of self-pity' (XXIII) and 'cynical self-indulgence' (XXII). It is built into the whole design of *Autumn Journal* that the protagonist should continually recognise and resist the temptation to wallow:

> I cannot lie in this bath for ever, clouding
> The cooling water with rose geranium soap. (XVII)

Earlier in the thirties there had been some divorce between MacNeice's 'monologue' and dialogue poems: between his lyrical 'monodrama' and the socially committed citizen-poet exacted by the times, by 'a world where one gambles upon practical ideals, a world in which one can take sides'.[7] For 'the quarrel with others', he chiefly employed his updated eclogue, although 'Eclogue from Iceland', the last and most political of the eclogues, also reflects the quarrel between MacNeice's two poetic selves. The Icelandic saga-hero Grettir, who rebukes the escapism of his visitors Ryan (MacNeice) and Craven (Auden), derives from Yeats's Cuchulain/man-of-action archetype; and the poem translates the Yeatsian issue of 'Responsibilities' (previously raised in 'Eclogue by a Five-Barred Gate') into fully contemporary terms:

> Minute your gesture but it must be made –
> Your hazard, your act of defiance and hymn of hate,
> Hatred of hatred, assertion of human values . . .

But this liberal-humanist agenda, although central to the assertions of *Autumn Journal*, seems at once incongruous and abstract, the climax of a debate rather than a drama: 'the mere deliberating what to do/ When neither the pros nor cons affect the pulses' (IV). Two other poems in *Letters from Iceland* show MacNeice approaching more nearly the fusion signalled by his Note to *Autumn Journal*: 'half-way between the lyric and the didactic poem'. 'Letter to Graham and Anna' modulates from personal chat – 'Hoping that Town is not the usual mess,/ That Pauli is rid of worms, the new cook a success' – to over-epigrammatic prescriptions for living, which again anticipate the didactic half of *Autumn Journal*: 'In short we must keep moving to keep pace/ Or else drop into Limbo, the dead place'. Yet Auden's epistolary 'airy manner' sits uneasily; nor is the heroic couplet, unlike the stanza of 'Letter to Lord Byron', a form 'large enough' for MacNeice 'to swim in'. In *Letters from Iceland*, as the 'Eclogue' indicates, 'Nations germinating hell' intermittently invade the poets' 'Time for soul to stretch and spit/ Before the world comes back on it'. MacNeice's 'Postscript to Iceland', source of my last two quotations, marks a full return to the world, while its quality confirms that imaginative refreshment has indeed taken place. Neither a debate nor (despite being addressed to Auden) a letter, but an overheard meditation, the poem inaugurates the persona and context of *Autumn Journal:*

> Here in Hampstead I sit late
> Nights which no one shares and wait
> For the 'phone to ring or for
> Unknown angels at the door.

The 'Commitments' double number of *New Verse* (Autumn 1938) contains two contributions from Geoffrey Grigson which are uncannily relevant both to 'Postscript' and the scenario of *Autumn Journal*. In his editorial note Grigson says: 'The only justified retreat is the loneliness from which everything and everybody is more visible, the loneliness in the centre and not on the edge';[8] and in 'Lonely, but not Lonely Enough': 'What we need now is not the fanatic, but the critical moralist; and the one loneliness which is justified is Rilke's loneliness *surrounded by everything* thorough, exact, without slovenliness, impressionable, and honest.'[9]

The first two sections of *Autumn Journal* establish this 'loneliness in the centre', together with its vast circumference. Section I shows, even shows off, the extent to which the poet proposes to be *'surrounded by everything'*. The inclusive compulsion of MacNeice's syntax and metre becomes almost exaggerated as he takes hold of his subject-matter. 'And', the ubiquitous conjunction which emphasises the many conjunctions of the poem, attaches various other endings to the ending of summer.

> Close and slow, summer is ending in Hampshire,
>> Ebbing away down ramps of shaven lawn where close-clipped yew
> Insulates the lives of retired generals and admirals
>> And the spyglasses hung in the hall and the prayer-books ready
>>> in the pew
> And August going out to the tin trumpets of nasturtiums
>> And the sunflowers' Salvation Army blare of brass
> And the spinster sitting in a deck-chair picking up stitches
>> Not raising her eyes to the noise of the 'planes that pass
> Northward from Lee-on-Solent. Macrocarpa and cypress
>> And roses on a rustic trellis and mulberry trees
> And bacon and eggs in a silver dish for breakfast

> And all the inherited assets of bodily ease
> And all the inherited worries, rheumatism and taxes,
>> And whether Stella will marry and what to do with Dick
> And the branch of the family that lost their money in Hatry
>> And the passing of the *Morning Post* and of life's climacteric
> And the growth of vulgarity, cars that pass the gate-lodge
>> And crowds undressing on the beach
> And the hiking cockney lovers with thoughts directed
>> Neither to God nor Nation but each to each . . .

These two largely unpunctuated sentences encompass a seasonal, geographical, historical and social transition. The 'insulated' lives of the rural gentry suggest an Edwardian order partially reasserted after 1918 (the image of summer recalls its nostalgic presence in First World War poetry), but now subject to disturbing tremors: 'the rebels and the young/ Have taken the train to town'. Four lines later the poet joins the poem and the trend: 'And I am in the train too now and summer is going/ South as I go north'. As he travels towards 'The harder life' – of winter, the metropolis and potential war – he has in fact 'surrounded' himself with multiple layers of the endangered, changing society. A symbolic encounter in the train focuses change within a shorter time-span. A woman with 'eyes/Patient beneath the calculated lashes,/ Inured forever to surprise' supplies an up-to-date image of insulation as compared with the earlier spinster. She inspires a song which parodies the popular idiom of the thirties: 'I loved my love with a platform ticket,/ A jazz song,/ A handbag, a pair of stockings of Paris Sand . . .' This farewell to the frivolities of the decade also obliquely introduces the personal plot of *Autumn Journal*. Another ending is that of MacNeice's first marriage ('two in a bed and patchwork cushions', VIII), and the ironic love-song thus adds the sphere of relationships to the general asset-stripping:

> I loved her between the lines and against the clock,
>> Not until death
> But till life did us part I loved her with paper money
>> And with whisky on the breath.

The zeugma dependent on 'loved' (zeugma, as in 'The passing of the *Morning Post* and of life's climacteric', is a pervasive ironic figure) cooperates with 'and' to create a more swiftly inclusive syntax than that of the 'Close and slow' start. 'And' can thus emphasise disjunction as well as conjunction. The metre too has increasingly stressed the shorter line, which eventually speeds up and fines down to one word: 'And so to London and down the ever-moving/ Stairs'. But the stairs and the poem move on, and the massed humanity that

MacNeice has collected disintegrates into its individual solitudes: 'Where a warm wind blows the bodies of men together/ And blows apart their complexes and cares'. These concluding lines condense the overall development from insulation to isolation.

Section II, in singling out MacNeice's own solitude, demonstrates the variety of his procedures. The poet-in-motion, who could at least manage a characteristic declaration of faith: 'no river is a river which does not flow', gives way to one statically caught in 'the web of night' and the web of his thoughts. The syntax of argument replaces that of progression (but, whether, why, if, only). Section II is the first and richest full soliloquy in *Autumn Journal*, setting the stage for others. At the start, details of MacNeice's flat near Regent's Park Zoo assume an aura of Shakespearean omen:

> I am afraid in the web of night
>> When the window is fingered by the shadows of branches,
> When the lions roar beneath the hill
>> And the meter clicks and the cistern bubbles
> And the gods are absent and the men are still . . .

Here 'when' and 'and' place the poet's loneliness at the centre of outward phenomena. Later, MacNeice explicitly draws on Shakespearean tragedy to strengthen his lyrical self-dramatisation:

> If you can equate Being in its purest form
>> With denial of all appearance,
> Then let me disappear – the scent grows warm
>> For pure Not-Being, Nirvana.

More laboriously than Hamlet – prototype of the artist/liberal facing the problem of constructive action in troubled times – MacNeice arrives at the same crux: 'Only there are always/ Interlopers, dreams,/ Who let no dead dog lie nor death be final'. As suicide falls short of a final solution, we are forced back on the questionable world. The world in fact still surrounds the poet as he deliberates whether to rejoin it. Images of 'quintessential dark' and paralysed faculties – 'Dumb and deaf at the nadir' – contrast with ripples of life and feeling: 'Some now are happy in the hive of home,/ Thigh over thigh and a light in the night nursery/ And some are hungry under the starry dome/ And some sit turning handles'. Robert the Bruce's exemplar, the spider, is the bridge to more positive involvement. Its animal persistence begins and binds the section: 'Spider, spider, twisting tight . . . Only the spider spinning out his reams/ Of colourless thread says Only there are always' . . . etc. A web, the poem itself, is a sequence as well as a tangle:

'Becoming is a match for Being.' The gesture which follows may be as minute as that proposed in 'Eclogue from Iceland', but it has certainly acquired more personal and symbolic flesh:

> I must go out tomorrow as the others do
> And build the falling castle;
> Which has never fallen, thanks
> Not to any formula, red tape or institution,
> Not to any creeds or banks,
> But to the human animal's endless courage.

It is not because 'lachrymose' Irishness qualified him to sing a swansong, that MacNeice could express 'the end-of-the-thirties mood'. The new situation, blurring issues of right and left, clarifying those of right and wrong, was simply more susceptible to his political and aesthetic individualism. Hynes rather caustically calls MacNeice's 'self-proclaimed role of common man' 'a kind of substitute for political commitment, a way of being apolitical with a good heart'[10] – or a waiting game that paid off poetically? In 1938 the equalising prospect of war validated an Everyman role. Similarly the poet-as-poet and the poet-as-citizen could be reconciled, since 'war spares neither the poetry of Xanadu nor the poetry of pylons'.[11] This observation appears in the introductory chapter to MacNeice's *The Poetry of W.B. Yeats,* in some respects a coda to *Autumn Journal.* From the perspective of late 1939 MacNeice makes amends to the breadth of Yeats's vision (queried in *Modern Poetry*), aligning his own generation with Yeats on behalf of 'system against chaos':[12] 'Where Eliot had seen misery, frustration, and ruins, they saw heroic struggle – or, sometimes, heroic defeat – and they saw ruins rebuilding.'[13] The link, *via* 'Lapis Lazuli' ('All things fall and are built again') with 'building the falling castle' is clear. Yet in *Autumn Journal* MacNeice does not assume the Yeatsian character of the artist or 'solitary soul' as tragic hero. He inhabits – whether as citizen, common man, Everyman or individual – what he says Yeats avoids, 'flux, the sphere of the realist proper'.[14] Nevertheless he follows the path recommended by Yeats when preferring Irish poets' methods (really his own) to English thirties approaches: 'Instead of turning to impersonal philosophy, they have hardened and deepened their personalities.'[15]

That *Autumn Journal* took shape as a 'living river' rather than a Tower is proved by the way in which the poem is conscious of its own medium. With a few exceptions, its self-commentary figures as a concern, not with Yeatsian 'art' (soul, imagination, spirit), but with language. And language in the sense on which MacNeice insisted during the thirties: as a 'community-product'.[16] Political, social, personal and intellectual life, all the spheres of the poem, produce words whose current function and fitness are in question. First comes the debased vocabulary of politics: 'travestied in slogans' (III); 'blank invective' in Spain (VI); 'Hatred scribbled on a wall' and 'Purblind manifestoes' in Ireland (XVI); 'Lies on the air endlessly repeated' (XVIII). (To the other affinities he finds between MacNeice and Orwell, Hynes might have added outrage at the propagandist violation of language.) From the ancient world to Ulster, truth has to fight for expression: 'free speech shivered on the pikes of Macedonia/ And later on the swords of Rome' (IX); 'Free speech nipped in the bud,/ The minority always guilty' (XVI). Education, which 'gives us too many labels/ And clichés' (XII), falls down on its preventive work. MacNeice questions the scope of the social and actual languages he learned at prep school, public school and Oxford: 'a heap of home-made dogma', 'Another lingo to talk' (X), 'a toy-box of hall-marked marmoreal phrases' (XIII). However, irony at the expense of one received doctrine:

> But the classical student is bred to the purple, his training in syntax
> Is also a training in thought (XIII)

is neutralised by MacNeice's own impressive Orwellian exhibition of the connection between clear thought and clear language – one of the implicit positives of the poem. In a sense there is a missing element in MacNeice's critique of language. He does not directly indict the now less relevant rhetoric of some literary-political intellectuals of the thirties. But his sarcasm in section XIII at the expense of abstraction covers many 'clever hopes', including his own:

> But certainly it was fun while it lasted
>   And I got my honours degree
> And was stamped as a person of intelligence and culture
>   For ever wherever two or three
> Persons of intelligence and culture
>   Are gathered together in talk
> Writing definitions on invisible blackboards
>   In non-existent chalk.

The language of love, initially degraded to 'every tired aubade and maudlin madrigal' (I), recovers its glory in a new relationship: 'Whose hair is twined in all my waterfalls/And all of London littered with remembered kisses' (IV); then abdicates at the end of the affair: 'The flowery orator in the heart is dumb' (XIX). But this kind of oratory carries a renewable poetic licence, and can never essentially be untrue like political jargon, or unreal like escapist literature. MacNeice's literary references again steer a course between cynicism and sentimentality. On the one hand he rules out the sophisticated decadence of the Greeks 'Who turned out dapper little elegiac verses/ On the ironies of fate, the transience of all/ Affections, carefully shunning an over-statement/ But working the dying fall' (IX). On the other, he refuses nostalgia for innocence: 'Sing us no more idylls, no more pastorals,/ No more epics of the English earth' (XVIII). Basically MacNeice wishes to replace all 'yesterday's magic coat of ragged words' (XVIII) – another echo of Yeats? – with the nakedness of admitted fact, as when 'protest/ Meetings assemble'

> simply to avow
> The need to hold the ditch; a bare avowal
> That may perhaps imply
> Death at the doors in a week but perhaps in the long run
> Exposure of the lie. (VII).

Voting in the Oxford by-election against the Munich agreement is 'a core/ Of fact in a pulp of verbiage' (XIV) – possibly a joke against the poem itself. In Spain, revisited at the new year, 'The white plane-trees were bone naked/ And the issues plain' (XXIII). More affirmatively, MacNeice's 'new Muse' is not really a siren of anodyne fantasy 'With false eyelashes and finger-nails of carmine' (XV), but his lover as celebrated in section IV. Her individuality and instinct for life set a stylistic as well as a moral standard: 'Whose words would tumble over each other and pelt/ From pure excitement'; 'And I shall remember how your words could hurt/ Because they were so honest/ And even your lies were able to assert/ Integrity of purpose.' She incarnates the self-dedication of section II ('To hit the target straight without circumlocution'): 'I should be proud if I could evolve at length/ An equal thrust and pattern.' MacNeice only occasionally deserts this living and linguistic aesthetic for symbols drawn from art, as when dance and music denote both the 'pattern' of the poem and the ideal harmony he desires for society: 'Where life is a choice of instruments and none/ Is debarred his natural music' (XXIV). But with his emphasis so overwhelmingly on the choice of words, on words and meaning, MacNeice evokes and continues the more clear-cut confrontation between two languages in First World War poetry:

> And we who have been brought up to think of 'Gallant Belgium'
> As so much blague
> Are now preparing again to essay good through evil
> For the sake of Prague;
> And must, we suppose, become uncritical, vindictive . . . (VII)

Autumn Journal is a pre-emptive strike against that 'must', as MacNeice completely answers Grigson's advertisement for a 'critical moralist'. His criticism of language merges naturally into the 'criticism of life' his Note desiderates: 'The Fool among the yes-men flashed his motley/ To prick their pseudo-reason with his rhymes' (X). He often pricks illusion or pretension with a phrase whose origin sharpens its point: 'The land of scholars and saints:/ Scholars and saints my eye' (XVI). One of his ideals, the Greek mind before it 'narrowed [its] focus', combines breadth of interests with a breadth of idiom mirrored in MacNeice's own language: 'talked philosophy or smut in cliques' (IX). (MacNeice and Auden effected a class-revolution in poetic diction, if in nothing else.) The critical dimension of *Autumn Journal* ranges from tragic self-questioning to a spectrum of ironic and satirical effects. If, as Hynes says, the poem belongs to 'a Literature of Preparation'[17] – to 'The dying that brings forth/ The harder life' (I) – the preparation involves a *post mortem* on unpreparedness:

> Nobody niggled, nobody cared,
>   The soul was deaf to the mounting debit,
> The soul was unprepared . . . (VIII)

MacNeice's hindsight is acceptable in that he casts himself as a representative scapegoat, yokes reminiscence to conscience. He mocks the irrelevance of his education – thanks both to class and the classics – and these sections interpret his inadequacy in relation to coming thirties events which have already entered the poem: the Depression and the Spanish Civil War. Sections VI ('And I remember Spain') and VIII ('We lived in Birmingham through the slump'), in adjusting perceptions *then* to perceptions *now*, exploit the habitual MacNeice contrast between surface and core: in Spain, 'the old/ Glory veneered and varnished/ As if veneer could hold/ The rotten guts and crumbled bones together'. Here, as in 'Eclogue from Iceland', he adopts the role of guilt-tripper ('we thought the papers a lark/ With their party politics and blank invective'), and *ipso facto* cannot hit home as in section VIII, where there is maximum co-incidence between the private and public plots of the poem. More contrast – 'Sunlight dancing on the rubbish dump' – but the sun image, ritualised into a mocking refrain, also carries over reverberations from MacNeice's spring-and-love poetry. Associated with his first wife in 'Mayfly' ('Daughter of the South, call the sunbeams home/ To nest between your breasts'), sunlight now connects what was wrong beneath the surface of their marriage with what was wrong beneath the surface of the time:

> We slept in linen, we cooked with wine,
>   We paid in cash and took no notice
> Of how the train ran down the line
>   Into the sun against the signal.

The climax of the section (which later winds down to Munich: 'The crisis is put off') powerfully fuses autobiography and history, criticism and drama in a negative 'bare avowal':

> No wife, no ivory tower, no funk-hole.

The road from marriage to divorce, and from the slump to Munich may also, however, have led to personal and artistic maturity or responsibility. All the critical/satirical passages in *Autumn Journal* feed into and out of the central issue of constructive 'Being' versus 'Non-Being'. Section XV, renewing the surreal method of 'Bagpipe Music', stages the most grotesque confrontation between surface and core. Exaggerated escapism: 'Give me a houri but houris are too easy,/ Give me a nun' yields to a 'nightmare' vision which unites the personal, communal, and universal terrors of the poem:

> Was it the murderer on the nursery ceiling
>   Or Judas Iscariot in the Field of Blood
> Or someone at Gallipoli or in Flanders
>   Caught in the end-all mud?

The most savage criticism in *Autumn Journal* is directed towards politics. For his sustained attacks, MacNeice uses neither ironic retrospect nor nightmare projection, but translates the scene to Ancient Greece (IX) and Ireland (XVI). But first of all, what *are* the politics of *Autumn Journal*? Is MacNeice still 'apolitical with a good heart'? Or now more aware 'that those who by their habit hate/ Politics can no longer keep their private/ Values unless they open the public gate/ To a better political system' (XIV)? Julian Symons perhaps said more about his own stance than MacNeice's, in calling the poem 'The Bourgeois's Progress'.[18] As elsewhere (in *I Crossed the Minch* and *The Strings Are False*), MacNeice frankly acknowledges his class status, Orwell's *sine qua non*. He often stresses the material 'ease' or 'cushiness' of his life up to now:

> Not but what I am glad to have my comforts,
>   Better authentic mammon than a bogus god;
> If it were not for Lit. Hum. I might be climbing
>   A ladder with a hod. (XII)

Yet section III, which begins with an evocation of 'the people/ Back from holiday', dismisses 'an utterly lost and daft/ System that gives a few at fancy prices/ Their fancy lives'. MacNeice then honestly admits, but 'suppresses', the selfish and conservative fear 'that in order/ To preserve the values dear to the élite/ The élite must remain a few'. *Laissez-faire* is a conspicuously recurrent term in *Autumn Journal*, its application shuttling from the economic through the political to the moral: 'The frost that kills the germs of *laissez-faire*' [I]; 'The autopsy of treaties, dynamite under the bridges,/ The end of *laissez-faire*' (VII); 'That Rome was not built in a day is no excuse/ For *laissez-faire*' (XIV). ('To be or not to be' might also be described as a struggle between '*laissez*' and '*faire*'.) MacNeice thus manifests the old thirties faith, more crudely proclaimed in 'An Eclogue for Christmas' (1933) and now reinforced by the imminence of war, that the present economic and social order is doomed: 'summer is ending in Hampshire', the gravy-train running 'Into the sun against the signal'. People must organise, not only 'against the beast/ That prowls at every door and barks in every headline' (XIV), but to change society. At the same time, the poem's Utopia is emphatically anti-totalitarian (the by-election prompts a cheer for democracy:[19] for 'this crude and so-called obsolete/ Top-heavy tedious parliamentary system'):

> a possible land
> Not of sleep-walkers, not of angry puppets,
> But where both heart and brain can understand
> The movements of our fellows . . . (XXIV)

MacNeice's social unity has elements in common with Yeats's unity of being and culture. Thus his ideal relation between the mass and the individual may seem *impossibly* poetic, as some far-fet imagery betrays: 'Where the individual, no longer squandered/ In self-assertion, works with the rest, endowed/ With the split vision of a juggler and the quick lock of a taxi' (XXIV). However, Orwell too was a better critic than inventor of systems. *Autumn Journal* strikes an Orwellian blow '*for* democratic Socialism',[20] or at very least for the political wing of liberal humanism, at a time when

> the individual, powerless, has to exert the
> Powers of will and choice
> And choose between enormous evils, either
> Of which depends on somebody else's voice. (V)

MacNeice voted at Oxford for the Popular Front (a Lib-Lab alliance) against the victorious pro-Munich candidate, Quintin

Hogg. His immediate reaction to Munich slams it as dishonourable last-ditch *laissez-faire*: 'Save my skin and damn my conscience . . . only the Czechs/ Go down and without fighting' (VIII). Section IX, on the basis of MacNeice's job 'As impresario of the Ancient Greeks', obliquely mounts his full attack: 'far from being objective about the Ancient Greeks, I see them in the light of the mood induced in me by Munich'.[21] A final irony, 'It was all so unimaginably different/ And all so long ago', underlines the similarities enforced by MacNeice's contemporary slanginess (satire again breaching a convention of discourse):

> And when I should remember the paragons of Hellas
>   I think instead
> Of the crooks, the adventurers, the opportunists,
>   The careless athletes and the fancy boys . . .
> And the trimmers at Delphi and the dummies at Sparta and lastly
>   I think of the slaves . . .

'The mood induced . . . by Munich' is an oppressive sense of corruption, tyranny and violence: 'And many died in the city of plague, and many of drouth/ In Sicilian quarries'. The mood develops to colour MacNeice's later reflections on Ireland: 'The blots on the page are so black/ That they cannot be covered with shamrock' – another image that removes veneer.

What *is* the function of this section, not essentially a memoir, and distinguished by an exceptional bitterness of tone – or by what MacNeice's Note calls 'overstatements'? In announcing '*Odi atque amo*', MacNeice of course sums up a lifelong tension, already explored at some length in 'Valediction' (1934). But, like the other echoes of earlier poems, this too bounces off the special receivers of *Autumn Journal*. Section XVI follows the 'houri'/'murderer on the nursery ceiling' phantasmagoria, and renews MacNeice's Hamlet-problem:

> Nightmare leaves fatigue:
>   We envy men of action
> Who sleep and wake, murder and intrigue
>   Without being doubtful, without being haunted.
> And I envy the intransigence of my own
>   Countrymen who shoot to kill and never
> See the victim's face become their own
>   Or find his motive sabotage their motives.

Irish 'men of action' are disturbing, in the way that Fortinbras disturbs Hamlet, or Yeats, after encountering 'An affable Irregular' and 'A brown Lieutenant and his men', silences 'the envy in my thought' ('Meditations in Time of Civil War'). MacNeice certainly has Yeats in mind, since he continues: 'So reading the memoirs of Maud Gonne . . ./ I note how a single purpose can be founded on/ A jumble of opposites.' But just as Yeats came to reject Maud Gonne's views, and 'Hearts with one purpose alone' ('Easter, 1916'), so MacNeice's catalogue of 'intransigence' and other black spots, eliminates even ironic 'envy'. If the ancient world cradled power-politics, Ireland has patented a peculiar brand of fanaticism and fratricidal violence. Yeats's 'Great hatred, little room' becomes MacNeice's 'And each one in his will/ Binds his heirs to continuance of hatred'. In fulfilling the 'Hatred of hatred' agenda of 'Eclogue from Iceland', MacNeice shows much more passion – born of 'family feeling' – than when either remembering or revisiting Spain. Irish questions rouse and raise his poetry; whereas his allegiance to the anti-Fascist cause in Spain has a dutiful tinge: 'not realising/ That Spain would soon denote/ Our grief, our aspirations' (VI). It is as if section XVI surfaces from the subconscious of *Autumn Journal* to interpret its whole political and moral stance. By embodying the deadly alternative to liberal or tragic 'doubt', MacNeice rescues it from charges of weakness. He brandishes his inoculations against extremism, against the plagues of all the Irish houses: 'the voodoo of the Orange bands/ Drawing an iron net through darkest Ulster'; (of the post-civil war South) 'Let them pigeon-hole the souls of the killed/ Into sheep and goats, patriots and traitors.' (MacNeice's remark during the thirties that Ulster 'has in our time had more experience of political violence than England, Scotland or Wales',[22] further explains his suspicion of Communist revolutionary fervour.) The reasons for departure given in 'Valediction' similarly include 'grandiose airs' ('Ireland is/ A gallery of fake tapestries') and blind violence ('minds/ Fuddled with blood'). With the exorcism of these attributes newly urgent, MacNeice now adds a clincher in the shape of backward-looking introversion, which prevents a responsible awareness of the European turmoil. Insularity compounds insulation: 'Let the round tower stand aloof/ In a world of bursting mortar!' (MacNeice's later poem 'Neutrality' frames this accusation still more savagely.) Despite lingering charms, chiefly of landscape, Ireland functions as an anti-Utopia, a kind of social and political original sin. Indeed, the whole 'To be or not to be' argument of *Autumn Journal*, intensifying that of a decade, might be referred on its political level to a conflict between the 'drug-dull fatalism' ('Valediction') encouraged by Irish politics, and the recurrent

English optimism about progress. The complexity of this conflict ensures that MacNeice shows fewer signs than formerly of his minor dose of a thirties disease: 'I . . . suffered . . . when I forced myself to feel things that in fact I merely thought; feelings are one's own but thoughts often come from the group.'[23]

In every long poem real structure diverges from imposed structure, the organic work from the prepared template. *Autumn Journal* falls loosely into three parts of eight sections each. The first part culminates in Munich, the second in the Irish outburst – both sections 'working the dying fall' (IX): 'only the Czechs . . .'; 'a faggot of useless memories'. Part one is more continuously set in the urgent present than part two, with Spain and Birmingham appearing as ghosts from the recent past. In part two the end, however shameful, of the immediate crisis seems to permit more (and more remote) retrospect, fuller background analysis, and some satirical changes of gear. Overall, part three attempts the difficult task of interweaving present and future into a Literature of more positive Preparation. Section XXIV, which contains the lovely resolving image 'The future is the bride of what has been', quite successfully blends within its lullaby-format the future tense and the optative/imperative moods. Still, too much of the last third of the poem is taken up with forward-looking speculation that merely paraphrases previous drama. (Some phrases serve almost too handily as commentary on the poem itself!) Section XXI, for instance, ponderously begins: 'And when we clear away/ All this debris of day-to-day experience,/ What comes out to light, what is there of value/ Lasting from day to day?' The great strength of *Autumn Journal* is of course the way in which it clings to such debris:

> Hitler yells on the wireless,
> The night is damp and still
> And I hear dull blows on wood outside my window;
> They are cutting down the trees on Primrose Hill.
> The wood is white like the roast flesh of chicken,
> Each tree falling like a closing fan;
> No more looking at the view from seats beneath the branches,
> Everything is going to plan;
> They want the crest of this hill for anti-aircraft,
> The guns will take the view
> And the searchlights probe the heavens for bacilli
> With narrow wands of blue.
> And the rain came on as I watched the territorials
> Sawing and chopping and pulling on ropes like a team
> In a village tug-of-war; and I found my dog had vanished
> And thought 'This is the end of the old régime,'
> But found the police had got her at St John's Wood station . . .

'They are cutting down the trees on Primrose Hill' indicates the ease with which MacNeice can abolish the frontier between detail and symbol. On the other hand, the first pathetic, then bathetic, dog-episode indicates his 'critical' wariness of doing the trick too slickly: 'all our trivial daily acts are altered/ Into heroic or romantic make-believe' (XVII). But after section XVI, the relation between detail and symbol tends to coarsen, while the situation of section II – poet meditating in his flat – becomes formulaic: 'I sit in my room in comfort/ Looking at enormous flowers –/ Equipment purchased with my working hours,/A daily mint of perishable metals' (XXI). Here he seems to be looking for – not at – an object that sparks off reflection. A smaller proportion of the last eight sections possess one or more of these vital ingredients: convincing 'trivial daily acts', developments in the love story, developments on the public front, particular memories, a distinctive mode like satire or love poetry. Thus, despite fine lines and passages (like the 'A week to Christmas' sequence), the didactic segment of the poem eats into the lyrical, the discursive into the evocative.

The genuine symbolism of *Autumn Journal* is neither abstract nor Utopian, but enriches the whole tapestry. The fate of 'the trees on Primrose Hill' belongs to a cornucopia of allusions that flow from Nature, the seasons, weather, day and night – the best register and measure of unnatural events: 'the dead leaves falling, the burning bonfire,/ The dying that brings forth/ The harder life' (I); 'Dumb and deaf at the nadir' (II); 'Whose nature prefers/ Trees without leaves and a fire in the fire-place' (IV); 'The year-god . . . shaping/ His gradual return' (XI); 'A sapling springs in a new country' (XXIV). MacNeice milks all the implications both of 'Autumn' and 'Journal'. But as well as suggesting universal patterns into which this local disturbance fits, the day-to-dayness, the nuances of seasonal change, also beguile us into accepting the poem as a diary, as if that 'and' really represented random jottings or free association. In larger transitions too, from section to section, the casual conceals the causal. *Autumn Journal* offers a Keatsian region, if a little straggly round the edges, inside which the reader partly believes he makes his own profuse chains of words and images. An image in section I: 'so many failures,/ The building of castles in sand, of queens in snow', after serving resolve in section II, becomes in XVI: 'The tide flows round the children's sandy fancy'. On a bigger scale, but again not too obviously, the lullaby of section XXIV answers the insomnia of section II. The range of the vocabulary and the metrical variations are subjects in themselves. And whether or not MacNeice, as his

Note claims, generally refrained from editing his impressions or reactions later on, the poem gives the sense of moving with the currents of life. Losing the dog and finding it, epitomises other twists and turns: outward changes, changes of mind, swings of mood, finding a lover and losing her. In fact, the process of growth that *Autumn Journal* recommends takes place within it. And the poet is not passively 'carried on the flood of history', as Hynes puts it.[24] Just as its metre is strong yet flexible, so *Autumn Journal* conveys a mixture of responsiveness and activity ('lyric' and 'didactic' again): the poet being shaped and shaping, man-in-history and history-in-man. MacNeice's empirical aesthetic matches his empirical philosophy: 'An "empiricist" may be someone who lives from hand to mouth. Or he may be someone who follows an ideal that is always developing, implicit rather than explicit.'[25]

'Shit or Bust': The Importance of Keith Douglas

In a recent poll Keith Douglas's *Complete Poems* received heartening votes as one of the best books of poetry since 1939.[1] However, the voters were mostly poets (compare the Edward Thomas lobby), and the "tradition", as manufactured by academies and anthologies, still leaves Douglas on the margin. What Geoffrey Hill, twenty years ago, called his 'ambivalent status – at once "established" and over-looked'[2] remains unresolved. And this, despite not only Hill's backing but Ted Hughes's splendid introduction to the *Selected Poems*: 'It is a language for the whole mind, at its most wakeful, and in all situations. A utility general-purpose style, as, for instance, Shakespeare's was, that combines a colloquial prose readiness with poetic breadth . . .'[3] Nor can all sins of omission be explained by Douglas's half-shunting into the 'war poetry' siding; although perhaps only in England would Michael Hamburger's point not be taken: 'In the era of total politics . . . war poetry has become continuous, ubiquitous and hardly distinguishable from any other kind of poetry.'[4] Roger Garfitt, reviewing Desmond Graham's helpful biography (1974), implies a deeper reason why English criticism and poetry lack the 'catholic belly' to digest Douglas: 'Critics have mistaken his masterly verse control for a cerebral detachment.'[5]

It is certainly ironical that Ian Hamilton should find 'reticence stiffening into the tight-lipped insensitivity of the officers' mess',[6] where Ted Hughes finds 'burning exploratory freshness'.[7] Yet even studies of Hughes – far more abundant than of Douglas – make little room for an obvious ancestor and inspiration.[8] That Douglas has not come through on Hughes's strong push may reflect an aesthetic conflict in England, not so much between Larkinians and Hughesians, as between the style-faction and the content-faction (which Hughes in this case straddles), cavaliers and puritans, Martians and down-to-earthers. At present battle-lines seem to be drawn up behind Craig Raine and Peter Porter, with Ulster poets sniped at in No Man's Land for not keeping their enviable raw material raw enough: '[The Ulster poets] . . . have more urgent matter to write about than most, but they commonly opt for style rather than message.'[9] Garfitt exposes this kind of false polarisation when he castigates Hamilton for

> valuing [Alun] Lewis's theorising on integrity above Douglas's realis-
> ation of it through form. Douglas's poetry is almost an imitation of
> action in the vigour and compactness of its language, yet fully human
> in its response.[10]

Such unity of creative being points back beyond Larkin, Hughes and Hill to Yeats. And in a very precise sense. Yeats and MacNeice envied men of action. Edward Thomas put his life where his poetry was; Wilfred Owen his poetry where his life was. But the symbiosis between Douglas's literary and military careers – soldier, poet, horseman – uncannily acted out the heroic aesthetic which Yeats constructed around Major Robert Gregory:

> Some burn damp faggots, others may consume
> The entire combustible world in one small room
> As though dried straw . . .

It is no sentimentality but well-documented fact that Keith Douglas conceived his short life-work in these terms, though without self-glorification. His 'terror of perishing into an ordinary existence',[11] 'hatred for wasted time',[12] desertion *to* the battle of Alamein (his batman commented 'You're shit or bust, you are'),[13] are inseparable from his poetry's imaginative courage.

Douglas told J.C. Hall, in a significant metaphor:

> Your talk of regrouping sounds to me – if you will excuse me for exhibiting a one-track mind – like the military excuse of a defeated general. There is never much need to regroup. Let your impulses drive you forward; never lose contact with life or you will lose the impulses as well. Meanwhile if you must regroup, do it by re-reading your old stuff.[14]

(The workshop advice is Yeatsian too.) All 'war poets' feel a special urgency to get things said: Owen to 'warn', Thomas 'to pack into that hour/ [His] unwilling hoard of song'.[15] Douglas, with his absolute 'conviction . . . that he would be killed in the war'[16] and compulsion from childhood to 'picture coming events' ('sing/ of what the others never set eyes on'),[17] tried to concentrate into his poetry all the experience he would ever and never have: 'The entire combustible world in one small room', A to Z. His hungry fore-imagining resembles the older Yeats's insatiability: 'I feel constantly if I were but twenty years old and not over sixty all I ever wanted to do could be done easily. One never tires of life and at the last must die of thirst with the cup at one's lip.'[18] For similar reasons, Douglas wanted to step on to 'the simple, central stage of the war' where 'the interesting things happen':

> To say I thought of the battle of Alamein as an ordeal sounds pompous: but I did think of it as an important test, which I was interested in passing . . . during two years or so of hanging about I

never lost the certainty that the experience of battle was something I must have . . .

But is is exciting and amazing to see thousands of men, very few of whom have much idea why they are fighting, all enduring hardships, living in an unnatural, dangerous, but not wholly terrible world, having to kill and to be killed, and yet at intervals moved by a feeling of comradeship with the men who kill them and whom they kill, because they are enduring and experiencing the same things. It is tremendously illogical – to read about it cannot convey the impression of having walked through the looking-glass which touches a man entering a battle.[19]

Hughes considers war 'in a sense [Douglas's] ideal subject: the burning away of all human pretensions in the ray cast by death'.[20] Hill argues for a different terminology: 'To say that "war was his ideal subject" implies a greater scope of freedom-in-choice than is, perhaps, called for. To do justice to Douglas one has to acknowledge how the virtù of his art arose from the necessity of his life as a soldier.'[21] Perhaps even this formulation omits Douglas's excitement and amazement, his theatrical sense, his 'lonely impulse of delight' or 'beast on my back'. And although Hill finally agrees with Hughes that 'the war brought his gift to maturity, or to a first maturity',[22] Douglas himself anticipated a last or only maturity, not phases in any Yeatsian master-plan of development.

Douglas's lust to say everything gives his imagery its cosmic thrust:

> The hand is perfect in itself – the five
> fingers, though changing attitude, depend
> on a golden point, the imaginary true focal
> to which infinities of motion and shape are yoked.
> There is no beginning to the hand, no end,
> and the bone retains its proportion in the grave.
>
> ('The Hand')

That microcosm might be an anatomy of his poetry. The love poems, for instance, progress from half-absorbed Donne ('You are the whole continent of love') to the true Donnean dimensions of 'The Knife' (1942):

> And in your body each minute I died;
> moving your thigh could disinter me
> from a grave in a distant city . . .

The body, the head, houses, cities, countries, the globe regularly metamorphose into each other. (In *Alamein to Zem Zem* Douglas first perceives the army 'as a body would look to a germ riding in its bloodstream'.)[23] Also, the organic and inorganic fuse with particular power in the face of death: 'the pockmarked house bleached by the glare/ whose insides war has dried out like gourds', 'the burst stomach like a cave'. Douglas constantly personifies the sun, moon, stars, time, death; and his cosmos includes angels and devils. The Shakespearean 'Time Eating' suggests the nature as well as the scope of his imagination. Both a portrait of the artist (creator-maker), and of what the artist is up against, Time comprehends what Douglas sets out to comprehend:

> That volatile huge intestine holds
> material and abstract in its folds . . .

All Douglas's images of art and the artist are on a large scale. His juvenilia yearn for 'The old free poets who talked to lustful kings', for Shelleyan 'unacknowledged rulers' who 'walk over the hilltop/ Into their rarer climate'. Despite the Yeats-like disillusionment of 'The Poets' (1940):

> For we are hated,
> known to be cursed, guessed to be venomous;
> we must advance for ever, always belated

'princely', if not regal, versions of the poetic activity persist. The poet 'lies in wait' for words 'by the white pillar of a prince', his ears 'admit princes to the corridors/ into the mind'. And Douglas continues to celebrate the imagination as having a universal design behind it or before it. The theoretic recommendation of 'Extension to Francis Thompson' – 'Look in earth and air to catch/ his mineral or electric eye' – becomes the practice of 'The Marvel', which affirms creation in more ways than one. Douglas's aristocratic 'baron of the sea, the great tropic/ swordfish' survives in spirit both the removal of his eye and an astonishing metamorphosis from animal to mineral:

> which is an instrument forged in semi-darkness
> yet taken from the corpse of this strong traveller
> becomes a powerful enlarging glass
>
> reflecting the unusual sun's heat.
> With it a sailor writes on the hot wood
> the name of a harlot in his last port.

The 'glass' also conjures up 'the querulous soft voice// of mariners who rotted into ghosts'. A focal, focusing point for the elements, for sea and sky, for unconscious and conscious powers, for life and death, for life and art, 'the burning eye' concentrates all the energies of creation as the poet does:

> And to engrave that word the sun goes through
> with the power of the sea,
> writing her name and a marvel too.

This naming proclaims a unified if awesome cosmos. It also proclaims a marvellously unifying imagination.

Keith Douglas's and Ted Hughes's images of poetry diverge. Hughes's early poetry also identifies the eye with poetic vision. A surrogate eye, his 'Drop of Water', is a 'without heart-head-nerve lens/ Which saw the first and earth-centering jewel/ Spark upon darkness'. Meanwhile the created world stares back into the eye of the beholder. The hapless ratiocinator of 'Meeting' shrinks under the gaze of a cosmic-eyed goat, '[Watching] his blood's gleam with a ray/ Slow and cold and ferocious as a star'. Or this too is the poet's eye, like that of 'The Thought-Fox': 'A widening, deepening greenness,/ Brilliantly, concentratedly,/ Coming about its own business'. Itself a flash of energy (ray, drill), Hughes's eye engages in an eyeball-to-eyeball exchange of sparks with the universe. He would not have detached the swordfish's eye. Douglas's eye, whether appropriated from a swordfish or not, does not go it alone but participates in a complex chain-reaction that includes 'heart-head-nerve':

> If at times my eyes are lenses
> through which the brain explores
> constellations of feeling . . .
>   ('Bete Noire')

'The Hand' lengthens the chain. Although not mentioned, the eye's rigorous scrutiny governs the 'transmutations' of the poem, 'this making a set of pictures, this drawing/ shapes within the shapes of the hand'. Douglas then moves from hand to brain, to 'arguments', to 'the centre of reason, the mainspring':

> To do this is drilling the mind, still a recruit,
> for the active expeditions of his duty
> when he must navigate alone the wild
> cosmos, as the Jew wanders the world:
> and we, watching the tracks of him at liberty
> like the geometry of feet
> upon a shore, constructed in the sand,
> look for the proportions, the form of an immense hand.

As the poem comes full circle it declares a humanistic confidence. The mind, in order to grapple with 'the wild/ cosmos', learns from the body, but is not thereby devalued like Hughes's 'Egg-Head'. (Douglas commonly uses 'mind' for imagination.) The military and mathematical language too, the repetitions of 'proportion' and 'form' align the poem's perspective with Yeats's Greek-Renaissance 'Measurement began our might'. The 'measured' deliberation of the syntax dramatises an 'instrumentation' crucial to Douglas's concept of art: 'This perfection slips/ through the hands to the instrument'; 'an instrument forged in semi-darkness'; 'Words are my instruments but not my servants'. Hughes, despite his brilliant summarising phrase, 'a language for the whole mind', might dispute the conclusion of 'Extension to Francis Thompson': 'analysis is worshipping'.

Keith Douglas does not always assert the order of creation. 'The Offensive', which echoes Owen's 'Spring Offensive', co-opts the constellations to express man's disorders: 'The stars dead heroes in the sky', 'The stars . . . are the heavenly symbols of a class/ dead in their seats'. Nevertheless, another component here – anger – reclaims Douglas for the humanism that Hughes would deny him:

> The truth of a man is the doomed man in him or his dead body . . . Douglas had no time, and perhaps no disposition, to cultivate the fruity deciduous tree of How to Live. He showed in his poetry no concern for man in society. The murderous skeleton in the body of a girl, the dead man behind the mirror, these items of circumstantial evidence are steadily out-arguing all his high spirits and hopefulness.[24]

It all depends what you mean by society – a word Hughes narrows till it indeed shrinks 'to a trinket shape' as compared with 'the whole/ Sun-swung zodiac of light'. Hughes and his admirers also shrink humanism to a version of the Movement. Thus Keith Sagar:

> The poet is a medium for transmitting an occult charge from the non-human world into the psyche and thence into consciousness . . . Most English poets have drifted into a rational humanism and arrogantly expect us to value their measured musings.[25]

Hughes's 'out-arguing', while acknowledging Douglas's dialectic, downgrades it even as a source of imaginative energy. Sagar's polarities accommodate neither dialectic nor 'the whole mind'.

Douglas of course radically criticised the socio-political emphases of thirties poetry, themselves worn out by 1939. Yet he also maintained much more continuity with the preceding generation than did Hughes with the Movement. *Autumn Journal* not only ended an era but inaugurated a new one, and a new poetry (for MacNeice himself too):

The New Year comes with bombs, it is too late
To dose the dead with honourable intentions.

At this time MacNeice (and Auden) was making amends to Yeats, and insisting that the war enforced a new aesthetic:

> Some of the poets who renounced the Ivory Tower were ready to enter a Brazen Tower of political dogma; where the Ivory Tower represents isolation from men in general, the Brazen Tower represents isolation from men as individuals (witness the typical entowered politician) and also from oneself as an individual. Bad logic demanded a choice between the Towers, but salutary self-deceit allowed many of the Brazen school to leave the door open. The impact of the war with its terrible threat of genuine spiritual imprisonment has brought them again out of doors. The poet is once more to be a mouth instead of a megaphone, and poetry, one hopes, is to develop organically from the organic premises of life – of life as it is lived, not of life when it is dried into algebra.[26]

Douglas's MacNeicean 'Invaders' (1939) resolves 'always to think, and always to indite/ of a good matter, while the black birds cry'. Although Douglas followed Yeats in repudiating a populist view of art (hence his kings and princes), he also followed him in not there-fore abandoning all interest in society. That magnificent letter (in 1943) to Hall, which resembles MacNeice's aesthetic, includes a social and human agenda within war's imaginative imperative:

> I don't know if you have come across the word Bullshit – it is an army word and signifies humbug and unnecessary detail. It symbolises what I think must be got rid of – the mass of irrelevancies, of "attitudes", "approaches", propaganda, ivory towers, etc., that stands between us and our problems and what we have to do about them . . . To be sentimental or emotional now is dangerous to oneself and to others. To trust anyone or to admit any hope of a better world is criminally foolish, as foolish as it is to stop working for it. It sounds silly to say work without hope, but it can be done; it's only a form of insurance; it doesn't mean work hopelessly.[27]

Having absorbed First World War poetry ('hell cannot be let loose twice . . . Almost all that a modern poet on active service is inspired to write, would be tautological')[28] Douglas addressed him-self to the unfinished business that had permitted the futility of one war to beget the illogic of another. His short essay 'Poets in this War' certainly raises the issue of 'How to Live' as well as 'How to Write':

> During the period "entre deux guerres" we were listening alternately to an emphasis of the horrible nature of modern war and to the vague remedies of social and political reformers. The nation's public char-

100

acter remained, in spite of all, as absurdly ignorant and reactionary as ever . . . the poets . . . who were accustomed to teach politics and even supposed themselves, and were supposed versed in the horrors of the current struggles in Spain, were curiously unable to react to a war which began and continued in such a disconcerting way.[29]

Michael Hamburger argues that 'Aristocrats', mourning a 'gentle/ obsolescent breed of heroes', writes off Keith Douglas as well as Rupert Brooke: 'Perhaps Douglas . . . knew in his heart that his own truthfulness in the face of corporate experience owed a good deal to his upbringing, to a liberalism and individualism that were no less in danger of becoming obsolete than the reliance on fair play which the same institutions served to inculcate.'[30] However, in this sense too Douglas swallowed the lessons of the thirties along with those of the twenties, and thus enlarged rather than abandoned the humane critique of war.

Yeats might have relished, not only a stance nearer to 'tragic joy' than to 'passive suffering', but also Douglas's importation of a phantasmagoria into the theatre of war. His poetry is much more populated than Hughes's, less anonymously populated than Owen's, its inhabitants falling somewhere between thirties type and Yeatsian archetype. In addition to his own interior drama, where love as well as life dices with death, the poetry, like *Alamein to Zem Zem*, observes others closely. Nor does Douglas confine his observation to Cairo 'vignettes', although the 'stained white town' consummates his concern with the city: not the socio-political laboratory of thirties poetry, but a timeless ferment (like MacNeice's Greek city-state in section IX of *Autumn Journal*). As sunlit landscape haunts First World War poetry, 'golden age' Oxford-Byzantium, home of 'leisurely immortals', haunts Douglas's:

> This city experiences a difficult time. The old bells
> fall silent, or are bidden to silence. The buildings lean
> inwards, watching the questionable sky,
> and across the meadows, where youth and age inhabit,
> exchange an austere opinion of foreboding.

'Soissons' (1940) and 'Enfidaville' (1943) also epitomise 'fallen' civilisation:

> Yet here something of the mind lived and died,
> a mental tower restored only to fall . . .

> In the church fallen like dancers
> lie the Virgin and St Thérèse
> on little pillows of dust.

'An Oration', with its Yeatsian cast of 'lovers', 'hucksters', 'ballad-mongers', 'beggars', 'saints and national heroes', opposes the vivid past to a living death: 'the people themselves are dead,/ wakeful and miserable in their dark graves'. Not to be fully alive (more horrifying to Douglas than 'the skull beneath the skin') receives subtler diagnosis in his Egyptian scenarios. For an Egyptian sentry 'There is no pain, no pleasure, life's no puzzle/ but a standing, a leaning, a sleep between the coasts// of birth and dying'. Cairo's 'stink of jasmin' symbolises all the sleeping sickness and corruption that allows the deaths 'in another place'. Egypt is

> the sick land where in the sun lay
> the gentle sloe-eyed murderers
> of themselves, exquisites under a curse . . .

Douglas's poetry concentrates less on compassion for death (Owen) than on a Shakespearean passion for the life which war highlights and destroys.

The image of a corrupt woman, Cleopatra, Dark Lady, Cressida ('Time Eating' also points to the influence of *Troilus and Cressida*) often accompanies rottenness in the state. The declaration of war coincided with Douglas's final rejection by his obsessively loved Yingcheng, 'Cressida could not match you':

> [Douglas] . . . visited the Cowley Road garage where Yingcheng had left the red sports car. Asking the girl there if she had news of Yingcheng, Douglas was told she was going to be married. Hatten remembers that he 'took this news with impassivity and then said to me, "Anyway, I had that week in Paris".' On 6 September Douglas reported to No. 15 Reception Unit, in Manor Road, to enlist in the 'Cavalry of the Line' . . . Afterwards . . . Douglas announced that he would join a good cavalry regiment and 'bloody well make my mark in this war. For I will not come back.'[31]

'I listen to the desert wind' identifies Yingcheng's cruelty and hardness with that of the desert world. 'Syria II', echoing Isaac Rosenberg's 'Returning, we hear the Larks', presents war in terms of sexual betrayal: 'fair apples where the snake plays', 'a murderer with a lover's face'. 'Egypt' personifies the country as a woman 'diseased and blind of an eye/ and heavy with habitual dolour'. 'Behaviour of Fish in an Egyptian Tea Garden' portrays decadent, commercial sex as a submarine region – often, for Douglas, symbolic of mortality. As in *Troilus and Cressida*, all this trafficking between love and war enriches a tragic perspective on perverted values:

> For here the lover and killer are mingled . . .

'Snakeskin and Stone', with its sharp antithesis between how to live and how to die, spells out Douglas's credo:

> I praise a snakeskin or a stone:
> a bald head or a public speech
> I hate: the serpent's lozenges
> are calligraphy, and it is
> truth these cryptograms teach,
> the pebble is truth alone.

Together, the 'complication' and 'subtlety' of the snake, the age and cruelty of the stone sum up life and death, establish a site for Byzantium:

> all the buildings truth can make,

> a whole city, inhabited by lovers,
> murderers, workmen and artists
> not much recognised: all
> who have no memorial
> but are mere men . . .

The human irreducibility of these citizens contrasts with the 'mask of words or figures' assumed by public life – like the bald head, 'a desert/ between country of life and country of death'. Again, it is the 'bullshit' of inbetween states that Douglas scorns. His attack on lifeless, yet deathly, rhetoric fuses, within another submarine vista, 'dead words' and dead bodies: 'Tangled they cruise/ like mariners' bodies in the grave of ships.' 'Snakeskin and Stone' confirms that Douglas's concept of death not only takes in 'dead bone', but attacks all that belies glowing skin. The end of the poem does not dismiss the social 'world' as separate and irrelevant, but hunts to their source, more ruthlessly than even Owen did, the origins of war:

> for you who think the desert hidden
> or the words, like the dry bones, living
> are fit to profit from the world.
> And God help the lover of snakeskin and stone.

'Landscape with Figures' – whether read as single poem or sonnet sequence[32] – channels this love and hatred into a more inward assumption of responsibility. In a parallel with 'Dulce et Decorum Est', the speaker moves from observer to participant ('I am the figure writhing on the backcloth') to scapegoat-redeemer:

> all these angels and devils are driven
> into my mind like beasts. I am possessed,
> the house whose wall contains the dark strife,
> the arguments of hell with heaven.

The pun on 'contain' and Douglas's recurrent sense of the mind as a house define an intensely feeling, densely peopled imagination, convulsed by, yet controlling, Yeatsian antinomies. 'Devils', those inside the mind divided by an 'unsubstantial wall' from those outside, dramatises a similar tension. 'Enfidaville' implicitly equates the poet's mind, desolated by 'the pain this town holds', with the war-emptied houses. Both beautifully fill up again at the end of the poem:

> But already they are coming back; to search
> like ants, poking in the débris, finding in it
> a bed or a piano and carrying it out.
> Who would not love them at this minute?
> I seem again to meet
> the blue eyes of the images in the church.

Antinomies or dualism? That reconciliation suggests the former. But dualistic himself, Hughes casts Douglas in the same mould – a mould which simplifies the reading of some poems. Thus the 'murderous skeleton in the body of a girl' may carry additional symbolic and dramatic layers. Addressed to Yingcheng 'The Prisoner' contrasts not only life and death, but love and the death of love, and perhaps again peace and war:

> But alas, Cheng, I cannot tell why,
> today I touched a mask stretched on the stone
>
> person of death. There was the urge
> to break the bright flesh and emerge
> of the ambitious cruel bone.

'Mask' (critical in 'Snakeskin and Stone') and 'cruel', a word associated with Yingcheng, indicate that the skeleton may stand for her real character. Or conversely, the poet's *memento mori* may take a 'cruel' revenge. Again, the 'dead men being eaten by dogs' appear in a context where Douglas offers a choice of 'attitudes', his irony implying their dualistic inadequacy:

> And the wise man is the lover
> who in his planetary love revolves
> without the traction of reason or time's control
> and the wild dog finding meat in a hole
> is a philosopher. The prudent mind resolves
> on the lover's or the dog's attitude forever.

'Dead Men', like 'Cairo Jag', bears out Geoffrey Hill's contention that war did not so much provide Douglas with 'a unifying generalisation', as introduce him to 'a world with its own tragi-comic laws, like *Alice* with all the sinister suggestions exaggerated. And much of the acuteness of the perception is in the recognition that not everyone has to go through with this; that two absolutely different worlds co-exist at about a day's journey from each other.'[33] At the end of 'Cairo Jag' these worlds collide: 'a man with no head/ has a packet of chocolate and a souvenir of Tripoli'. However, Cairo has its 'somnambulists and legless beggars'. And while the whole gaze of Douglas's poetry widens towards extremes, its effort is to comprehend – though without squinting reconciliations – their 'coexistence'. Dualism would preclude 'the arguments of hell with heaven'. Douglas's self-portrayal after reaching the Alamein army, fits Hill's distinction: 'a scepticism that is not so much metaphysical doubt as the willingness to lay the mind completely open to experience':[34]

> Perhaps betrayed by the spectacle of the stars as clear as jewels on black velvet into a mood of more solemnity, I suddenly found myself assuming that I was going to die tomorrow. For perhaps a quarter of an hour I considered to what possibilities of suffering, more than of death, I had laid myself open. This with the dramatic and emotional part of me: but my senses of proportion and humour, like two court jesters, chased away the tragic poet, and I drifted away on a tide of odd thoughts, watching the various signs of battle in the lower sky.[34]

But if not dualism, double vision certainly shapes Douglas's perceptions and methods. 'Negative Information', a poem about travelling to war, about passing through the looking-glass, ends without reconciliation:

> To this there's no sum I can find –
> the hungry omens of calamity
> mixed with good signs, and all received with levity,
> or indifference, by the amazed mind.

As with Robert Frost, the question of 'seeing' is crucial to any sceptical poetic procedure. However, in the absence of 'metaphysical doubt' (whether *a priori* or *a posteriori*) Douglas's eye differs from Frost's as well as Hughes's. It does not so much look from alternative angles, as aim at progressive penetration: 'lenses/ through which the brain explores . . .' (Exploration is another favourite idea.) Different perspectives extend rather than qualify each other, strive towards the total comprehension of a camera obscura blended with a microscope: a kind of analytic synthesis. The early stages of *Alamein to Zem Zem*, particularly abundant in metaphors of visual display, outline an aesthetic for the desert war: 'the spectacle of the stars', 'the silhouettes of men and turrets',[36] 'the view from a moving tank is like that in a camera obscura or a silent film',[37] 'Against a backcloth of indeterminate landscapes of moods and smells, dance the black and bright incidents'.[38] Verbs of seeing had rehearsed in 'The House' (of the imagination): seems (3), inspect (2), ('like a conjured spectacle'), appear (3), see, scrutinising, prospecting, 'my incredulous eyes/ discern her'. Such verbs function actively and dramatically: 'I watch with interest, for they are ghosts'; 'Look. Here in the gunpit spoil . . .'; 'I see my feet like stones/ underwater', 'I look each side of the door of sleep'. Neither in prose nor poetry does this resemble the 'spectatorial' attitude condemned by Edward Thomas.[39] Douglas uses techniques – verbal as well as imagistic – of montage, collage, silhouetting, juxtaposition, the two-way telescope to elicit the incongruities and complexities of what he perceives. 'Russians' (1940), written before he had witnessed the 'triumphant silence' of the dead,[40] suggests how experimental metaphors of mime, ballet and tableau trained him for the desert theatre:

> How silly that soldier is pointing his gun at the wood:
> he doesn't know it isn't any good.
> You see, the cold and cruel northern wind
> has frozen the whole battalion where they stand.

Later, anticipating an image in *Alamein to Zem Zem*,[41] the poem asks us to 'Think of them as waxworks'. The frozen pose, sustained by a tone and syntax of faux-naif understatement, chills, then pains when emotional 'thaw' arrives in an injunction which ostensibly rules it out:

> Well,
> at least forget what happens when it thaws.

As double vision becomes single here, 'Russians' sets a pattern for later poems where, in Roger Garfitt's words, 'the detachment is not cerebral but is rather a strategy deployed against the strength of feeling'.[42]

Three poems which proceed by still finer gradations of focus are 'Syria II', 'How to Kill' and 'Landscape with Figures'. Syria, 'this two-faced country', is presented in terms not only of contradictory images and ambiguous perspectives ('you think you see a devil stand/ fronting a creature of good intention'), but of linguistic surprise: 'a movement of live stones/ the lizards with hooded eyes/ of hostile miraculous age'. Oxymorons culminate in the images of 'a mantrap in a gay house,/ a murderer with a lover's face'. Athough the poem in a sense remains dualistically unresolved ('devil and angel do not fight,/ they are the classic Gemini'), Douglas's final irony holds this

kaleidoscope in a single frame that partly 'accounts' for all contra-
dictions:

Curiously

> though foreigners we surely shall
> prove this background's complement,
> the kindly visitors who meant
> so well all winter but at last fell
> unaccountably to killing in the spring.

What oxymoron is to 'Syria II', contracting, enjambed, sometimes
inverted sentences are to 'How to Kill':

> The wires touch his face: I cry
> NOW. Death, like a familiar, hears
>
> and look, has made a man of dust
> of a man of flesh. This sorcery
> I do.

Everything in the poem helps Douglas to get death as accurately into
his sights, 'my dial of glass', as the speaker his victim (for here the
poet and killer are mingled). The exact hit, the instant proximity of
life and death, are captured by radii towards a verbal centre, the
delicate 'touch' of sounds and images:

> A shadow is a man
> when the mosquito death approaches.

Like the mosquito, Douglas's imagination hovers over the
invisible point or frontier where extremes meet; where life becomes
death; flesh, dust or bone; love, indifference; Cairo, the desert;
man's creativity, destruction (the 'excellent smooth instruments' of
war). In 'Desert Flowers' he 'looks each side of the door of sleep'. In
'On a Return from Egypt' he lays his whole life and poetry, his dark
Muse, on the line:

> The next month, then, is a window
> and with a crash I'll split the glass.
> Behind it stands one I must kiss,
> person of love or death
> a person or a wraith,
> I fear what I shall find.

Does the incomplete rhyming of 'find' with 'window' stop just this
side of the glass? The thinly dividing walls, doors, glass in Douglas's

house of the imagination reflect a scrutiny as finely balanced as a coin on its edge; or the situation between wartime lovers who 'can never lean/ on an old building in the past/ or a new building in the future', but must

> balance tiptoe on a pin,
> could teach an angel how to stand.
>
> ('Tel Aviv')

Yet the amount of touching, meeting, sudden synchronisations at the end of poems – for good or ill – again suggests an ultimate integrity of vision. 'Landscape with Figures' constitutes Douglas's most comprehensive desert panorama and two-way looking-glass, his sharpest etching of human puniness and lunacy against cosmic spaces. Before section III contains the whole situation, the poet's imagination swoops from being 'Perched on a great fall of air', to a close-up which traps the speaker into the picture as 'the figure writhing on the backcloth'. Just through the looking-glass from 'How to Kill', the poem catches death while it still mimics life. The particular visual tactic of section I uses distance to create a surreal pathetic fallacy. Military vehicles seem the *disiecta membra* of violated insects or plants: 'stunned/ like beetles', 'the steel is torn into fronds/ by the lunatic explosive'. After that 'eccentric chart', Douglas's metaphor of art fuses with his metaphor of theatre. Oxymoron again reinforces a life-death paradox: 'the dead men wriggle', 'express silence', 'this prone and motionless struggle', 'the one who opens his mouth and calls/ silently', and climactically 'stony actors' (compare 'live stones'). In contrast with the violent action arrested in the past participles of section I (squashed, stunned, scattered, torn) the feeble active verbs of section II (wriggle, express, enacting, crawling) have the shocking impact of life continuing as a reflex action. As the stage language moves in from 'scenery' to 'maquillage', the collisions between artifice and reality underline a terrifying unreality. Douglas's 'cosmetic blood and hectic/colours death has the only list of' wounds as deeply as Owen's 'hurt of the colour of blood'. The last line of section II – 'I am the figure writing on the backcloth' – thaws like the end of 'Russians', since 'writhe' is a verb of emotion as well as motion, and prepares for the protean empathy of section III.

Some poems isolate a particular 'stony actor'. 'John Anderson', like 'How to Kill', expresses a life at the moment of death: 'his creative brain whirled'. But it is the enemy soldier of 'Vergissmeinnicht' (how different a poem from 'Strange Meeting') who most completely characterises the unbridgeable nearness of life and death. His eloquent soliloquy indeed 'calls/ silently':

> Look. Here in the gunpit spoil
> the dishonoured picture of his girl
> Who has put: *Steffi. Vergissmeinnicht*
> in a copybook gothic script.
>
> We see him almost with content
> abased, and seeming to have paid
> and mocked at by his own equipment
> that's hard and good when he's decayed.
>
> But she would weep to see today
> how on his skin the swart flies move;
> the dust upon the paper eye
> and the burst stomach like a cave.

By displacing his own feeling into the girl's hypothetical reaction, Douglas combines the intimate ('how on his skin') with the universalised: 'lover and killer' (which includes loved and killed). Hughes narrows Douglas's 'nightmare ground' in defining it as 'the burning away of all human pretensions in the ray cast by death'. Despite 'abased' and 'mocked', the poem's tone encompasses human waste and human dignity. Or Douglas 'burns away' in the sense of exposing essentials rather than of reducing to nothing. His imagination works in the way 'Simplify me when I'm dead' demands of posterity. It is the difference between Hughes's 'Relic' and Douglas's 'Time Eating'. Hughes's evolutionary, zoological perspectives – 'Time in the sea eats its tail, thrives' – are too long for grief. 'Time Eating', with its Shakespearean love story, inhabits historical and psychological time – if with fierce stringency: 'and though you brought me from a boy/ you can make no more of me, only destroy'. The last two lines of 'Vergissmeinnicht', where double vision again becomes 'single', prove the indivisibility of 'mortal hurt' and Douglas's art:

> And death who had the soldier singled
> has done the lover mortal hurt.

'Vergissmeinnicht' also exemplifies Douglas's unusual blend of statement and mimesis. His technique is consistent with the philosophical refusal of 'The Hand' to prefer mind over matter or matter over mind. On the side of statement, his debt to Yeats and Auden appears most strikingly in emphatic adjectives: 'That volatile huge intestine', 'The logical little fish', 'the querulous soft voice// of mariners'. 'The Marvel' combines abstract polysyllabic adjectives – 'one most curious device/ of many, kept by the interesting waves' – with strong basic monosyllables: great, bright, sharp, dim, strong, hot, soft. As regards rhetorical demonstratives, 'this' outscores the Yeatsian 'that': 'This sorcery/ I do', 'this prone and motionless struggle', 'this strong traveller', 'this making a set of pictures, this drawing/ shapes within the shapes of the hand'. The structural role of 'this' in 'The Hand' clarifies its function of uniting close-up and distance, distilling the essence of a phenomenon which it holds out for inspection. More broadly, by mixing in various strengths evocation and declaration, Douglas's syntax pursues his analytical synthesis. The first line of 'Devils', 'My mind's silence is not that of a wood' (for Keith Douglas the verb 'to be' is never weak) prepares for a dialectic, indeed a poem about dialectics. 'A baron of the sea', on the other hand, plunges us into physical experience. Yet there is no hard and fast distinction between the poems. 'Devils' illustrates the link between Douglas's adjustment of sights and redefinition of images. In Geoffrey Hill's words: 'It would seem that he possessed the kind of creative imagination that approached an idea again and again in terms of metaphor, changing position slightly, seeking the most precise hold'.[43] Thus 'Devils' proceeds: 'not that of a wood', 'but this deceptive quiet', 'Only within they make their noise'. But 'The Marvel' too moves over a track of argumentative syntax, if more deeply embedded. Mimesis and statement, material and abstract, cooperate most delicately in the sphere of sound and rhythm. In 'Vergissmeinnicht' Douglas not only consonantally imitates the thick intricacy of 'a copybook gothic script', or increases horror through dynamic assonance ('the burst stomach like a cave'), but in the 'mingled' r, l and t sounds of the last quatrain makes his final statement sensuously and musically incontrovertible.

The war governed Douglas's aesthetic as well as his content, and he saw it as conscripting music and imagery into the service of 'significant speech':

> my object (and I don't give a damn about my duty as a poet) is to write true things, significant things in words each of which works for its place in a line. My rhythms, which you find enervated, are carefully chosen to enable the poems to be *read* as significant speech: I see no reason to be either musical or sonorous about things at present. When I do, I shall be so again, and glad to. I suppose I reflect the cynicism and the careful absence of expectation (it is not quite the same as apathy) with which I view the world . . . perhaps one day cynic and lyric will meet and make me a balanced style. Certainly you will never see the long metrical similes and galleries of images again.[44]

110

This, in 1943, was too modest. Give or take a few immaturities, a few incompletions ('time is all I lacked'), Douglas achieved syntheses, both thematic and stylistic, since unmatched in English poetry. And within his fine balances speech and music, cynicism and lyricism *do* meet. As an aesthetic his economical prescription of economy – 'every word must work for its keep'[45] – is not nearly as well known as it should be, in comparison with many inflated twentieth-century poetic manifestoes. One of Douglas's rich wartime economies is a rigorous paring of phrase, clause and sentence to create a new kind of music as well as a 'sharp enquiring blade':

> A baron of the sea, the great tropic
> swordfish, spreadeagled on the thirsty deck
> where sailors killed him, in the bright Pacific,
>
> yielded to the sharp enquiring blade
> the eye which guided him and found his prey
> in the dim place where he was lord.

'The Marvel' begins with an apposition, a participial phrase, an adverbial clause, pivotal main verb ('yielded'), relative clause, adverbial clause, several prepositional phrases: a great deal of information and implication packed into six lines. Also, the last line of the second stanza reverses syntactically the last line of the first. This reinforces a temporal reversal that resurrects the fish, 'lord' restoring 'baron', and sets up its double role in the poem's cycles of destruction and creation. Douglas's syntax further works for its keep by levelling out historic sequence into a deceptively uniform past tense. His lean periodicity, like MacNeice's ampler rhetoric, may have benefited from classical studies. Not skeletal poetry, but poetry with no superfluous flesh, fighting fit, the cadence of energy.

Two poems called 'Words', by Keith Douglas and Edward Thomas, at once overlap and contrast – as did two wars. They agree on the poet's necessary submission to language. Thomas's appeal 'Choose me,/ You English words' accords with Douglas's strategy:

> Words are my instruments but not my servants;
> by the white pillar of a prince I lie in wait
> for them.

They agree too on the chemistry between language and life, and on consequent artistic responsibilities; even if Thomas's 'earth which you prove/ That we love' is less bleak than Douglas's version:

the pockmarked house bleached by the glare
whose insides war has dried out like gourds
attracts words.

Both poems feature the paradoxical age-youth of words: Thomas's 'Worn new', Douglas's word-butterflies 'hot-coloured, or the cold scarabs a thousand years/ old'. Douglas's metaphor of a butterfly-catcher projects the poet more actively than does Thomas's negative capability before 'natural' language. But his model resembles neither Thomas's dreaded 'murderous' entomologist with a dictionary,[46] nor Hughes's hunter:

There are those who capture them
in hundreds, keep them prisoners in black
bottles, release them at exercise and clap them back.
But I keep words only a breath of time
turning in the lightest of cages – uncover
and let them go: sometimes they escape for ever.

This balancing act (compare Thomas's 'Fixed and free/ In a rhyme') interprets all Douglas's others. The poem's own form – tightly rhymed or half-rhymed yet unpredictable in stress-placing and syllable-count – makes a light cage indeed for vigorously 'significant speech'. Hughes says of Douglas's language: 'Its air of improvisation is a vital part of its purity.'[47] Speaking from the First World War, Thomas celebrates the poet's language as a living medium of continuity and renewal. Speaking from the Second World War, Keith Douglas insists that the poet's basic job is to keep words alive, out of prison camps. His own poetry's immortality is that it 'escapes for ever'.

'Any-angled Light': Philip Larkin and Edward Thomas

Donald Davie's *Thomas Hardy and British Poetry* seems to emerge from his own unresolved mid-Atlantic dilemmas. Like a government spokesman lauding British products in the export-market (his American audience) while urging industry at home to pull its socks up, Davie argues with himself as to whether British poetry should be reasonably satisfied with the more limited role he feels it has chosen in the twilight of empire. Thus, on Hardy's influence as he detects it in the contemporary scene, Davie alternately blows hot and cold, praises with faint damns: 'Are not Hardy and his successors right in severely curtailing for themselves the liberties that other poets continue to take? Does not the example of the Hardyesque poets make some of those other poets look childishly irresponsible?'[1] and damns with faint praise: 'For it begins to look as if Hardy's engaging modesty and his decent liberalism represent a crucial selling short of the poetic vocation, for himself and his successors.'[2] Fixing on Philip Larkin as Hardy's most obvious heir, although 'he sells out or sells off a great deal of his inherited estate',[3] Davie continues to pay back-handed compliments to a 'poetry of lowered sights and patiently diminished expectations'.[4] In an ultimate sense Davie may be right, but penultimately I feel that he ignores certain factors. Firstly, his nomination of Larkin as 'for good or ill the effective unofficial laureate of post-1945 England' sells out poetry to its sociological surfaces: 'the England in [Larkin's] poems is the England we have inhabited . . . We all know that England still has bullfrogs and otters and tramps asleep in ditches; yet because in the landscape of Hughes's poems these shaggy features bulk so large, it may strike us as more an Irish landscape than an English one.'[5] It might easily be maintained that between them Larkin and Hughes exhibit very nearly the full inherited imaginative and linguistic wealth of English poetry. Secondly, Davie swallows too unquestioningly Larkin's own avowals that Hardy is his master. I will suggest later that more of Yeats – if only as Anti-self – and therefore more that is 'Blindingly undiminished' survives in Larkin's poetry than he would have had us believe. Can a writer ever obliterate the memory of his first literary love? And Larkin's 'infatuation with [Yeats's] music' was a three-year *affaire*. Thirdly, and most importantly, I want to introduce a new actor into Davie's scenario. If there is a missing link between Hardy and Larkin, it is surely Edward Thomas.

Thomas, who preferred Hardy's poetry to his novels, understood its special qualities as did few other critics in the first decade of the century: 'He would abide with equanimity and certainty of ultimate approval any too nice questioning as to whether his verses are poetry.'[6] Thomas notes Hardy's 'unvarying sadness',[7] as Larkin calls sadness his poetry's 'dominant emotion';[8] but is less at home than Larkin with 'that most tyrannous obsession of the blindness of Fate, the carelessness of Nature, and the insignificance of Man, crawling in multitudes like caterpillars, twitched by the Immanent Will hither and thither'.[9] Thomas also, although in an analytical rather than critical spirit, finds Hardy's poetry without some dimensions of form and mystery:

> though he indulges in many varieties of rhyme and stanza form, it is hard to believe that it is for any sensuous quality . . .[10]

> Seldom does anything creep in from Nature or the spirit of humanity to give his work a something not to be accounted for in what he actually says.[11]

Thomas wrote his most Hardyesque cluster of poems in the weeks before he left for the trenches, when his life, like 'The Long Small Room', 'narrowed up'. The figure in these poems becomes more a twitched pawn of fate. The vocabulary and monotonous rhyme of 'Out in the Dark' (which bears a strange relation to Hardy's 'The Fallow Deer at the Lonely House') almost quote Hardy, and its vision supports Paul Fussell's contention that Hardy's imaginative structures foreshadowed the experience of the First World War:[12]

> And star and I and wind and deer
> Are in the dark together, – near,
> Yet far, – and fear
> Drums on my ear
> In that sage company drear.
>
> How weak and little is the light,
> All the universe of sight,
> Love and delight,
> Before the might,
> If you love it not, of night.

'If you love it not', however, complicates the poem's attitude as compared with the end of Larkin's 'The Building':

> nothing contravenes
> The coming dark, though crowds each evening try
>
> With wasteful, weak, propitiatory flowers.

Apart from specific thematic or technical convergence, or revealing divergences, the poetry of Hardy, Thomas and Larkin shares a close connection with prose – a connection which helped them to renew poetry. In 1909, still five years away from writing poetry himself, Thomas began a review of *Time's Laughingstocks* by speculating:

> It would be interesting to learn how a great prose writer regards his verse. He will have a tenderness for it as for the fairer and perhaps the elder child; but in what frame of mind does he who can say so much in prose and denies himself no subject or mood in it, turn to verse? Is it an instinct for finality in form, a need of limitation and strict obedience to rule, or a desire to express but not to explain, or is it partly for the sake of the royalty of the robes and the great tradition?[13]

Both Thomas and Larkin (accurately) judge their own prose less complete than Hardy's – which may have impelled them towards a greater 'finality' of poetic form. As Larkin partly disqualifies himself as a novelist on grounds of lyrical solipsism ('novels are about other people and poems are about yourself'[14]), so Thomas asked Gordon Bottomley: 'What will you say of my 25,000 words of landscape [*Beautiful Wales*], nearly all of it without humanity except what it may owe to a lanky shadow of myself . . .?'[15] And just as Thomas compared his first poems to 'quintessences of the best parts of my prose books',[16] some of Larkin's poems resemble quintessential novels or short stories. He draws a distinction akin to Thomas's 'express' and 'explain': 'whereas the poet relies on the intensity with which he can say it, the novelist relies on the persuasiveness with which he can show it'.[17] Nevertheless, a line such as 'And Christmas at his sister's house in Stoke', one of the saddest lines in English poetry, speaks volumes. Similarly, Thomas's many attempts to capture Autumn culminate in the quintessential 'green elm with the one great bough of gold'. Although Hardy's fiction may incline more to 'showing', and his poetry to 'saying', his poems rarely transmute the characteristics of his prose with such intensity. As for more direct links between Thomas and Larkin: Larkin includes Thomas (and Robert Frost) in a list of twelve exemplars; and gives him nine interestingly chosen poems in his *Oxford Book of Twentieth-Century English Verse*, though surprisingly not 'Old Man'. His review of William Cooke's *Edward Thomas: A Critical Biography* takes a compassionate there-but-for-the-grace-of-God interest in Thomas's thraldom to Grub Street and domesticity ('Oh, no one can deny/ That Arnold is less selfish than I'). And one can hear him cheering Thomas's escape from his 'stalemate of temperament and circumstance' to 'a serene and unquestionable climax' once war and other changes had brought 'his proper subject, England, into focus'[18]. But I am less concerned with any possible 'influence' of Thomas on Larkin than with a significant coincidence and continuity of effort. I want to consider the strength and centrality of an approach which, concentrating rather than lowering its sights, exposes these two poets imaginatively naked to their experience and the world, walking their different 'solitary' tightropes between light and dark, all balance dependent on a scrupulous fidelity to observation, feeling and language.

It sometimes looks as if Larkin, like Thomas, has to live down affiliations with the wrong minor poetic school. In contrast, Imagists, like Etonians, used to be excused every incompetence. The similarities between Georgian poetry and Movement poetry have been much canvassed, especially by those who dislike both. But if one does not accept "Georgian" and "neo-Georgian" as necessarily pejorative terms, these similarities seem worth pursuing in a more positive spirit. From a cultural point of view, before one war and after another, the Georgians and the Movement signalled, if nothing else, an important sensibility-shift. As the Georgians rejected Victorian rhetoric, 'Hectoring large-scale verses' on public themes, the propaganda of Kipling: so the Movement poets reacted in part against the propaganda of Auden and the socio-political orientation of much thirties poetry. At the other end of the spectrum they repudiated the oddly equivalent psychic wallowings of the *fin de siècle* and the Apocalypse. If this shift involved contraction, it also involved precision. The cutting back of undergrowth and overgrowth is perhaps a recurrently necessary *reculer pour mieux sauter*. This is Edward Marsh on his team (whom Thomas had discovered a decade earlier):

> The vague iridescent ethereal kind [of poetry] had a long intermittent innings all through the nineteenth century, especially at the end, and Rossetti, Swinburne, and Dowson could do things which it is no use trying now. It seems a necessity now to write either with one's eye on an object or with one's mind at grips with a more or less definite idea.[19]

And Robert Conquest on his:

> If one had briefly to distinguish this poetry of the fifties from its predecessors, I believe the most important general point would be that it submits to no great systems of theoretical constructs nor agglomerations of unconscious commands. It is free from both mystical and logical compulsions and – like modern philosophy – is empirical in its attitude to all that comes.[20]

116

As Thomas's dominant personae 'only look into the water', 'prefer the truth/ Or nothing', so Larkin's 'Lines on a Young Lady's Photograph Album' sets its aesthetic sights on 'a real girl in a real place,// In every sense empirically true'. Robert Graves and Laura Riding once contemptuously characterised the original Georgian aesthetic as 'resulting in a poetry that could rather be praised for what it was not than for what it was',[21] but Conquest argues that 'a negative determination to avoid bad principles' is in itself 'a good deal'.[22] Whereas the 'empirical' base to which the Georgians returned was observation of Nature; the Movement was more grounded in observations on human nature – after Auden and Graves (and Yeats) the emphasis was bound to be on placing rather than places, statement not evocation – and this difference is reflected in the different textures of Thomas's and Larkin's poetry. Larkin has been as firmly prised apart from the Movement by well-intentioned critics as Thomas from the Georgians. Although qualitative distinctions must be made, this sundering could one day leave him vulnerably solitary like Thomas, credited with anomalous excellence, a shrine to be routinely saluted on one's way to the big altars, while his central contribution to modern poetry is ignored. Of course the link with Hardy – and, I hope, Thomas – may help to prevent this. In a radio interview with Anthony Thwaite concerning his editorship of the *Oxford Book*, Larkin accounted for the generous space he accords the Georgians in terms of a (revealing) curiosity on his part to discover whether 'there might have been an English tradition coming on from the nineteenth century begun by Hardy'. He admitted, however, that the Georgians 'didn't resuscitate themselves in my own mind' and that he found their language 'stale'. But if instead of flogging the dead horses of Gibson and Squire, Larkin had placed a more limited selection from the minor figures in relation to a doubled representation of Thomas and of Owen, he might have found what he was looking for, and filled in his own genealogy.

The most obvious common factor between Thomas and Larkin is of course "Englishness". It has long been apparent that Thomas's poetry is 'English as this gate, these flowers, this mire', although the implications of this, and the complex *earned* nature of Thomas's Englishness, have not been fully pursued. The speaker in 'The Importance of Elsewhere' seems to carry Larkin's sanction in acknowledging 'These are my customs and establishments', and Davie observes: 'we recognise in Larkin's poems the seasons of present-day England, but we recognise also the seasons of an English soul'.[23] A peculiarly indigenous quality has been preserved by their wariness about the Modernist invader. Thomas, infinitely better informed about his contemporaries than Larkin, may have sensed something both alien and unworkable in Pound's aesthetic (see page 30 above). But Thomas and Frost wrestled with the challenge of Modernism at an early stage, when all poetry was in the wars, and the bout strengthened their own theory and practice. When Larkin dismisses Parker, Pound and Picasso in the introduction to *All What Jazz* (perhaps his absent preface to the *Oxford Book*), he paints himself into a right-wing corner; thus undermining the real authority of his attack on 'irresponsible exploitations of technique in contradiction of human life as we know it', on art that 'helps us neither to enjoy nor endure'.[24] Nor did Thomas's regard for England allow him to defend Newbolt, for instance – 'all his verse might be described as an elaborate corollary to "Rule Britannia"'[25] – as Larkin out of insecurity over-protects Betjeman. Larkin all too correctly titles his essay on Betjeman 'It Could Only Happen In England'. The cult, like the poetry, is a cosy tribal ritual which bewilders outsiders. Betjeman's Marlborough contemporary Louis MacNeice failed even then to 'understand his passion for minor poetry and misbegotten ornament'.[26]

Extolling Betjeman's 'defiant advocacy of the little, the obscure, the disregarded', and his preservation of 'what I should want to remember' 'if I were a soldier leaving England',[27] Larkin expends energy better put to broadcasting Edward Thomas's higher versions of these matters, his much less comfortable 'seasons of an English soul'. Thomas's twin rootedness in the English countryside and English literature enabled him to discover – though by hard, lonely work – a genuine continuity, instead of desperately appropriating charming fossils. It is perhaps the struggle between Larkin's doubts as to whether a native tradition exists, and his instinct that it must, which to some extent distorts his attitudes and tastes. It may indeed denote some crisis of confidence that Larkin nowhere *positively* relishes his cultural roots, as Thomas celebrates in 'Words' the very language which affords a living proof of continuity: 'Worn new/ Again and again,' – although every line of his poetry declares that English words have also chosen him.

It would be literal-minded, however, to labour the contrast between the train-window epiphany of 'Adlestrop' (a poem included in the *Oxford Book*) and its failed counterpart in 'I Remember, I Remember':

                    What I saw
Was Adlestrop – only the name

And willows, willow-herb, and grass,
And meadowsweet, and haycocks dry,
No whit less still and lonely fair
Than the high cloudlets in the sky.
                    (Thomas)

I leant far out, and squinnied for a sign
That this was still the town that had been 'mine'
So long, but found I wasn't even clear
Which side was which. From where those cycle-crates
Were standing, had we annually departed

For all those family hols? . . .
                    (Larkin)

Coventry transmits no 'sign' from what should have been 'roots'; for
Thomas, an unfamiliar place, 'only the name', opens up spiralling
vistas which eventually evoke an English microcosm and Muse: 'all
the birds/ Of Oxfordshire and Gloucestershire'. But although
Larkin's poetry comes up England by a different, mid-century, line
than Thomas's, it *does* include areas 'Where sky and Lincolnshire
and water meet'. Davie rather curiously sees Larkin as limited by
being 'one sort of extreme humanist' who 'makes himself numb to
the non-human creation in order to stay compassionate towards the
human'.[28] 'Myxomatosis' hardly bears this out:

You may have thought things would come right again
If you could only keep quite still and wait.

Admittedly Larkin's brilliant animal-miniatures are in various
degrees consciously emblematic of The Human Situation – but then
so are most Nature poems. Davie seems to contradict his own thesis
when he asserts:

near the end of 'The Whitsun Weddings', when

I thought of London spread out in the sun,
Its postal districts packed like squares of wheat . . .

the collision between the organicism of wheat and the rigidity of
'postal districts' is calculated. It is the human pathos of the many
weddings he has seen from the train which spills over to sanctify, for
the poet, the postal districts of London, the train's destination; the
human value suffuses the abstractly schematised with the grace of an
organic fertility.[29]

After diagnosing 'collision', he in fact describes fusion. And some of the richest moments of release and blossoming in Larkin's poetry, his 'kneeling as cattle by all-generous waters', seem to demand natural imagery for their expression:

> Earth's immeasurable surprise

> Spring, of all seasons most gratuitous,
> Is fold of untaught flower, is race of water,
> Is earth's most multiple, excited daughter

> A sense of falling, like an arrow-shower
> Sent out of sight, somewhere becoming rain.

Although Larkin does not plot psychic weather and seasons as minutely as Thomas, these are often sensed in oppositions between 'seasonal decrease' and increase: weeds, stalks, falling or fallen leaves, snow, 'Summer is fading', 'cold sun'; petalled flowers, Whitsun, wheat, 'punctual spread of seed', 'breed', 'It will be spring soon', 'spring-woken trees', 'unmolesting meadows', 'And that high-builded cloud/ Moving at summer's pace'. Larkin's 'Spring' and Thomas's 'October' turn on a precisely similar anguish that the poet, man, is cut off from the organic annual cycle, though his longing to participate finally establishes a paradoxical identification. After feeling himself to be 'An indigestible sterility', the speaker in 'Spring' finally recognises:

> And those she has least use for see her best,
> Their paths grown craven and circuitous,
> Their visions mountain-clear, their needs immodest.

'Visions mountain-clear' invokes Wordsworth, for whom by implication Nature has more use than for Larkin. Yet just as one level of Larkin's poetry explores a problematic relation to 'customs and establishments' (marriage, society, religion, England), so a sub-stratum conducts Hughesian negotiations with 'what is out there' (and in there). Two poems of Thomas's which firmly earth all human life are paralleled by two of Larkin's. Thomas's 'There's Nothing Like the Sun' and Larkin's 'Solar' certainly aim at comprehensiveness:

> There's nothing like the sun as the year dies,
> Kind as it can be, this world being made so,
> To stones and men and beasts and birds and flies,
> To all things that it touches except snow
> Whether on mountain side or street of town.
>
> (Thomas)

Suspended lion face
Spilling at the centre
Of an unfurnished sky
How still you stand
And how unaided,
Single stalkless flower
You pour unrecompensed.

(Larkin)

In fact 'There's Nothing Like the Sun' carries a sting in its tail which the sunflowering, sexual 'Solar' (compare Lawrence's 'Sun') lacks: 'There's nothing like the sun till we are dead'/ 'You give for ever'. 'The Word' and 'Forget What Did' assign similar priority to universal seasons, as opposed to social, political or national annals:

I have forgot, too, names of the mighty men
That fought and lost or won in the old wars,
Of kings and fiends and gods, and most of the stars.
Some things I have forgot that I forget.
But lesser things there are, remembered yet,
Than all the others. One name that I have not –
Though 'tis an empty thingless name – forgot
Never can die because Spring after Spring
Some thrushes learn to say it as they sing.

The speaker in 'Forget What Did' less passively suppresses an unhappy past into a nullity,

Like the wars and winters
Missing behind the windows
Of an opaque childhood.

And the empty pages?
Should they ever be filled
Let it be with observed

Celestial recurrences,
The day the flowers come,
And when the birds go.

Both poems also identify the Muse with Nature: Thomas's 'say' and 'sing'; Larkin's hidden agenda for future poems 'filled . . . with . . . Celestial recurrences'. (None of this, incidentally, sells poetry short, but consigns all that is not poetry to Thomas's 'undefiled/ Abyss of what will never be again'.) Far from making himself numb to the non-human creation, Larkin like most English Nature poets hungers for it, but entertains the possibility that it may be numb to him.

Both Thomas and Larkin also of course relate themselves to a specific countryside, Larkin's inevitably much more peopled and built-up. Davie argues that Larkin makes no evaluative distinctions between what he observes out of a train window: 'There is no meaning, no "placing", in the way pre-industrial things like farms, cattle, hedges and grass are interspersed with industrial things like chemical froth and dismantled cars.'[30] Colin Falck too has remarked: 'the view from the train window, with its complete randomness and detachment is at the heart of Larkin's vision . . . There are no epiphanies'.[31] If Larkin's train journeys perform an equivalent function to Thomas's walks, then the contrast may indeed denote the two poets travelling at different distances from 'Lob'; though both *set out* as solitary observers. Up to a point too I agree with Davie that 'the tone of the describing voice is scrupulously neutral'[32] – in 'The Whitsun Weddings' and elsewhere – yet this resembles Thomas's anxiety to fill in the whole picture: 'Twig, leaf, flint, thorn,/ Straw, feather, all that men scorn' ('November'). But even if Larkin is careful not to let the power of the rural images overwhelm the others in a way that would falsify the real contours of his and the contemporary English experience, he also seems interested in trying to bring the urban into some kind of significant relation with the rural, whereby the former might be revalued or revitalised. After all, his trains do not simply commute between city stations, they traverse representative stretches of landscape, just as Thomas mapped the 'copses, ponds, roads, and ruts', villages and counties of his England. (MacNeice often gets overlooked as an intermediary, as a pioneer of the poetic train-window panorama – see the first section of *Autumn Journal*). And Larkin discovers bridging 'epiphanies' in suburbia: 'An Odeon went past, a cooling tower,/ And someone running up to bowl'; 'A thrush sings,/ Laurel-surrounded/ In the deep bare garden,/ Its fresh-peeled voice/ Astonishing the brickwork' – as Larkin's voice can astonish it.

In 'Here', where Davie seems to feel that Larkin abandons his neutrality, detecting 'a perverse determination that the ultimate ("terminate") pastoral shall be among the cut-price stores, and nowhere else',[33] the underlying rhetoric in fact moves in the opposite direction. On top of the neutral basis which impartially assigns appreciative and depreciatory epithets to the natural and the man-made ('rich industrial shadows'/ 'raw estates'; 'thin and thistled'/ 'The piled gold clouds, the shining gull-marked mud'), there is an attempt to connect town and country ('grain-scattered streets', 'a terminate and fishy-smelling/ Pastoral of ships up streets'). Davie says 'every nonurban thing comes along with a negating or cancelling epithet'[34] at the conclusion:

> And out beyond its mortgaged half-built edges
> Fast-shadowed wheat-fields, running high as hedges,
> Isolate villages, where removed lives
>
> Loneliness clarifies. Here silence stands
> Like heat. Here leaves unnoticed thicken,
> Hidden weeds flower, neglected waters quicken,
> Luminously-peopled air ascends;
> And past the poppies bluish neutral distance
> Ends the land suddenly beyond a beach
> Of shapes and shingle. Here is unfenced existence:
> Facing the sun, untalkative, out of reach.

But the 'ultimate pastoral' is surely 'here'. And the poem has significantly come full circle, enclosing and including the townscape of the two middle stanzas, 'fenced existence', within the 'widening' perspectives provided by river and sea. 'Luminously-peopled air ascends' and 'Facing the sun' (images of light, sun, heat often appear to tilt the balance in Larkin) shine out without qualification, as do the verbs of increase: 'thicken' 'flower' 'quicken', which contrast with the earlier 'dead straight miles' and 'slave museum'. The 'terminate' streets seem to be a dead end, this vista, despite 'Ends the land suddenly', open-ended: 'distance', 'unfenced'. Rather than signifying 'noncommittal, unhelpful'[35] (Davie), 'untalkative' speaks for the landscape. It asserts latent instinctive wisdoms, however disregarded or difficult of access, potential 'clarifications' for the 'cut-price crowd, urban yet simple'. Through a Thomas-like paradox, whereby the real conclusion in part runs counter to what is overtly stated, Larkin reaches out towards Thomas's landscape. Thomas's 'The Path', which like 'Here' may also track poetry itself, mysteriously ends 'sudden, it ends where the wood ends'.

For both poets, the conditions of epiphany are frequently sun, solitude, and silence. In 'The Whitsun Weddings', more continuously affirmative and inclusive, Larkin brings the 'cut-price crowd' on the journey with him 'through the tall heat that slept/ For miles inland'. Leaving Hull, setting off from a cameo of 'Here', the poem dramatises a solitary's growing involvement with society, and traverses a representative stretch of England, even while admitting its own 'frailty' as a 'travelling coincidence'. Nevertheless, a combined sense of movement and marriage, acceleration and

increase, weds poet, people, town and country, 'holding' and ordering them within a harnessed vitality –

> and what it held
> Stood ready to be loosed with all the power
> That being changed can give

– that throws off cultural as well as personal reverberations.
Thomas's 'Good-night', which portrays a solitary journey to the
London streets of the poet's childhood, to Larkin's England perhaps,
where 'the call of children in the unfamiliar streets' is 'Sweet as the
voice of nightingale or lark', registers a similar coincidence or
unexpected sense of belonging ('homeless, I am not lost'): 'Never
again, perhaps, after tomorrow shall/ I see these homely streets,
these church windows alight,/ Not a man or woman or child among
them all:/ But it is All Friends' Night, a traveller's good-night.' In
addition, 'Here' and 'The Whitsun Weddings', like Thomas's poetry
more pervasively, may be just tinged by what Thomas calls Blake's
'mystic patriotism':[36] a phantom Jerusalem 'luminously-peopled',
an 'arrow-shower' achieving its desire.

Some of Larkin's landscapes then do follow Thomas's in holding
out a promise of coherence to what Thomas called 'those modern
people who belong nowhere'.[37] Another way of making them feel at
home is to connect them with their past. Davie commends Larkin
for, unlike other post-*Waste Land* poets, refusing to 'measure our
present (usually seen as depleted) against our past (usually seen as
rich)', and his lack of Betjemanesque 'nostalgia'.[38] I don't believe
that Thomas is nostalgic either, although or because he could more
often and more confidently detect the visible and living presence of
the past: 'Safe under tile and thatch' ('The Manor Farm'). When
Larkin captures it in 'MCMXIV' he does so, significantly, by entering Thomas's era (though Thomas removed the haze from place-
names):

> And the countryside not caring:
> The place-names all hazed over
> With flowering grasses, and fields
> Shadowing Domesday lines
> Under wheat's restless silence . . .

and adding his own further dimension:

> Never such innocence,
> Never before or since,
> As changed itself to past
> Without a word . . .

124

Although 'hazed over', 'Shadowing', and 'changed itself to past' suggest the increasing faintness of the horizons, Larkin's zoom-lens works like Thomas's layering in 'Digging' – another line of doomed soldiers:

> What matter makes my spade for tears or mirth,
> Letting down two clay pipes into the earth?
> The one I smoked, the other a soldier
> Of Blenheim, Ramillies, and Malplaquet
> Perhaps. The dead man's immortality
> Lies represented lightly with my own,
> A yard or two nearer the living air
> Than bones of ancients . . .

In fact certain vistas already haze over in Thomas's 'Haymaking'. The archetypal scene 'Under the heavens that know not what years be' is fixed by an ambiguous final couplet:

> All of us gone out of the reach of change –
> Immortal in a picture of an old grange.

As with Larkin's enlistment photographs, and the exploded view of 'Digging', the shutter clicks on the question: death or immortality? 'Haymaking' frames and distances pastoral as actuality, pastoral as art: 'Older than Clare, and Cobbett, Morland and Crome'. Thomas of course constantly registers his position on the cusp of change, though with residual hopes for 'an England beautiful/ And like her mother that died yesterday'. Larkin's 'Going, Going', with no such obvious justification, forecloses the cultural recession of 'Church Going', to write an epitaph less open-ended than Thomas's despite its future tense:

> And that will be England gone,
> The shadows, the meadows, the lanes,
> The guildhalls, the carved choirs.

This lament for a church of England contracts Larkin's formerly 'rich industrial shadows' into Betjeman country, just as 'Homage to a Government' contracts 'MCMXIV' into Kipling country and removes Blake from the map:

> Next year we shall be living in a country
> That brought its soldiers home for lack of money.

'At Grass', in Blake Morrison's reading, more sensitively takes the temperature of 'post-imperial *tristesse*'.[39] Thomas was too near 'the word [and deed] Imperialism'[40] ever to confuse cultural with

125

political Nationalism, introverted love of country with an external patriotism. Thomas perceives the leviathan of war and oppression as a constant. His 'ancients' in 'Digging' see 'Almighty God erect the mastodon'; the same God who in 'February Afternoon' 'sits aloft' with Hardyesque indifference 'in the array/ That we have wrought him, stone-deaf and stone blind'.

Larkin's true imaginative archaeology (as opposed to antiquarian aberrations) is directed, like Thomas's, towards the common humanity and inhumanity that links the ages. Both endeavour to trace, sometimes in derelict or deserted places, man's footprints or landmarks; to excavate and construe 'Bone-riddled ground'. They take in the dead that 'lie round' in 'Church Going' or 'that never/ More than half hidden lie' in Thomas's 'Two Houses'. 'An Arundel Tomb' spans the centuries, as elsewhere Larkin spans the industrial wastelands: 'Snow fell, undated. Light/ Each summer thronged the glass . . . And up the paths/ The endless altered people came . . .' The paradoxical endurance of 'The stone fidelity/ They hardly meant' suggests as does Thomas's 'Women He Liked' where 'Bob Hayward' devotedly plants elms which have the effect of 'turning the lane to slough/ And gloom' until 'the name alone survives, Bob's Lane', that although man cannot influence or properly interpret the selective processes of history, something 'survives'. Further, 'What will survive of us' is likely to reflect in some way individual acts of 'love', and derive its permanence from associations with art or language. In each case, the poet himself completes the transformation of history into myth, adds the 'final blazon'.

As a preliminary to comparing the more psychological and metaphysical aspects of Larkin's and Thomas's poetry, here are some broad parallels. There is the preoccupation with finding a 'home' in a profounder sense, the post-Romantic self-projection as spiritually displaced person:

> This is my grief. That land,
> My home, I have never seen;
> No traveller tells of it,
> However far he has been.
>
> (Thomas, 'Home')

> No, I have never found
> The place where I could say
> *This is my proper ground,*
> *Here I shall stay . . .*
>
> (Larkin, 'Places, Loved Ones')

Such statements crystallise an atmosphere of indefinable 'desire', often quickly nipped in the bud. Thomas's 'Melancholy' almost self-parodyingly announces 'What I desired I knew not, but whate'er my choice/ Vain it must be, I knew'. Larkin's 'Sparkling armada of promises' 'leave us holding wretched stalks/ Of disappointment'. Thomas's pursuit of 'Health', 'happiness', 'content', 'The Glory', 'Beauty', 'the unseen moving goal', corresponds to Larkin's of 'joy', 'happiness', 'that much-mentioned brilliance, love', 'Intensely far, that padlocked cube of light', 'purer water/ Not here but anywhere'. For both desire is occasionally located in the figure of a woman. Thomas's 'Unknown' 'is to be kissed/ Only perhaps by me . . . she/ May not exist'. Larkin more ironically conjures up in 'Essential Beauty' 'that unfocused she/ No match lit up, nor drag ever brought near,/ Who now stands newly clear,/ Smiling, and recognising, and going dark'. Larkin includes one of Thomas's poems of this type, 'Celandine', in the *Oxford Book*: 'For a short swift eternity back she came' only to be 'Gone like a never perfectly recalled air'. Both poets also record darker desires and loves:

> Beneath it all, desire of oblivion runs
> (Larkin, 'Wants')

> Like me who have no love which this wild rain
> Has not dissolved except the love of death . . .
> (Thomas, 'Rain' – included in the *Oxford Book*)

The balance oscillates between desire and foreboding anticipation of what ends desire. For Larkin 'Only one ship is seeking us', 'There is an evening coming in'. For Thomas 'The tall forest towers', night gradually encroaches on 'All the universe of sight'. At low ebb his poetry reduces life and itself to 'this my right hand// Crawling crab-like over the clean white page,/ Resting awhile each morning on the pillow,/ Then once more starting to crawl on towards age' ('The Long Small Room'). Larkin in the persona of 'Death-suited' visitor looks forward to 'age, and then the only end of age' ('Dockery and Son').

Here I can do no more than suggest that Thomas's exploration of all these issues is a little more subtle and affirmative than Larkin's. The questing, questioning *movement* of his poetry occasionally enables the seeker to touch his goal (as in 'I Never Saw that Land Before'), or at any rate closes the distance between him and it – for instance in the terrier-like self-inquisition of 'The Glory'. It is possible that Larkin included this poem in the *Oxford Book* for its final admission 'I cannot bite the day to the core', but at least Thomas probes all the likely reasons for failure and thus to some extent alleviates it:

> Or must I be content with discontent,
> As larks and swallows are perhaps with wings?
> And shall I ask at the day's end once more
> What beauty is, and what I can have meant
> By happiness? And shall I let all go,
> Glad,weary, or both?

In contrast, Larkin's 'Home is so Sad' and 'As Bad as a Mile' unravel backwards – the latter to 'The apple unbitten in the palm'. Larkin's pendulum swings more violently between sending images of the ideal on ahead in arrow-showers or 'joyous shots at how things ought to be', and announcing an iron *status quo*: 'Electric limits to their widest senses.' Thomas always tries to push back limits and cross frontiers. In the epiphanic 'Ash Grove' his imagination passes through a wall 'at either end without noticing' and wins one of the unexpected bonuses of its persistence:

> the moment unveiled something unwilling to die
> And I had what most I desired, without search or desert or cost.

Even Thomas's fascination with death figures as more an active curiosity to penetrate the unknown than a passive yielding to the inevitable: 'There is not any book/ Or face of dearest look/ That I would not turn from now/ To go into the unknown'. One would rather wander with Thomas along 'The green roads that end in the forest' than limp with Larkin 'down Cemetery Road'.

The combination of 'nostalgia', desire and death-wish in the work of both poets has, however, aroused rather similar hostility in critics with a 'maturer' outlook. Colin Falck, who speaks disparagingly of Larkin bathing everything in 'the same general wistfulness', also remarks: 'The ideal, for Larkin, has become inaccessible, and being inaccessible it can only throw the real world into shadow instead of lighting it up from within.'[41] H. Coombes finds 'something *relatively* immature in the way Thomas often refers to happiness and beauty as "goals" that can conceivably be reached and retained, as if he hoped a golden land existed at the end of the journey'.[42] In 'A Note on Nostalgia' D.W. Harding observes: 'It would be a mistake to complain because Edward Thomas refused to account for his moods and label them. But it is a defect that, through a failure to probe his unhappiness, he implied that its causes were remoter, less tangible and more inevitable than in fact they were.'[43] This kind of psychoanalytical criticism is (was?) the modern heir of the Victorian and Edwardian moralising over Shelley or Keats which so amused Thomas:

> I am not attempting to answer the man who should say that after boiling the 'Ode to a Nightingale', he found only peevishness at the bottom of it. I do think, however, that melancholy (in spite of the ode) is too disparaging a name for this mood, and that we have been deceived into suspecting evil of the poem because it is beautiful and attributes divinity to what we think a weakness. None today would complain if the thought had remained in this lyrical form:

> > *Welcome joy, and welcome sorrow,*
> > *Lethe's weed and Hermes' feather!*
> > *Come today, and come tomorrow;*
> > *I do love you both together;*

> we should begin to talk earnestly of the gospel of pain.[44]

Poetry 'In every sense empirically true' must fluctuate between the poles of nightmare and dream, between 'Electric limits' and 'What so soon will wake and grow/ Utterly unlike the snow' ('First Sight'). Thomas's poems more often than Larkin's incubate the gyre of a contrary movement, instead of falling into Manichean contradiction (like 'Wires' and 'First Sight'). This may define their different distances from Romanticism as an aesthetic of transcendence. Whereas Thomas and Frost could subject a still-breathing spirit to severe tests without terminal damage, Larkin alternately switches on and off its life-support system. Thus in 'Dublinesque' Romanticism itself becomes an object of desire:

> A voice is heard singing
> Of Kitty, or Katy,
> As if the name meant once
> All love, all beauty.

Thomas tries on Romantic attitudes only to discard them ('rid of this dream, ere I had drained/ Its poison'). The waker of 'Cock-Crow' clothes his imagination in 'twin trumpeters . . ./ Heralds of splendour' whom the last line banishes: 'The milkers lace their boots up at the farms'. Yet this line, the essence of Thomas's true aesthetic, is not exactly an anti-climax, partly because it retains an aura from its heralds. Larkin's poems sometimes explicitly proclaim the incongruity of such costumes: 'swagger the nut-strewn roads', 'where I did not invent/ Blinding theologies of flowers and fruits'. However he *does* sun-worship and endow his hypothetical religion of water, perhaps his own poetry, with a high-Romantic altar 'Where any-angled light/ Would congregate endlessly'. Larkin also oscillates between two masters, between Hardy who mourned at the graveside of Romanticism and Yeats who resurrected it – hence 'Dublinesque'. Despite a public demeanour which (like his poetry's strategies) obfuscates the solitary prophet or *vates*, his sensibility secretes an extreme Romanticism within its capacity for extreme disappointment: 'If the worst/ Of flawless weather is our falling short.' Yet the honesty with which he turns in faithful and disappointing snapshots, itself underwrites the occasional all-transcending winners: 'what grace/ Your candour thus confers upon her face!' A 'romantic loiterer who recalls the days when poetry was condemned as sinful',[45] Larkin also laments: 'The days when one could claim to be the priest of a mystery are gone . . . Yet writing a poem is still not an act of the will.'[46]

'All love, all beauty' apart, Anthony Thwaite's term for the attitude and tone of some of Larkin's poems, 'agnostic stoicism',[47] also applies to Thomas (though he is at once more thoroughly agnostic and more often epicurean), and might most comprehensively denote their common starting-point. Both are agnostic in the ordinary sense of the term. Thomas slips in the passing dig at 'God' (see above); and although 'The Mountain Chapel' recognises a certain value in a ritual from which the protagonist remains excluded ('Men behind the glass/ Stand once a week, singing, and drown/ The whistling grass/ Their ponies munch') it bows to the wind as the real power in the land: 'When gods were young/ This wind was old'. Thomas's feelings for Nature do provide him with a quasi-religious, quasi-mythological, if not particularly reassuring, faith that the wind and the rain, natural forces, preceded and will succeed man and his monuments: 'the roar of towns/ And their brief multitude'. He enjoyed the prospect of Jefferies's *After London*. Larkin in 'Church Going', without putting forward any alternative perspective, also implies that all religious formulations, 'belief' and 'disbelief', are much of a muchness and so can identify even his own scepticism with the 'compulsions' that have brought people to 'this accoutred frowsty barn', 'Since someone will forever be surprising/ A hunger in himself to be more serious,/ And gravitating with it to this ground'. Compare 'The Mountain Chapel': 'And yet somewhere,/ Near or far off, there's a man could/ Live happy here . . .'. Larkin's occasional translations of *his* feeling for Nature on to a religious plane ('any-angled light') cannot consistently dissolve the fear of mortality within larger mysteries, as happens in Thomas's poetry. Larkin's 'Aubade', written after *High Windows*, maintains:

This is a special way of being afraid
No trick dispels. Religion used to try,
That vast moth-eaten musical brocade
Created to pretend we never die . . .

Larkin and Thomas, like MacNeice, are also more broadly agnostic in their acceptance of what is "given" (though Larkin feels he has been given less than Thomas does) as all we have to go on. This is their ultimate empiricism, to which the path through the self, the sensed, England and history leads, or from which it derives. Again, Thomas's settling for 'life and earth' is rather more affirmative and mythological, and thus takes us further. For him, life emerges from the forest, the 'unknown', 'an avenue, dark, nameless, without end', only to pass back into it (the swallow through a banquet-hall parable). Larkin's apprehension of life as intersecting perspectives of past and future, also central to Thomas's vision, is rather more contracted and less mysterious. It begins in what we consciously remember and ends in what we consciously expect – 'Extinction's alp':

For borne away in deadened air
May go the sudden shut of loss
Round something nearly at an end,
And what cohered in it across
The years, the unique random blend
Of families and fashions, there

At last begin to loosen.
                    ('Ambulances')

As for stoicism, Thomas has in addition subtler strategies for coping with a situation which in any case he more positively embraces, and even celebrates ('And yet I still am half in love with pain'). He is not so ready to 'sense the solving emptiness/ That lies just under all we do', or postulate life as 'first boredom, then fear' or 'slow dying'. However, his bleakest poems fall back on stoicism:

Until blindness come, I must wait
And blink at what is not good.
                    ('Home')

I am something like that:
Not one pane to reflect the sun,
For the schoolboys to throw at –
They have broken every one.
                    ('Gone, Gone Again')

Since the agnostic's 'element is time', there remains the problem of getting, or hopefully coming, through it. 'What are days for?' 'What does it mean?' The agnostic is immediately involved in questions, decisions, choices, 'Horny dilemmas', unknown to the believer whose creed promises salvation or the poet whose system guarantees solution. I believe that the complexities and strength of Thomas's and Larkin's poetry have their origin in such necessities:

> Strange to know nothing, never to be sure
> Of what is true or right or real,
> But forced to qualify, *or so I feel*,
> Or *Well, it does seem so:*
> *Someone must know.*
>
> (Larkin, 'Ignorance')

> There's none less free than who
> Does nothing and has nothing else to do,
> Being free only for what is not to his mind,
> And nothing is to his mind.
>
> (Thomas, 'Liberty')

But Thomas's seeker after truth standing under 'The Signpost' enquiring 'Which way shall I go?' receives more guidance than does Larkin's 'Standing under the fobbed/ Impendent belly of Time' demanding *'Tell me the truth . . . Teach me the way things go'.* Thomas's 'voice' advises the questioner not to rush his fences and to enjoy the rich intricacies of even this moment of doubt, which defines human existence: 'your wish may be/ To be here or anywhere talking to me,/ No matter what the weather, on earth,/ At any age between death and birth'. In 'Send No Money' Time 'booms' brutally: *'watch the hail/ Of occurrence clobber life out'.* There is again a contrast, which should probably not be overstressed, in the framing of the questions: the preparedness for active engagement in 'I go', and the implied acceptance that circumstance prevails in *'things go'.* Yet Larkin is undeniably Hardyesque in his recurrent perception, if subtler in its presentation, that 'something', 'something hidden from us', controls the shape of our lives at perhaps some point beyond choice. Thomas's imagination never opts out of choice. He keeps options open, refusing to foreclose or close doors or let them 'warp tight-shut', never permitting himself the luxury of complaining to the management. The conclusion of 'The Other' recognises that the struggle to solve, the pursuit of truth or the self, is infinite: 'no release/ Until he ceases. Then I also shall cease.'

Backing up the dialectical structure of so many poems, the syntax and diction of agnosticism also conducts the poets' lyrical drama: questions, rhetorical and unrhetorical, the subjunctive mood *passim*, all the niggling army of qualifiers and modifiers: but, yet, if, as if, but if, only, whether, unless, less, although, almost, just, rather, hardly, perhaps. Larkin's un- dis- in- im- words have become bywords: 'unrecommended', 'unspent', 'unworkable', 'unanswerable', 'disappointing', disproved', 'imprecisions', the incompletely self-cancelling 'incomplete unrest'. Less obtrusively, Thomas can almost match him with 'unfroze', 'unswerving', 'unpromised', 'unwontedly', 'unaccomplished', 'disappoint', 'discontent', *half* in love with pain,/ With what is imperfect'. For Larkin's, 'scentless', 'natureless', 'shadeless', 'shoreless', 'birdless', Thomas has 'lightless', 'thingless', 'flowerless', 'houseless', 'beeless' (they share 'sunless'). It has also been pointed out how often Larkin's very words of celebration and affirmation carry negative prefixes: 'Blindingly undiminished', 'Unvariably lovely there'. However, they at least hinge on possibility; just as Larkin's coinage 'unwelcome' (as noun) proves less final than Hardy's 'unhope'. This trait is less marked in Thomas – who does not invest so much of his energies in the single word – though we do find 'season of bliss unchangeable'. Both go in for the qualified hyperbole: Larkin's 'and to prove/ Our almost-instinct almost true' is nearly equalled in its embarrassed teetering on the brink of 'an enormous yes' by Thomas's 'And I am nearly as happy as possible' in 'It Rains' (which Larkin chose for the *Oxford Book*). As well as the qualified hyperbole, there is, again and again, the undercut climax:

> It becomes still more difficult to find
> Words at once true and kind,
> Or not untrue and not unkind.
>
> (Larkin, 'Talking in Bed')

> And myself, too, if I could find
> Where it lay hidden and it proved kind.
>
> (Thomas, 'And You, Helen')

Or, vice versa, the 'unexpected ebullition' (Thomas's phrase for his poetry's emergence) from a pressure-cooker of reservations. Larkin's 'Born Yesterday', quoted below, resembles the prolonged syntactical dramatic suspense of Thomas's 'Beauty':

> But, though I am like a river
> At fall of evening while it seems that never
> Has the sun lighted it or warmed it, while

> Cross breezes cut the surface to a file,
> This heart, some fraction of me, happily
> Floats through the window even now to a tree
> Down in the misting, dim-lit, quiet vale,
> Not like a pewit that returns to wail
> For something it has lost, but like a dove
> That slants unswerving to its home and love.

Such a battery of resources for understatement, or complex statement, argues a formidable command of syntax and its interplay with metre. Litotes becomes a rhetorical strategy for poetry that 'slants unswerving'. After what appears to be a series of glancing blows, the reader finds himself unexpectedly on the canvas. It is at this point that labels like "minor" become totally insulting.

It is at this point too that Yeats comes back into the picture. Larkin certainly did not learn *his* rhetoric from Hardy, even if he adjusted it to fit Hardyish situations – and this is where his technique diverges from Thomas's. The climax of 'Old Man' (see page 38) transposes Thomas's tactics of 'listening, lying in wait' into the major rhetorical key. This is a key in which Larkin is more frequently at home. The fine climax of 'Reference Back' outlines equivalent if less mysterious dark avenues or 'long perspectives':

> Truly, though our element is time,
> We are not suited to the long perspectives
> Open at each instant of our lives.
> They link us to our losses: worse,
> They show us what we have as it once was,
> Blindingly undiminished, just as though
> By acting differently we could have kept it so.

Statement predominating over evocation, Larkin much more conspicuously controls the horizons he presents – 'Truly', 'worse', 'just as though'. He is generalising, abstracting (as Thomas rarely does), taking an assertive grip of his material. And Larkin's 'affirmative capability' (Ellmann's term for Yeats) is particularly shown in his masterly, mastering organisation of the big stanza. Above (as in 'Church Going', 'The Whitsun Weddings' and other poems) the impulsion from one sentence or clause to another, pointed alliteration, dramatic caesura and enjambement add up to a brilliant calculating of syntactical organisation in relation to rhythmical and metrical climax. The inversion and break in the syntax of the last line and a half works with the rhythmical hiatuses to provide an appropriate movement of rising, dipping, then rising to a lower pitch. Such tricks with the couplet are noticeable in Yeats:

134

'And not a fountain, were the symbol which/ Shadows the inherited glory of the rich'. Like Larkin's stanza-ending this also stars the usually unobtrusive relative or conjunction. And I wonder whether Larkin's seven-line stanza here – in a poem of uneven stanza-division – like the nine-line stanza of 'Church Going' (nine and a half in 'The Whitsun Weddings', ten in 'Faith Healing') marks some wariness of Yeats's habitual eight-liner, though he adopts it elsewhere. Davie astonishingly observes: 'the stanzaic and metrical symmetries which [Larkin] mostly aims at are achieved skilfully enough, but with none of that bristling expertise of Hardy which sets itself, and surmounts, intricate technical challenges'.[48] I suppose I prefer the close-shaven, modern precision machine-tooling, muscles smoothly controlled rather than ruggedly flexed. Nostalgia for the steam-engine should not inhibit our admiration of the diesel.

The more pliable texture of Thomas's metres derives from his aesthetic's natural orientation, as Larkin's forms recall Yeatsian architecture. The difference can be seen in their short poems: a mode in which they are among the century's champions. Larkin's *Oxford Book* contains two four-line poems by Thomas: 'In Memoriam (Easter, 1915)' and 'Thaw'. The last sentence of Larkin's review of *Edward Thomas: A Critical Biography*, pays an indirect tribute to 'In Memoriam' as a feat of concentration: 'the England of his poems is not a Georgian dream, but the England of 1915, of farms and men "going out", of flowers still growing because there were no boys to pick them for their girls':[49]

> The flowers left thick at nightfall in the wood
> This Eastertide call into mind the men,
> Now far from home, who, with their sweethearts, should
> Have gathered them and will do never again.

This single sentence unfolds so that 'should' constitutes a metrical climax and syntactical hiatus, hanging with dramatic appropriateness over an abyss. 'Thaw' is also one sentence:

> Over the land freckled with snow half-thawed
> The speculating rooks at their nests cawed
> And saw from elm-tops, delicate as flower of grass,
> What we below could not see, Winter pass.

Syntactically and metrically (couplets) more serial, 'Thaw' releases 'Winter pass' from a complex of precisely angled perspectives and phrases which finally intersect. That the third line is an alexandrine intensifies the culmination before release, as does the sound-sequence 'freckled . . . speculating . . . delicate'. Without any disproportion between form and subject, these poems reduce two of Thomas's most essential thematic tensions *to* their essentials: historical change, psychological seasons. Compared with Thomas's crafty reversals, Larkin's antinomial structural tendency seems to require at least two units for his short poems, as in 'Wires':

> The widest prairies have electric fences,
> For though old cattle know they must not stray
> Young steers are always scenting purer water
> Not here but anywhere. Beyond the wires
>
> Leads them to blunder up against the wires
> Whose muscle-shredding violence gives no quarter.
> Young steers become old cattle from that day,
> Electric limits to their widest senses.

The metrical chiasmus is of course organic to the meaning of the poem, which takes shape as emblematic statement: contrast Thomas's invisible elisions from fact to symbol. End-stopping and strong distinctions ('For though', 'Not here but') make us more aware of 'Wires' as a metrical, syntactical and moral construction, harder-edged than Thomas's sinuosities. 'Cut Grass' in *High Windows*, which faintly echoes 'Adlestrop', holds a softer line 'Moving at summer's pace'.

Larkin is also Yeatsian in his mastery of the big words: 'element', 'perspectives' 'undiminished', juxtaposed with the colloquial phrase: 'suited', 'worse', the monosyllabic simplicity and starkness of 'They show us what we have as it once was'. Although in Larkin's poetry Yeatsian rhetoric is domesticated, democratised, or integrated with Thomas's conversational idiom, it reserves the right to move closer to its original pitch, especially at the climax of a poem. 'Church Going' *ascends* to 'A serious house on serious earth it is'. 'Truly though our element is time' and 'Blindingly undiminished' also exhibit Larkin's crucial, Yeats-like capacity to endow polysyllabic abstractions with sensuous texture, by means of subtle assonances and by giving their strongest stresses maximum opportunity within the line. (This earths the rhythm of 'Wires', otherwise less mimetic than those of 'In Memoriam' and 'Thaw'.) Effects like 'Earth's immeasurable surprise', 'The stone fidelity/ They hardly meant', 'Such plainness of the pre-baroque', 'nutritious images', the gravitational pull between 'gravitating' and 'ground' in the last stanza of 'Church Going' look back to Yeats's 'measureless consummation that he dreamed', 'murderous innocence of the sea', 'Monuments of its own magnificence', 'pieced our thoughts into philosophy'. But Larkin's grand manner of course more pervasively surfaces as a sudden injection of the resonant adjective, adverb or rhetorical construction into quieter surroundings: 'How overwhelmingly persuades', 'Unvariably lovely there' (compare Yeats's 'So arrogantly pure'), 'Uncalled-for to this day', 'Such attics cleared of me! Such absences!' The favourite 'that' and 'how' might epitomise Larkin's scaling-down of Yeatsian rhetoric (from 'That is no country for old men', 'And that enquiring man John Synge comes next') to fit a more conversational – defining not definitive – but still heightened context: 'that lifted, rough-tongued bell', 'And how remote that bare and sunscrubbed room', 'That vase'. He also adapts the inclusive Yeatsian 'all' to his own purposes: giving it its full weight in his only fully dramatic mask-poem 'Wedding-Wind': 'All's ravelled', 'all-generous waters', more often deploying its restrictive implications: 'All they find, outside the fold,/ Is a wretched width of cold'.

Larkin must have absorbed from Yeats the adjectival habit fundamental to declarative or declamatory poetry: Yeats's 'high and solitary and most stern', 'Many ingenious lovely things', 'Monstrous familiar images', 'great ebullient portrait'; Larkin's 'light, unanswerable and tall and wide', 'huge remembering pre-electric horn', 'bluish neutral distance', 'sweet commissioned grace', 'earth's most multiple, excited daughter'. Even the compounds to which Thwaite draws attention ('Laurel-surrounded', 'muscle-shredding violence', 'Luminously-peopled air', 'Vast Sunday-full and organ-frowned-on spaces', 'grain-scattered streets, barge-crowded water') surely owe at least as much to 'The salmon-falls, the mackerel-crowded seas', 'World-famous golden-thighed Pythagoras', 'wave-whitened', 'haystack- and roof-levelling wind', as they do to Thwaite's suggestion, Hopkins.[50] What differentiates the compounds of Yeats and Larkin from those of Hopkins and Hardy ('neutral-tinted haps') is the beautiful synchronisation of these potentially unwieldy units with the movement of the iambic line. As Thomas says, Hardy's stanzas lack sensuousness. And as Larkin says: 'Yeats and Auden, the management of lines, the formal distancing of emotion . . .'[51]

Larkin's adjectival tendency is seen at its most extreme in 'Born Yesterday', a poem which maintains a significant dialogue with Yeats's 'A Prayer for my Daughter':

> In fact, may you be dull –
> If that is what a skilled,
> Vigilant, flexible,
> Unemphasised, enthralled
> Catching of happiness is called.

While seeming to go out of his way to contradict the terminology of Yeats's ideal: 'Not the usual stuff/ About . . . running off a spring/ Of innocence and love' – Yeats's 'innocence' and 'glad kindness' perhaps – and insisting on 'dull', 'ordinary', Larkin goes on both to accept and qualify it in a revealing fashion. 'And may her bridegroom bring her to a house/ Where all's accustomed, ceremonious' becomes 'Nothing uncustomary/ To pull you off your balance'; and neither poet wishes 'beauty' or unbalancing exceptional gifts for the child. The lines quoted might also describe and defend Larkin's own procedure as a poet, its rhetorical and rhythmical ambitions defying the label "minor" as it redefines the adjective "dull". Compare the thrust of Thomas's 'Beauty'. And yet Davie talks of Larkin's 'grayly constricting world',[52] of his 'selling poetry short' (everybody sells it shorter than Yeats). His style at least exhilaratingly sings of hope; and, as Larkin should not have to remind critics: 'A good poem about failure is a success'.[53]

In 'Born Yesterday', as elsewhere, Larkin is unable or unwilling to supply the resounding positives with which Yeats heroically wards off disillusionment and chaos: 'custom', 'ceremony', 'the rich horn', 'the spreading laurel tree', all his proclaimed resources of 'imagination' and 'soul'. Nevertheless we *do* find 'Catching of happiness', 'grace', 'what must be joy', 'A serious house', 'destinies', 'all-generous waters' and, in other contexts, 'innocence and love'. Even if the qualities he sees as transcending 'time's eroding agents' are more directly, painfully and infrequently deduced from empirical observation, and cannot reinforce each other, they carry a mythic sanction in their individual contexts. Nor is Larkin above or below more emphatic and emblematic transcendence of flux: the photograph-album holds the girl 'like a heaven', the light 'Would congregate endlessly', while in 'An Arundel Tomb' the 'supine stationary voyage' of the earl and countess completes at least part of the journey to Byzantium. Looked at in this light perhaps, Larkin's representations of the ideal, his 'joyous shots at how things ought to be', again do not function entirely in the same way as Thomas's 'unseen moving goal'. In 'Born Yesterday', 'An Arundel Tomb' and 'Church Going' they emerge as literally irrational, 'overwhelmingly persuasive' Yeatsian affirmations, which do not disregard the difficulties but hold them magnificently at bay from some superior inch of imaginative height. And, as I have indicated, Larkin's Manichean thematic starting point, his struggle between a fallen world and an 'inaccessible' ideal is as closely related to Yeats's original anguish that 'The woods of Arcady are dead', as to Hardy's that 'Sportsman

Time but rears his brood to kill'. Larkin is a richer, stranger poet than appears from the 'sunless glare' at first sight. Witness the contents of the head in 'If, My Darling': a poem which (like 'Age') uncovers a Symbolist Larkin, just as Seamus Heaney detects a powerful 'Imagist Larkin' in 'Going'.[54] In any case, Larkin's 'Look, no masks, no myth-kitty, no exotic technical imports!' is itself a mask or sleight of hand. Thomas's and Larkin's attitude to their material, like Yeats's 'walking naked', goes back to and forward from Keats's own movement from beauty to truth, and places them all in the context of the Romantic inheritance.

There are other links between Larkin and Thomas. Both write poems 'to preserve things' – perhaps their most fundamental affinity; both exhibit an extraordinary delicate understanding of the possible variations on the iambic line; both conceal a considerable range of tone and approach under an apparent consistency of texture. They distrust organised literature or music, as they do organised religion. As jazz is Larkin's 'natural noise of good,/ Scattering long-haired grief and scored pity', so Thomas 'preferred "All round my hat" . . . to Beethoven',[55] and drew on the improvisations of folk-song. The 'Crescent City' that rises as Larkin listens to Bechet is related to the 'spark' that Thomas discovers 'In the Gypsy boy's black eyes as he played and stamped his tune,/ "Over the hills and far away," and a crescent moon'. (None of this is worlds away from Yeats's pipers and fiddlers!) They also share, unfortunately, a capacity to be underrated or to have their excellence taken for granted. This may be partly their own fault. Besides eluding the reader who takes their postures and gestures too literally, they maintain a self-deprecatory or, more accurately, "Take it or leave it" attitude: Thomas's 'But need not listen, more than to my rhymes'. Nevertheless, it is not quite enough that many will always desert 'The clink, the hum, the roar, the random singing' of poetry's more publicised hostelries for Thomas's aspen, or that 'someone will forever be surprising/ A hunger in himself to be more serious,/ And gravitating with it' to the 'ground' of Larkin. Although neither sets off 'bristling' with equipment and intentions, 'Stubbly with goodness', to scale the big peaks, or promises to revolutionise poetry by some 'audacious, purifying,/ Elemental move', they cover a surprising amount of ground, as well as 'preserving' the most central and essential qualities of the art and its tradition. Apart from Yeats, and throwing back that red herring "greatness", have there been any *better* poets this century? Certainly few such congregations of 'any-angled light'.

'Inner Emigré' or 'Artful Voyeur'?
Seamus Heaney's *North*

Seamus Heaney himself sees *North* (1975) as a culmination: 'I'm certain that up to *North*, that that was one book; in a way it grows together and goes together.'[1] While broadly agreeing that the collection indeed crowns Heaney's previous poetry – in terms of merit as well as development – British and Irish commentators have diverged in their emphases. Anthony Thwaite, for instance, praises both style and content:

> These new poems have all the sensuousness of Mr Heaney's earlier work, but refined and cut back to the bone. They are solid, beautifully wrought, expansively resonant. They recognise tragedy and violence without despairingly allowing them to flog human utterance into fragments . . .[2]

But he does not probe the content more particularly or more politically, falling back on the blurb ('Seamus Heaney has found a myth which allows him to articulate a vision of Ireland' etc). Five years later Blake Morrison was to note: 'with the exception of Conor Cruise O'Brien in the *Listener*, hardly anyone seemed interested in what it was that Heaney had to "say" about Northern Ireland'[3]. There is nothing new in divergent perceptions on either side of the Irish Sea. (Or, conversely, in Irish writers simultaneously transmitting different messages to different audiences.) Still, O'Brien's informed response established a native line of comment on *North*, including contributions by its author, that raises the most fundamental questions about the relationship between literature and politics. He begins: 'I had the uncanny feeling, reading these poems, of listening to the thing itself, the actual substance of historical agony and dissolution, the tragedy of a people in a place: the Catholics of Northern Ireland.'[4] Being so locally tuned in, O'Brien can dismiss simplistic comparisons between Heaney and Yeats: 'Yeats was free to try, and did splendidly try, or try on, different relations to the tragedy: Heaney's relation to a deeper tragedy is fixed and pre-ordained.'[5]

Is Heaney then, like 'The Tollund Man', 'Bridegroom to the goddess'? His reaction to the Man's photograph deserves the much-abused term "epiphany", with its full Joycean connotations: a revelation of personal and artistic destiny expressed in religious language.

140

Glossing the poem, he figures as pilgrim-acolyte: 'My sense of occasion and almost awe as I vowed to go to pray to the Tollund Man and assist at his enshrined head';[6] or as initiate into an order:

> when I wrote that poem I had a sense of crossing a line really, that my whole being was involved in the sense of – the root sense – of religion, being bonded to something, being bound to do something. I felt it a vow . . .[7]

The three parts of the poem itself might be tabulated as evocation ('his peat-brown head,/ The mild pods of his eye-lids'), invocation ('I could . . . pray/ Him to make germinate/ The scattered, ambushed/ Flesh of labourers'), and vocation ('Something of his sad freedom . . . Should come to me'). If nothing else, 'The Tollund Man' certainly germinated *North*. Insofar as Heaney's own role in the poems parallels that of the bridegroom-victims, does he really attain 'sad freedom', or in fact sacrifice some imaginative liberty to that 'dark-bowered queen', Cathleen ní Houlihán? Has tribal pre-ordination, or ordination, any petrifying effect on poetic life?

Part of the answer must lie in the distinctive strengths of Heaney's earlier poetry: in whether certain approaches to 'historical agony' go against the grain of these strengths. From the outset his poems have travelled a rich boundary between conscious and unconscious, or instinctual, experience; between the farm and 'The great slime kings' of wild Nature. His imaginative adventures take place upon the brink that 'Personal Helicon' leans over:

> I loved the dark drop, the trapped sky, the smells
> Of waterweed, fungus and dank moss.

Symbolically summarising *Death of a Naturalist*, the wells with their varying depths and contents represent different entries into different parts of the hidden self. The poem evokes both Robert Frost's 'For Once, Then, Something', and Heaney's comment on another Frost poem, 'The Most of It':

> a poem housing power of some kind. It's not discourse, analysis, judgment, display, it moves by instinct, moves itself, moves the reader; a sense of connection and perhaps not much deliberation.[8]

'Personal Helicon' partly exemplifies, partly describes such strategic semi-consciousness. Key-verbs – savour, hover, pry, finger – fuse physical and metaphysical exploration. John Wilson Foster criticises the continuation of these methods in *Door into the Dark*: 'the dark remains unchallenged by the end of the book. Heaney has a marked reluctance to strike inwards, to cross the threshold, to explore the emotional and psychological sources of his fear'.[9] But many of the best poems in the language depend on signs, hints, mysteries. Indeed 'The Most of It' refuses to go further than 'and that was all'. Heaney 'rhymes . . . to set the darkness echoing', rather than switch on lights. It will be part of my further argument that his poetry suffers when he forsakes the hovering suggestiveness of thresholds, the actual process of discovery, a slowly opening door, and comes to or from political conclusions. In *Door into the Dark* 'The Plantation', like Thomas's 'Lights Out', implies the poet's mystery-tour:

> You had to come back
> To learn how to lose yourself,
> To be pilot and stray – witch,
> Hansel and Gretel in one.

When Heaney evolved this productive strategy his Helicon was still largely personal. Interviewed (1977) by Seamus Deane about the relationship of the Ulster poets 'to the Northern crisis', he first volunteers the wise minimum: 'The root of the troubles may have something in common with the root of the poetry'; then adduces some revealing autobiography:

> the very first poems I wrote, 'Docker' and one about Carrickfergus Castle for instance, reveal this common root. The latter had William of Orange, English tourists and myself in it. A very inept sort of poem but my first attempts to speak, to make verse, faced the Northern sectarian problem. Then this went underground and I became very influenced by Hughes and one part of my temperament took over: the private county Derry childhood part of myself rather than the slightly aggravated young Catholic male part.[10]

The 'slightly aggravated young Catholic male' did, however, occasionally surface before *Wintering Out* and his complete emergence from hibernation in *North*. As well as 'Docker' ('That fist would drop a hammer on a Catholic'), *Death of a Naturalist* contains two poems, 'At a Potato Digging' and 'For the Commander of the "Eliza"', written in reaction to Cecil Woodham-Smith's *The Great Hunger*. The Commander, obliged by orders to withhold food from starving men in a rowing-boat, is haunted by an image that anticipates the boneyard of *North*: 'Next day, like six bad smells, those living skulls/ Drifted through the dark of bunks and hatches.' Heaney's private imagery of rot and smells spills over into the public domain, perhaps also sniffing something rotten in the state of Northern Ireland. In 'At a Potato Digging' a rather awkward metamorphosis changes potatoes as 'live skulls, blind-eyed' into the real thing:

> Live skulls, blind-eyed, balanced on
> wild higgledy skeletons
> scoured the land in 'forty-five,
> wolfed the blighted root and died.

This transition is the hinge on which the poem turns from present to past (a better-oiled process in *North*). 'At a Potato Digging' starts out like an echo of Patrick Kavanagh's *The Great Hunger*: 'Clay is the word and clay is the flesh/ Where the potato-gatherers like mechanised scarecrows move/ Along the side-fall of the hill' (Kavanagh); 'A mechanical digger wrecks the drill,/ Spins up a dark shower of roots and mould./ Labourers swarm in behind . . .' (Heaney). But Kavanagh's title symbolises the starvation of the spirit in twentieth-century rural Ireland; his perspective on servitude to the land is local in place and time, whatever historic deprivations lurk in the background. As Heaney says, 'The "matter of Ireland", mythic, historical or literary forms no significant part of [Kavanagh's] material.'[11] And again, 'At the bottom of Kavanagh's imagination there is no pagan queen, no mystique of the national, the mythic or the tribal.'[12] (Does this make Kavanagh paradoxically more forward-looking than Heaney – a function of the North-South timelag?) Heaney's potato-diggers undoubtedly guide him towards 'the matter of Ireland', and towards his first embryonic fusion of Catholic experience in the North with the longer national history: 'A people hungering from birth'; 'and where potato diggers are/ you still smell the running sore' (rottenness in the state again). In another portent of the procedures of *North*, Heaney resolves the poem by drawing on a mixture of Christian and pagan ritual. The diggers who make 'a seasonal altar of the sod', finally propitiate 'the famine god' by spilling 'Libations of cold tea'.

'Requiem for the Croppies', the historical poem in *Door into the Dark*, joins the centuries more seamlessly and achieves a more organic, indeed germinal, resolution: 'And in August the barley grew up out of the grave'.

> [It] was written in 1966 when most poets in Ireland were straining to celebrate the anniversary of the 1916 Rising. That rising was the harvest of seeds sown in 1798, when revolutionary republican ideals and national feeling coalesced in the doctrines of Irish republicanism and in the rebellion of 1798 – itself unsuccessful and savagely put down. The poem was born of and ended with an image of resurrection based on the fact that some time after the rebels were buried in

common graves, these graves began to sprout with young barley, growing up with barley corn which the 'croppies' had carried in their pockets to eat while on the march. The oblique implication was that the seeds of violent resistance sowed in the Year of Liberty had flowered in what Yeats called 'the right rose tree' of 1916. I did not realise at the time that the original heraldic murderous encounter between Protestant yeoman and Catholic rebel was to be initiated again in the summer of 1969, in Belfast, two months after the book was published. [13]

Heaney speaks in the poem as one of the 'fatal conclave', a more effective tactic than his use of the Commander's voice as a semi-ironic filter. However, in 'Bogland', a threshold-poem like 'The Tollund Man' ('I wrote it quickly . . . revised it on the hoof' [14]), he abandons both straight history and the dramatic monologue. He opens his proper door into 'the matter of Ireland', by imagining history as an experience rather than a chain of events, by dramatising his own imaginative experience of history, by discovering within his home-ground a myth that fits the inconclusiveness both of memory and of Irish history, and by fusing the psychic self-searching of poet and nation:

> Our pioneers keep striking
> Inwards and downwards . . .

The qualities and contents of bog, as before of wells and plantation, represent an unconscious – this time collective. But it is the movement of the poem, in Heaney's Frostian sense, that counts. Metre, sound, and rhythms enact a descent through layers. The poem alternates ampler development with sharp insertions. Thus the abrupt 'They'll never dig coal here' interrupts assonances which imitate the wet softness of bog 'Melting and opening underfoot'. 'Bogland' might be called not so much 'a prospect of the mind' (to use Heaney's favourite Wordsworthian phrase for poetic landscape) as a prospecting of the mind.

1969 thus coincided with Heaney's readiness to pioneer the frontiers of Irish consciousness: 'From that moment the problems of poetry moved from being simply a matter of achieving the satisfactory verbal icon to being a search for images and symbols adequate to our predicament.' Again, 'those language and place-names . . . poems [in *Wintering Out*] politicise the terrain and the imagery of the first two books.' [15] The poem that most literally, and perhaps most richly, 'politicises the terrain' is 'The Other Side', in which Heaney intertwines land, religion, and language to characterise, and tentatively close, the distance between Catholic and Protestant neighbours in Ulster:

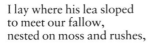

> I lay where his lea sloped
> to meet our fallow,
> nested on moss and rushes,
>
> my ear swallowing
> his fabulous, biblical dismissal,
> that tongue of chosen people.

This new kind of exploratory relation to Mossbawn complements the Belfast terrain of 'A Northern Hoard', a sequence that puts the question to which the surrounding poems respond: 'What do I say if they wheel out their dead?' 'Tinder', whose prehistoric imagery connects with that of 'The Tollund Man', might be described as Heaney's 'Easter, 1916'. But his before-and-after contrast displays little even of Yeats's qualified excitement. The underprivileged 'tribe' who have lit the tinder of revolution, wonder what to do with their 'new history', while the poet simultaneously wonders about his role:

> Now we squat on cold cinder,
> Red-eyed, after the flames' soft thunder
>
> And our thoughts settle like ash.
> We face the tundra's whistling brush . . .

Both the rhetorical questions of 'A Northern Hoard', and the answering probes into rural local history, develop the prospecting of 'Bogland'. Heaney's 'Inwards and downwards' strike also turns up anonymous ancestors, deprived even of 'scraggy acres': servant boy ('Old work-whore, slave-/ blood'), mummer (though this model of the vanishing tribal artist has English origins), 'mound-dwellers', Spenser's 'geniuses who creep/ "out of every corner/ of the woodes and glennes"'. Occasionally such figures convey a thinner, more romantic, more literal version of history: not so much active prospecting as nostalgic retrieval: 'how/ you draw me into/ your trail'. 'The Tollund Man' himself and two poems with no explicit historical ties, 'Limbo' and 'Bye-Child', embody more powerfully the same structure of feeling. 'Bye-Child', which might symbolise 'A people hungering from birth', expresses Heaney's most intense empathy with deprivation:

> Little henhouse boy,
> Sharp-faced as new moons
> Remembered, your photo still
> Glimpsed like a rodent
> On the floor of my mind.

The 'language and place-names poems' too sometimes resort to ready-made history. 'Traditions', for instance, exchanges the multi-layered socio-linguistics of 'The Other Side' for a narrower focus: 'Our guttural muse/ was bulled long ago/ by the alliterative tradition.' However these poems excitingly pioneer, in the context of Ulster English, the kind of resonance that Edward Thomas's parallel researches found more traditionally latent. And they give Heaney a valid 'political' role within his profession of poet. An aesthetic brand of revolutionary action, perhaps more linguistic reclamation than decolonisation, takes on the English language itself, with mixed declarations of love and war:

> But now our river tongues must rise
> From licking deep in native haunts
> To flood, with vowelling embrace,
> Demesnes staked out in consonants.
>
> ('A New Song')

As a group the poems insinuate that the ghost of Gaelic, local idiom, the sound of the land itself, all united in Heaney's own utterance, are compelling the tradition of Shakespeare and Spenser to go native.

He puts this, and other things, more bluntly in Part II of *North*:

> Ulster was British, but with no rights on
> The English lyric

— or so they thought. Perhaps Heaney's poetry was always a form of revolution, like negro jazz:

> Between my finger and my thumb
> The squat pen rests; snug as a gun.

In Berkeley (1970-71) he became aware 'that poetry was a force, almost a mode of power, certainly a mode of resistance'.[16] To Seamus Deane he says: 'I think that my own poetry is a kind of slow, obstinate, papish burn, emanating from the ground I was brought up on.'[17] 'Obstinate' is a favourite and favourable word of Heaney's, signifying the immovable object or objection that reverses 'No Surrender'. (John Hewitt's oft-repeated 'stubborn' may represent the Protestant cultural equivalent.) Up to and including *Wintering Out* his poetry may have been poetry-as-protest or protest-as-poetry in an extraordinarily profound sense: unjust Ulster 'hurt' him into poetry. However, in *North* this subtext whereby Heaney makes up for the lost time of those lost 'geniuses', the mute inglorious Spensers, coarsens as it becomes text. 'The Ministry of Fear' and 'Freedman' turn the tables with too much relish for the effect to be wholly ironic:

146

> Those hobnailed boots from beyond the mountain
> Were walking, by God, all over the fine
> Lawns of elocution . . .
>
> Then poetry arrived in that city –
> I would abjure all cant and self-pity –
> And poetry wiped my brow and sped me.
> Now they will say I bite the hand that fed me.

Such speaking-out by the 'slightly aggravated young Catholic male', or poet, accords with Heaney's view elsewhere in Part II, that artificial balance distorts: '"One side's as bad as the other," never worse' ('Whatever You Say Say Nothing'). Much of the aggravation continues as a portrait of the artist, especially in the sequence 'Singing School' which begins with 'The Ministry of Fear'. The third poem, 'Orange Drums, Tyrone, 1966', was written before the Troubles – a pointer to how throughout *North* Heaney's creative maturity catches up on his youthful pieties and impieties. Combining aural and visual menace, the drums define Unionist hegemony in terms of 'giant tumours', of a claustrophobic violence that afflicts its inflictor:

> The pigskin's scourged until his knuckles bleed.
> The air is pounding like a stethoscope.

'A Constable Calls' (the second poem) lacks the same ultimate impact, the caller's bike becoming, even from the child's eye view, an implausibly melodramatic time-bomb: 'His boot pushed off/ And the bicycle ticked, ticked, ticked.' However, both poems explore their own subjects; we infer the effect on Heaney's developing sensibility. 'The Ministry of Fear' and 'Summer 1969' (4) seem written largely for the sake of the sequence, and to fill in a poetic curriculum vitae (down to the provision of dates). Again, the nods to Yeats and Wordsworth in Heaney's titles and epigraphs (one of which is 'Fair seedtime had my soul') look self-conscious as well as satirical. 'The Ministry of Fear' veers from the sharply specific:

> In the first week
> I was so homesick I couldn't even eat
> The biscuits left to sweeten my exile.
> I threw them over the fence one night
> In September 1951 . . .

to the archly literary: 'It was an act/ Of stealth.' Heaney's theme may contrast the boy and the 'sophisticated' author ('Here's two on's are sophisticated'), but his language need not divide them. Also sophisticated, 'Summer 1969' forces home-thoughts from Spain: 'stinks from the fishmarket/ Rose like the reek off a flaxdam'; cites Lorca and Goya as exemplars in the context of trying 'to touch the people'; and finally applies too much local colour to the latter's portrait:

> He painted with his fists and elbows, flourished
> The stained cape of his heart as history charged.

This is elementary stuff from the proven matador of *Wintering Out*.

The two remaining poems, 'Fosterage' (5) and 'Exposure' (6), withdraw towards the centre of Heaney's own art. The former quotes the anti-heroic advice of Ulster short-story writer Michael McLaverty ('Don't have the veins bulging in your biro'), although the manner and content of the last line partially disregard it: 'and sent me out, with words/ Imposing on my tongue like obols'. 'Exposure' (to which I shall return) sets up a much more genuine inner conflict than 'Summer 1969', and falls a long way short of confidently identifying the artist with the man of action:

> I walk through damp leaves,
> Husks, the spent flukes of autumn,
>
> Imagining a hero
> On some muddy compound,
> His gift like a slingstone
> Whirled for the desperate.

This truly is the doubtful mood and mode of Yeats's 'Meditations in Time of Civil War':

> I turn away and shut the door, and on the stair
> Wonder how many times I could have proved my worth
> In something that all others understand or share.

But if 'Exposure' casts second thoughts back over *North* as a whole, most of Part II underwrites Part I – in the sense of paraphrase as well as of explaining its motivation. A few critics indeed have found Heaney's personal and documentary explicitness more to their taste than the mythic approach of Part I. Colin Falck considers it 'a relief . . . that he can still call on some of his old directness in dealing with the Ulster conflicts'.[18] But is the directness of 'Whatever You Say Say Nothing' either equal or equivalent to the sensuous immediacy of Heaney's first three books?

> The times are out of joint
> But I incline as much to rosary beads

As to the jottings and analyses
Of politicians and newspapermen
Who've scribbled down the long campaign from gas
And protest to gelignite and sten,

Who proved upon their pulses 'escalate',
'Backlash' and 'crack down', 'the provisional wing',
'Polarisation' and 'long-standing hate'.
Yet I live here, I live here too, I sing,

Expertly civil tongued with civil neighbours
On the high wires of first wireless reports,
Sucking the fake taste, the stony flavours
Of those sanctioned, old, elaborate retorts:

'Oh, it's disgraceful, surely, I agree,'
'Where's it going to end?' 'It's getting worse' . . .

Heaney too seems to practise a kind of shorthand: 'gas/ And protest to gelignite and sten' cannot be offloaded on to 'newspapermen', while 'the provisional wing' is a hasty reference that carries its own 'backlash'. His subsequent anatomy of Ulster evasiveness ('Smoke-signals are loud-mouthed compared with us . . ./ O land of password, handgrip, wink and nod,/ Of open minds as open as a trap'), labours the point in comparison with Derek Mahon's bleak earlier indictment:

[We] yield instead to the humorous formulae,
The spurious mystery in the knowing nod.
Or we keep sullen silence in light and shade,
Rehearsing our astute salvations under
The cold gaze of a sanctimonious God.

('In Belfast')

The mood of Heaney's poem comes over as irritation, impatience, rather than grand indignation (perhaps partly a result of his difficult gear change from poetic smoke-signaller to loud-speaker). The concluding vision of a petty society leaves a sour taste, because it admits empathy but excludes sympathy: 'Coherent miseries, a bite and sup,/ We hug our little destiny again.' His blanket dismissal of cliché is more palatable, indeed a cliché itself. Yet it may have something to do with the fact that Heaney's own poetry – unlike, say, MacNeice's *Autumn Journal* – has among its many rich resources no means of accommodating, transforming, criticising such idiom. The inadequacy of media jargon, or of everyday commonplace, invalidates neither the political process nor 'civilised outrage'. However, 'Whatever You Say Say Nothing' – which Heaney did not include in his *Selected Poems* – essentially voices the same sentiment as Edward Thomas's 'This is No Case of Petty Right or Wrong'. Just as Thomas during the First World War insisted on expressing England in his own way ('I hate not Germans, nor grow hot/ With love of Englishmen, to please newspapers'), so Heaney is justifying the language, aesthetic and perspective of the greater part of his book.

The lecture 'Feeling into Words', from which I have already quoted, coincided with the completion of *North*. By 'a search for images and symbols adequate to our predicament', Heaney

> [does] not mean liberal lamentation that citizens should feel compelled to murder one another or deploy their different military arms over the matter of nomenclatures such as British or Irish. I do not mean public celebrations or execrations of resistance or atrocity – although there is nothing necessarily unpoetic about such celebration, if one thinks of Yeats's 'Easter, 1916'. I mean that I felt it imperative to discover a field of force in which, without abandoning fidelity to the processes and experience of poetry . . . it would be possible to encompass the perspectives of a humane reason and at the same time to grant the religious intensity of the violence its deplorable authenticity and complexity. And when I say religious, I am not thinking simply of the sectarian division. To some extent the enmity can be viewed as a struggle between the cults and devotees of a god and goddess. There is an indigenous territorial numen, a tutelar of the whole island, call her Mother Ireland, Cathleen Ní Houlihán, the poor old woman, the Shan Van Vocht, whatever; and her sovereignty has been temporarily usurped or infringed by a new male cult whose founding fathers were Cromwell, William of Orange and Edward Carson, and whose god-head is incarnate in a rex or caesar resident in a palace in London. What we have is the tail-end of a struggle in a province between territorial piety and imperial power.
>
> Now I realise that this idiom is remote from the agnostic world of economic interest whose iron hand operates in the velvet glove of 'talks between elected representatives', and remote from the political manoeuvres of power-sharing; but it is not remote from the psychology of the Irishmen and Ulstermen who do the killing, and not remote from the bankrupt psychology and mythologies implicit in the terms Irish Catholic and Ulster Protestant. The question, as ever, is 'How with this rage shall beauty hold a plea?' And my answer is, by offering 'befitting emblems of adversity'.[19]

My contention will be that 'this idiom' can represent as unreal an extreme as the other: that Part I of *North* (unlike *Wintering Out*) often falls between the stools of poetry and politics instead of building a mythic bridge.

After the passage quoted above, Heaney tells how he found 'befitting emblems' in P.V. Glob's *The Bog People*, and swore his vow to the Tollund Man. What is the precise 'emblematic' relevance of these mummified figures to the 'man-killing parishes' of Northern Ireland? The prototype developed by 'The Tollund Man' is a scapegoat, privileged victim and ultimately Christ-surrogate, whose death and bizarre resurrection might redeem, or symbolise redemption for,

> The scattered, ambushed
> Flesh of labourers,
> Stockinged corpses
> Laid out in the farmyards . . .

Here Heaney alludes particularly to Catholic victims of sectarian murder in the 1920s. His comment to James Randall interprets the amount of family as well as religious feeling in the poem: 'The Tollund Man seemed to me like an ancestor almost, one of my old uncles, one of those moustached archaic faces you used to meet all over the Irish countryside.'[20] Thus related to 'the moustached/ dead, the creel-fillers' elsewhere in *Wintering Out*, the Man becomes the logical conclusion, the terminal case, the *reductio* of ancestral dispossession and oppression. In 'Feeling into Words', having summarised Glob's account of 'ritual sacrifices to the Mother Goddess' for the sake of fertility, Heaney asserts: 'Taken in relation to the tradition of Irish political martyrdom for that cause whose icon is Cathleen ní Houlihán, this is more than an archaic barbarous rite: it is an archetypal pattern. And the unforgettable photographs . . . blended in my mind with photographs of atrocities, past and present, in the long rites of Irish political and religious struggles.'[21] Heaney does not distinguish between involuntary and voluntary 'martyrdom', and the nature of his 'archetype' is such as to subsume the latter within the former.

If 'The Tollund Man' and its glosses lay down a 'pattern' for *North*, as it seems reasonable to suppose, how do the later Bog poems compare with the original model? 'The Grauballe Man' obviously invites such a comparison; even the inference that the poems typify successive books (after the manner of 'Sailing to Byzantium' and 'Byzantium', or 'Toads' and 'Toads Revisited'). Whereas 'The Tollund Man' varies its angle of approach and moves with the dynamic of a pilgrimage, 'The Grauballe Man' has more the air of a set-piece, arrival, its subject celebrated because he's there, rather than summoned into being by the poet's need:

As if he had been poured
in tar, he lies
on a pillow of turf
and seems to weep

the black river of himself.
The grain of his wrists
is like bog oak,
the ball of his heel

like a basalt egg.

A difference in quality issues from the difference in stance; emotion anticipated in excitement gives way to tranquil contemplation; the intensity of conversion to ritual observance; crucifixion to resurrection. Almost too dutifully the poem venerates wrists, heel, instep, hips, spine, chin, throat, hair – inclining to rosary beads indeed. The chain of inventive similes reinforces the point that the Man has been translated into the element of the bog, and is thus at one with faintly healing Nature, but the Tollund Man somehow remains the *human* face of the Bog People. The less elaborate physical detail in the first poem counts for more, especially 'The mild pods of his eye-lids'. 'Mild' combines physical suggestiveness with a subliminal reference to Jesus ('Gentle Jesus, meek and mild'), while its last three letters set up a soothing assonance within the line, which ratifies the union. The two humanising images in 'The Grauballe Man': 'And his rusted hair,/ a mat unlikely/ as a foetus's', 'bruised like a forceps baby', compete with each other and retain a chiefly visual quality. (Again, the simple 'stained face' of 'The Tollund Man' says more.) The climax of the poem, following on the latter simile, appears unduly self-referring, pointed towards the 'perfection' with which the rosary has been told:

but now he lies
perfected in my memory,
down to the red horn
of his nails,

hung in the scales
with beauty and atrocity . . .

Beauty on the whole has outweighed atrocity by the time we reach 'the actual weight/ of each hooded victim,/ slashed and dumped'. In fact the poem almost proclaims the victory of metaphor over 'actuality':

Who will say 'corpse'
to his vivid cast?
Who will say 'body'
to his opaque repose?

Possibly someone should. The ultimate difference between the two poems is that between Christ on the Cross and a holy picture: the urgent presence of 'The Tollund Man' worked 'to a saint's kept body'. Heaney may have mistaken his initial epiphany for a literal signpost, when it was really a destination, a complete emotional curve that summed up profound feelings and wishes about the situation in Northern Ireland. The ambiguous resolution – 'lost,/ Unhappy and at home' – may be as far as he can genuinely go, and it resembles other reactions in his poetry to tragic circumstances. 'Elegy for a Still-born Child' (*Door into the Dark*), for instance, ends: 'I drive by remote control on this bare road . . . White waves riding home on a wintry lough.'

Heaney's contracted or 'perfected' perception of the Bog People in *North* renders their emblematic function, as well as his poetry, less complex. If what was hypothetical in 'The Tollund Man' – the consecration of 'the cauldron bog' – has hardened into accepted doctrine, do these later images imply that suffering on behalf of Cathleen may not be in vain, that beauty can be reborn out of terror: 'The cured wound'? The females of the species also attain a 'leathery beauty'. For the girl in 'Punishment', the wind 'blows her nipples/ to amber beads', and the tone of love-making compensates for any deficiencies:

Little adulteress,
before they punished you

you were flaxen-haired,
undernourished, and your
tar-black face was beautiful.

As women cannot be 'bridegrooms', Heaney must find them a different place in the 'archetypal pattern'. The final moral twist of 'Punishment' has attracted a good deal of comment:

I who have stood dumb
when your betraying sisters,
cauled in tar,
wept by the railings,

who would connive
in civilised outrage

yet understand the exact
and tribal, intimate revenge.

This is all right if Heaney is merely being 'outrageously' honest about
his own reactions, if the paradox 'connive . . . civilised' is designed
to corner people who think they have risen above the primitive, if the
poem exposes a representative Irish conflict between 'humane
reason' and subconscious allegiances. But can the poet run with the
hare ('I can feel the tug/ of the halter') and hunt with the hounds?
Ciarán Carson observes:

> Being killed for adultery is one thing; being tarred and feathered is
> another . . . [Heaney] seems to be offering his 'understanding' of the
> situation almost as a consolation . . . It is as if he is saying, suffering
> like this is natural; these things have always happened; they happened
> then, they happen now, and that is sufficient ground for understand-
> ing and absolution. It is as if there never were and never will be any
> political consequences of such acts; they have been removed to the
> realm of sex, death and inevitability.[22]

Perhaps the problem is one of artistic, not political, fence-sitting.
The conclusion states, rather than dramatises, what should be
profound self-division, one of Heaney's most intense hoverings over
a brink. In any case it remains unresolved, unless the poem does in a
sense make a political point by endorsing the 'idiom', of something
deeper than politics. (Although today's anthropology may only be
yesterday's politics.) Blake Morrison argues:

> It would be going too far to suggest that 'Punishment' in particular and
> the Bog poems generally offer a defence of Republicanism; but they
> are a form of 'explanation'. Indeed the whole procedure of *North* is
> such as to give sectarian killing in Ulster a historical respectability
> which it is not usually given in day-to-day journalism.[23]

In fact Heaney grants no licence to the latter. He excludes the
intersectarian issue, warfare *between* tribes, by concentrating on the
Catholic psyche as bound to immolation, and within that immolation to savage tribal loyalties. This is what he means by
'slaughter/ for the common good' ('Kinship'), and by 'granting the
religious intensity of the violence its deplorable authenticity and
complexity' – and, of course, no apologia for the 'male cult' of
imperial power. 'Kinship' defines the battlefield in astonishingly
introverted Catholic and Nationalist terms:

Our mother ground
is sour with the blood
of her faithful,

they lie gargling
in her sacred heart
as the legions stare
from the ramparts.

If *North* doesn't cater for 'liberal lamentation', neither does it offer a universal, Wilfred Owen-style image of human suffering. It is a book of martyrs rather than of tragic protagonists. Only 'Strange Fruit' questions its own attitude, challenges inevitability:

Murdered, forgotten, nameless, terrible
Beheaded girl, outstaring axe
And beatification, outstaring
What had begun to feel like reverence.

The frank adjectives capsize what has previously been rather a decorative dawdle of a sonnet ('Pash of tallow, perishable treasure'; 'Diodorus Siculus confessed/ His gradual ease among the likes of this'). They also capsize a good deal else in *North*. Heaney told John Haffenden: '['Strange Fruit'] had ended at first with a kind of reverence, and the voice that came in when I revised was a rebuke to the literary quality of that reverent emotion.'[24]

'Bog Queen' has the advantage of dealing directly with the goddess herself, so that questionable behaviour on the part of her acolytes may be ignored. The female figures in the poems, perhaps understandably, bear a family resemblance to one another: 'The pot of the skull,/ The damp tuck of each curl'; 'My skull hibernated/ in the wet nest of my hair'; 'They unswaddled the wet fern of her hair'; 'my brain darkening'; 'your brain's exposed/ and darkened combs'. However 'Bog Queen', although over-amplified like 'The Grauballe Man', renews that well-worn genre the aisling by presenting Ireland as her landscape, weather, geography, and history, and by pushing her 'old hag' incarnation to an extreme:

My diadem grew carious,
gemstones dropped
in the peat floe
like the bearings of history.

Since this is the one Bog poem with true Irish antecedents,[25] it can begin with an apt analogue of dormant nationhood ('I lay waiting/ between turf-face and demesne wall'), and end with an equally plausible 'rising':

and I rose from the dark,
hacked bone, skull-ware,
frayed stitches, tufts,
small gleams on the bank.

These lines, and the poem's clearly shaped symbol speak for themselves. But Heaney sometimes asks too much of his myth, as if all statement has been shunted off to Part II, as if 'archetypes' remain above or below argument. ('Punishment' suggests the contrary.) A number of his comments on poetry nudge it towards the visual arts – a surprising development from such a rhythmic prodigy: 'the verbal icon'; 'a search for images and symbols'; 'The poetry I love is some kind of image or visionary thing'; 'a painter can lift anything and make an image of it'.[26] The notion of 'befitting emblems' also requires examination. Their original context is section II of 'Meditations in Time of Civil War', where Yeats defines the purpose of his art in terms of 'founding' his Tower:

that after me
My bodily heirs may find,
To exalt a lonely mind,
Befitting emblems of adversity.

Yeats's 'emblems' are the many facets of the Tower and of his poetry as a whole. Heaney seems to regard a symbol or myth as sufficiently emblematic in itself: 'beauty' pleading with 'rage' within the icon of 'The Grauballe Man' – Man and poem synonymous – rather than through any kind of dialectic. Nor does the myth, as the resemblances between the poems suggest, undergo much evolution. Before the publication of *North*, John Wilson Foster said of the language poems in *Wintering Out*: 'Heaney's conceit (landscape = body = sex = language) and the way it sabotages emotion leads him into . . . difficulties'.[27] In *North* the addition of = Ireland, of the aisling element, makes it still harder to determine which level is primary, or whether they are all just being ingeniously translated into each other. Presumably 'Come to the Bower' signifies the poet's imaginative intercourse with his country, but does the conceit do more than consummate itself?

I reach past
The river bed's washed
Dream of gold to the bullion
Of her Venus bone.

When England participates in the landscape-sex-Ireland poems,

Heaney's edifice and his artifice wobble. In 'Bone Dreams' the poet's lady uneasily assumes foreign contours:

> I have begun to pace
> the Hadrian's Wall
> of her shoulder, dreaming
> of Maiden Castle.

'Ocean's Love to Ireland' overworks phallic symbolism: Ralegh 'drives inland'; 'his superb crest . . . runs its bent/ In the rivers of Lee and Blackwater'; 'The Spanish prince has spilled his gold// And failed her'. Love poetry in political language risks even more than the reverse:

> And I am still imperially
> Male, leaving you with the pain,
> The rending process in the colony,
> The battering ram, the boom burst from within.
> The act sprouted an obstinate fifth column
> Whose stance is growing unilateral.

This poem, 'Act of Union', pursuing the parallel between sexual and political union, and between imperialism and maleness, casts the speaker in a role which fits uneasily. And the allegory could apply to begetting Loyalism as much as 'obstinate' Republicanism. In any case, the poem hardly persuades as a man's emotion towards his wife or child: 'parasitical/ And ignorant little fists'.

Given Heaney's previous successful explorations of landscape, water, femaleness, what has gone wrong this time? His prose comments support the view that an obsession with stacking up parallels has replaced flexible 'soundings'. And in the case both of sex-and-landscape and of Bogland regions, Ireland is the straw that breaks the poems' backs. The Jutland connection does achieve certain archetypal dimensions but, as 'Punishment' indicates, the moral and political ground beyond the self-contained emblem is boggy indeed. With reference to the process in 'Kinship', whereby the poet finds 'a turf-spade' and quickly ends up 'facing a goddess', Ciarán Carson points out:

> The two methods are not compatible. One gains its poetry by embodiment of a specific, personal situation; the other has degenerated into a messy historical and religious surmise – a kind of Golden Bough activity, in which the real differences between our society and that of Jutland in some vague past are glossed over for the sake of the parallels of ritual.[28]

Whereas 'Bogland' enacted the stages of the poet's thrust into the past, he now obtains ready access: 'Kinned by hieroglyphic peat . . . to the strangled victim' ('Kinship');

> To lift the lid of the peat
> And find this pupil dreaming
> Of neolithic wheat!
>
> ('Belderg')

That exclamation (at quernstones) represents a kind of elementary archaeological awe, borne out by the poem's Irish, Planter, and Norse 'growth rings' which express simply 'A congruence of lives'. In *Wintering Out* Heaney worked from present to past, interpreting (the historic congruence and incongruity of 'The Other Side'); in *North* he works from past to present – equating. The book appears fascinated more by bones, fossils, relics, archaisms – 'antler combs, bone pins,/ coins, weights, scale-pans' – than by those things which they are emblems of. 'Bone Dreams', as perhaps its title candidly admits, loses all contact with the thing itself: 'I wind it in// the sling of mind/ to pitch it at England'. An ecumenical gesture, despite the metaphor, but 'England' soon becomes an amalgam of history, geography, literary and linguistic tradition ('Elizabethan canopies./ Norman devices'; '*ban-hus* . . . where the soul/ fluttered a while'; 'I am . . . a chalk giant'; 'Hadrian's Wall'; etc.). Apart from section VI, a beautifully exact poem about a mole – and moles do focus differences between the Irish and English terrains – the poem turns the tables on Romantic versions of Ireland in English literature.

But the real costume-drama imports into *North* are the Vikings. The title-poem begins with the poet searching for a kindred revelation to that of 'The Tollund Man':

> I returned to a long strand,
> the hammered shod of a bay,
> and found only the secular
> powers of the Atlantic thundering.
>
> I faced the unmagical
> invitations of Iceland,
> the pathetic colonies
> of Greenland, and suddenly
>
> those fabulous raiders . . .

The somewhat abstract adjectival sequence – 'secular', 'unmagical', 'fabulous' – gives the show away. Why not write a 'secular' or nature poem about the sea? (Like 'Shoreline' in *Door into the Dark*, where the Danes are a notional and mysterious 'black hawk bent on the sail'.) Why dismiss Iceland as 'unmagical', unless because Heaney is not Auden? 'Suddenly' (at the end of a stanza) introduces 'fabulous raiders' to fable-hungry poet too much on cue. They also open communication with remarkable speed, and the word 'epiphany', deeply implicit in 'The Tollund Man', is actually used:

> ocean-deafened voices
> warning me, lifted again
> in violence and epiphany.
> The longship's swimming tongue
>
> was buoyant with hindsight –
> it said Thor's hammer swung
> to geography and trade,
> thick-witted couplings and revenges,
>
> the hatreds and behindbacks
> of the althing, lies and women,
> exhaustions nominated peace,
> memory incubating the spilled blood.

This is Heaney's own 'hindsight', a 'relevant' historical summary which hardly requires such elaborate sponsorship. (May he be forgiven the zeugma 'lies and women'!). And does the idea of the North really provide an umbrella for the not very Nordic north of Ireland, fertility rites and capital punishment in prehistoric Denmark, and the conquests of the Vikings in Ireland – coming to or from the north? Although all these different places, time-zones and moral worlds clearly strike genuine imaginative chords in Heaney, why attempt to unify them into a mythic confederation? Perhaps again in order to stress the obvious: 'these things have always happened', as Carson says, and as Morrison finally puts it: 'His allusions to former cultures amount to a sort of historical determinism.'[29] Yet determinism, the plundering of the past for parallels, circular thinking (all incidentally features of Republican and Loyalist ideology) once more insist on 'territorial piety', on a religious-anthropological, even slightly glamorous way of apprehending the conflict, beside which 'talks between elected representatives' indeed look dull. In the last three quatrains of 'North' the longship adds an aesthetic to the subject-matter it has already supplied:

> It said, 'Lie down
> in the word-hoard, burrow

the coil and gleam
of your furrowed brain.

Compose in darkness.
Expect aurora borealis
in the long foray
but no cascade of light.

Keep your eye clear
as the bleb of the icicle,
trust the feel of what nubbed treasure
your hands have known.'

This self-dedication hints at a purpose – 'long foray' – beyond 'befitting emblems', and to which Heaney's sensuous intimacy with his world ('nubbed treasure') might contribute a value as well as an 'explanation'. Like D.H. Lawrence and Ted Hughes before him, he edges towards turning his instinctive sureties into a philosophy.

Ritual is undoubtedly a value and a method, as well as a subject, in *North*. It sets and sets off the emblems. While of course aware that some rituals have more in their favour than others, Heaney employs the term a little oddly at times: 'the long rites of Irish political and religious struggles'. A struggle is not a rite, just as murder like that at Vinegar Hill is not 'heraldic' when it happens. The decorative tinge that Heaney imparts to violence and to history derives from a ritualising habit, which itself derives from his religious sensibility. The continual catalogues in *North* – whether details of the Bog People, inventories of objects like 'antler-pins', or historical summaries as in the message of the longship – level disparate experience into a litany, a rosary, a faintly archaic incantation: 'neighbourly, scoretaking/ killers, haggers/ and hagglers, gombeen-men,/ hoarders of grudges and gain'. In those lines from 'Viking Dublin' alliteration swamps meaning. 'Funeral Rites' declares Heaney's love for the positive function of ritual:

Now as news comes in
of each neighbourly murder
we pine for ceremony,
customary rhythms . . .

(An echo of Yeats there.) Carson praises the poem's initial evocation of remembered funerals:

their eyelids glistening,
their dough-white hands
shackled in rosary-beads

but then comments: 'all too soon, we are back in the world of megalithic doorways and charming, noble barbarity'.[30] The worthy root-emotion of 'Funeral Rites' is that of 'The Tollund Man' – Heaney's passionate desire to 'assuage'[31] – but he goes to such ritualistic lengths as to obliterate his starting-point:

> I would restore
>
> the great chambers of Boyne,
> prepare a sepulchre
> under the cupmarked stones . . .
>
> Somnambulant women,
> left behind, move
> through emptied kitchens
>
> imagining our slow triumph
> towards the mounds.

An affirmation of 'custom' and 'ceremony' – especially as a kind of mass trance – cannot in itself earn 'the cud of memory/allayed for once'. Heaney's 'rites', ancient, modern or imagined, are profoundly 'Catholic' in character:

> My sensibility was formed by the dolorous murmurings of the rosary, and the generally Marian quality of devotion. The reality that was addressed was maternal, and the posture was one of supplication . . . Irish Catholicism, until about ten years ago, had this Virgin Mary worship, almost worship. In practice, the shrines, the rosary beads, all the devotions were centred towards a feminine presence, which I think was terrific for the sensibility. I think that the 'Hail Mary' is more of a poem than the 'Our Father'. 'Our Father' is between chaps, but there's something faintly amorous about the 'Hail Mary'.[32]

The sense in *North* that something is to be gained by going through the ritual, telling the beads, adopting a posture of supplication or worship, curiously aligns Heaney with the early rather than the later Yeats (the Catholic ethos of the Rhymers' Club). 'A Prayer for my Daughter', on the other hand, is not only a prayer but a contest in which 'custom' and 'ceremony' engage with their opposites.

The whole design of *North*, including its layout, proclaims a more punctilious patterning than that of Heaney's first three books: 'I had a notion of *North*, the opening of *North*: those poems came piecemeal now and again, and then I began to see a shape. They were written and rewritten a lot.'[33] In contrast with the fecund variety of *Wintering Out* there is system, homogenisation. Certain poems seem

161

dictated by the scheme (rather than vice versa), commissioned to fill in the myth or complete the ritual. Conspicuous among these are three first-person quatrain sequences, all in six parts: 'Viking Dublin: Trial Pieces', 'Bone Dreams' and 'Kinship'. Neatly spanning the Vikings, England and Bogland, the sequences present the poet in a somewhat self-conscious physical and imaginative relation to each mythic territory: 'a worm of thought// I follow into the mud'; 'I push back/ through dictions'; 'I step through origins'. Such announcements seem again a substitute for action, for genuine prospecting. 'Land' and 'Gifts of Rain' in *Wintering Out* began this kind of open quest, which owes a debt to the Ted Hughes of *Wodwo*. But the further back Heaney pushes, in default of a specific impulse, the more specialised or specialist he in fact becomes; so that the sequences exaggerate the book's anthropological, archaeological and philological tendency. The evolution since *Wintering Out* of the theme of language typifies other contractions. The place-name poems, if occasionally too calculated, stir mutual vibrations between landscape and language. But in 'Viking Dublin' Heaney's phonetic fantasy drives a huge wedge between word and thing: a longship's 'clinker-built hull' is 'spined and plosive/ as *Dublin*'. 'Kinship', already off to a sign-posting start ('Kinned by hieroglyphic/peat') that has travelled far from 'We have no prairies' ('Bogland'), eventually goes into a swoon of synonyms:

> Quagmire, swampland, morass:
> the slime kingdoms,
> domains of the cold-blooded,
> of mud pads and dirtied eggs.

> But *bog*
> meaning soft,
> the fall of windless rain . . .

'Bone Dreams', perhaps because of the poet's outsider position, relies more heavily on linguistic keys to unlock England: 'Elizabethan canopies,/ Norman devices,// the erotic mayflowers/ of Provence/ and the ivied latins/ of churchmen', 'the scop's/ twang, the iron/ flash of consonants/ cleaving the line'. This comes uncomfortably close to the way Heaney talks about English in his lecture 'Englands of the Mind' (1976). In Geoffrey Hill's poetry: 'The native undergrowth, both vegetative and verbal, the barbaric scrollwork of fern and ivy, is set against the tympanum and chancel-arch, against the weighty elegance of imperial Latin';[34] '[Hughes's] consonants . . . take the measure of his vowels like calipers, or stud

162

the line like rivets.'[35] That the gap has narrowed between Heaney's creative and critical idioms, while widening between word and thing, underlines the extent to which the artist's own specialism also figures in these poems. Every poet worth his salt imprints his poetry with a subtext about poetry itself – as Heaney does, profoundly and skilfully, in 'The Forge' or 'Bogland'. A minority, because of the particular nature of their art, go public like Yeats as the poet-artist, taking on all comers. The protagonist's high profile in the *North* sequences, however, reveals him almost incestuously involved with the contents of his own imagination:

> My words lick around
> cobbled quays, go hunting
> lightly as pampooties
> over the skull-capped ground.
>
> ('Viking Dublin')

> I grew out of all this
> like a weeping willow
> inclined to
> the appetites of gravity.
>
> ('Kinship')

(Contrast: 'As a child, they could not keep me from wells' in 'Personal Helicon'.) Heaney's appetite for abstraction has certainly grown: 'ceremony', 'history', 'violence and epiphany', 'memory', 'dictions', 'the cooped secrets/ of process and ritual'. Several commentators on *North* have headlined 'Hercules and Antaeus' as symbolising the different approaches of Parts II and I. Mark Patrick Hederman follows up such an attribution with this analysis:

> Hercules and Antaeus represent two different kinds of poet: the first composes his own poetry; the second is composed by his own poetry. The first is the self-assertive poet, the political poet, who has a definite vision of things, who chooses his style and his words, who decides what kind of poet he is going to be. The second kind of poet is he whom Martin Heidegger calls the 'more daring' . . . because he works from the heart and . . . articulates a song 'whose sound does not cling to something that is eventually attained, but which has already shattered itself even in the sounding . . .'[36]

The poem certainly dramatises a conflict in Heaney (amply evidenced by *Preoccupations*) between an instinctive, 'feminine' artesian procedure ('the cradling dark,/ the river-veins, the secret gullies/ of his strength'), and an ordering, 'male' architectonic 'intelligence' ('a spur of light,/ a blue prong graiping him/ out of his element'). However, Hercules may be quite as responsible for the prescribed rituals of Part I as for the outbursts of Part II: telling yourself to 'Lie down/ in the word-hoard' makes it less likely that you have done so. Stylistic examination suggests that Heaney has upset his strategic brinkmanship, his former complex creative balance, by applying architectonic methods to artesian matters, by processing his rich organic resources into hard-edged blocks, by forgetting 'They'll never dig coal here.'

Heaney should have been the last poet to turn 'the word-hoard' into a dragon-hoard: 'the coffered/ riches of grammar/ and declensions'. The burnishing by repetition of certain words is an allowable consequence of recurrent subjects; other instances serve the grand design, as in the shot-gun marriages of berg and bog: 'the black glacier/ of each funeral'; 'gemstones dropped/ in the peat floe/ like the bearings of history.// My sash was a black glacier/ wrinkling'; 'floe of history'. But repeated rhythms and constructions do more than words to reinforce the ritual or cement the architecture. Metre, the skinny quatrain, is the most obvious formal unifier: 'those thin small quatrain poems, they're kind of drills or augers for turning in and they are narrow and long and deep'.[37] The narrowness of the line, in conjunction with that of the stanza, makes immense demands on both local variation and overall rhythm, if prefabricated cadences are to be prevented. As Heaney himself said later, 'The shortness of a line constricts, in a sense, the breadth of your movement'.[38] In fact, the quatrain often falls into two iambic pentameters, each harshly severed at the caesura:

> Come back past
> philology and kennings,
> re-enter memory
> where the bone's lair . . .

It can dwindle to mere layout unjustified by stress or sense:

> . . . is a love-nest
> in the grass.

The method really amounts to a ribbon-developed sentence where the enjambement of line and stanza quickly becomes itself a convention, and the basic unit must be a phrase that will fit into something more like a passive receptacle than an active drill. This form blurs climaxes and by-passes terminuses, while also letting the sequences divide too tidily into equal sections. Nevertheless Heaney stiffens the backbone of the poems by drawing on the 'alliterative tradition'. His comments on its importance to Ted Hughes interpret his own motives: 'Hughes relies on the northern deposits, the pagan Anglo-Saxon and Norse elements, and he draws energy also from a related constellation of primitive myths and world-views. The life of his language is a persistence of the stark outline and vitality of Anglo-Saxon that became the Middle English alliterative tradition . . .'[39] The 'iron/ flash of consonants' undoubtedly strikes sparks, as in the dedicatory 'Sunlight' ('the scone rising/ to the tick of two clocks'), but can also be overdone ('haggers/ and hagglers') and pepper a poem with hard little pellets, for which the Anglo-Saxon compound word is the model: 'Earth-pantry, bone-vault,/ sunbank', 'oak-bone, brain-firkin' (an empty interchange of images). Consonantal monosyllables are conspicuous – taking their cue from 'bone' and 'skull' – especially those with an archaic cast: shod, scop, bleb, coomb, crock, glib (as a noun), nubbed. Heaney's fondness for the hard -ed ending as participle/adjective (often with a co-opted noun) has developed into infatuation: 'the tomb/ Corbelled, turfed and chambered,/ Floored with dry turf-coomb'; 'Their puffed knuckles/ had unwrinkled, the nails/ were darkened, the wrists/ obediently sloped.' Sometimes the participles seem to involve a shortcut as well as shorthand: 'the cud of memory/ allayed'. The ending of 'The Grauballe Man', 'each hooded victim,/ slashed and dumped', is less poignantly precise than 'the scattered, ambushed/ Flesh of labourers' and 'Stockinged corpses' of 'The Tollund Man'. Constant asyndeton helps to compress the pellets, but the conjunction 'and' sets up its own syntactical orthodoxy: 'geography and trade,/ thick-witted couplings and revenges'; 'ancestry and trade'; 'pinioned by ghosts/ and affections,// murders and pieties'. The prominence of paired abstractions in the Viking poems underlines their anxiety to connect. Thus the form and sound of the quatrain exert pressure on syntax and meaning to the point where 'customary rhythms' may indeed take over.

And yet *North* is framed by three poems that avoid or transcend such mannerisms. 'Mossbawn: Two Poems in Dedication' occupies a truly timeless zone within which 'calendar customs' of domesticity and agriculture inoculate against the more barbaric 'rites' to come. Two emotionally and rhythmically expansive endings emphasise how much Part I cuts down, and cuts out, in pursuit of 'the matter of Ireland':

And here is love
like a tinsmith's scoop
sunk past its gleam
in the meal-bin.

('Sunlight')

O calendar customs! Under the broom
Yellowing over them, compose the frieze
With all of us there, our anonymities.

('The Seed Cutters')

The first stanza of 'Sunlight' does contain 'helmeted', 'heated' and 'honeyed', but their varied physicality shows up 'slashed and dumped'; just as the last four lines show up the periphrastic sensuousness of 'Kinship': 'The mothers of autumn/ sour and sink,/ ferments of husk and leaf// deepen their ochres'. Consummating a sequence of diversely rendered 'customary rhythms', the subtle chiastic assonance 'gleam' – 'meal' dramatises the complete sub-jugation both of 'love' and the poem – and the poem because of its love – to what they work in. These poems are Heaney's real, unceremonious assertions of 'custom' and humanity, his most important refusal to let 'human utterance' be flogged 'into frag-ments'. Carson observes that in the opening of 'The Seed Cutters':

They seem hundreds of years away. Brueghel,
You'll know them if I can get them true . . .

'the apostrophe works perfectly; we realise how Brueghel's realism, his faithfulness to minutiae, are akin to Heaney's, and what could have been portentousness takes on a kind of humility'.[40] Compare the strained self-introduction to Tacitus in 'Kinship': 'And you, Tacitus,/ observe how I make my grove/ on an old crannog/ piled by the fearful dead' – this he doesn't know and doesn't get true. *Field Work* makes a significant return to Mossbawn, to 'that original townland', for visionary renewals.

From composure to 'Exposure', from sunlit suspended moment or Grecian Urn 'frieze' to 'It is December in Wicklow'. With day, season, Nature, the weather, the heavens all in a state of exhausted flux – 'Alders dripping, birches/ Inheriting the last light', Heaney wonders about the lasting usefulness of his own enterprise, about perfection of the life or of the work. The poem asks why he sits

weighing and weighing
My responsible *tristia*.
For what? For the ear? For the people?

Anguished dialectic, recalling that of 'A Northern Hoard', banishes both the polished icon of Part I, and the top-of-the-head arguments in the rest of 'Singing School'. The contrast between images of dripping, falling, darkening, 'let-downs and erosions', and 'The diamond absolutes', dramatises a profound self-searching a 'sad freedom', which goes beyond the aesthetic politics of 'Hercules and Antaeus' into the moral and emotional priorities of the artist. Fundamentally, the poem asks whether departure from Ulster, for which the writing of *North* may be an over-compensation ('blowing up these sparks'), has precluded some personal or poetic revelation (akin to that of 'The Tollund Man', perhaps):

> Who, blowing up these sparks
> For their meagre heat, have missed
> The once-in-a-lifetime portent,
> The comet's pulsing rose.

In 'Exposure' the poet earns the label he gives himself – 'inner émigré', inwardly examining his emigration – which conflicts with another, bestowed not quite self-critically enough in 'Punishment':

> I am the artful voyeur
>
> of your brain's exposed
> and darkened combs . . .

Is this objective correlative, or substitute, for an interior journey?

Heaney's move South between *Wintering Out* and *North* must indeed have shifted the co-ordinates of his imagination: distanced some things, brought others closer. In an essay of 1975 Seamus Deane found Heaney (and Derek Mahon) apolitical in comparison with John Montague, whose *The Rough Field* (1972) had 'politicised the terrain' of his native Tyrone: 'it is in Montague, with his historical concentration, that this fidelity [to the local] assumes the shape of a political commitment'.[41] Interviewing Heaney after *North*, Deane encourages him to 'commit' himself: 'Do you think that if some political stance is not adopted by you and the Northern poets at large, this refusal might lead to a dangerous strengthening of earlier notions of the autonomy of poetry and corroborate the recent English notion of the happy limitations of a "well-made poem"?' Heaney replies:

> I think that the recent English language tradition does tend towards the 'well-made poem', that is towards the insulated and balanced statement. However, major poetry will always burst that corseted and

decorous truthfulness. In so doing, it may be an unfair poetry; it will almost certainly be one-sided.[42]

('One side's as bad as the other, never worse.') This interchange logically, but oddly, ties in the espousal of a Nationalist attitude with divorce from 'English' modes. The combination marks a step across the border, away from 'vowelling embrace'. Similarly, whereas *Wintering Out* was written from the perspective of Belfast/South Derry, Heaney's hinterland interpreting the 'plague'-ridden city, *North* was written from the perspective of Wicklow/Dublin, and a broader Nationalism:

> I always thought of the political problem – maybe because I am not really a political thinker – as being an internal Northern Ireland division. I thought along sectarian lines. Now I think that the genuine political confrontation is between Ireland and Britain.[43]

The vision of 'The Other Side' is absent from *North*: 'the legions stare/ from the ramparts'. The 'Mossbawn' poems (though not the learned debate about the place-name's origin in 'Belderg') prove the local textures that Heaney's panoptic view omits. 'The Seed Cutters' also shows how the English dimension of his technique lives on in a concreteness and empiricism reminiscent of nothing so much as Edward Thomas's 'Haymaking' (written during the First World War): 'All of us gone out of the reach of change –/ Immortal in a picture of an old grange'. *Preoccupations* salutes the varied influences that have fertilised Heaney's imagination, and which render irrelevant the false distinction between 'well-made' and 'major' poetry, rather than good and bad. (No *real* poem is 'well-made' in any limited sense; no major poem ill-made.) Heaney here seems to join ranks with Montague and Thomas Kinsella, who in different ways, and often too self-consciously, have stressed the European and transatlantic alliances which should be reflected in the outlook and technique of Irish poetry.

The Deane interview epitomises the intensive pressure on Heaney, including his own sense of duty: to be more Irish, to be more political, to 'try to touch the people', to do Yeats's job again instead of his own. Printed in the first issue of the journal *Crane Bag*, it heralds successive, obsessive articles on the relevance of his poetry to the Northern conflict. Again, Deane sets the tone with an attack on Conor Cruise O'Brien:

> But surely this very clarity of O'Brien's position is just what is most objectionable. It serves to give a rational clarity to the Northern position which is untrue to the reality. In other words, is not his

humanism here being used as an excuse to rid Ireland of the atavisms which gave it life even though the life itself may be in some ways brutal?[44]

Heaney demurs ('O'Brien's . . . real force and his proper ground is here in the South'[45]); nor is he responsible for the conscription of his poetry to bolster pre-set Nationalist conceptual frameworks, to endorse 'an Irish set of Archetypes, which form part of that collectivity unearthed by Jung, from which we cannot escape'.[46] But one of O'Brien's 'clarities' is his distrust of the 'area where literature and politics overlap'.[47] If they simply take in one another's mythological laundry, how can the former be an independent long-term agent of change? *North* does not give the impression of the urgent 'matter of Ireland' bursting through the confines of 'the well-made poem'. Heaney's most 'artful' book, it stylises and distances what was immediate and painful in *Wintering Out*. It hardens a highly original form of procedure ('pilot and stray') into a less original form of content ('imperial power' *versus* 'territorial piety'). By plucking out the heart of his mystery and serving it up as a quasi-political mystique, Heaney temporarily succumbs to the goddess, to the destiny feared in Derek Mahon's 'The Last of the Fire Kings'[48] where the people desire their poet-king

> Not to release them
> From the ancient curse
> But to die their creature and be thankful.

The Singing Line: Form in Derek Mahon's Poetry

'I think you read too much with the eye perhaps'
(Edward Thomas to Edward Garnett)

Most critics of contemporary poetry neglect form. By form I mean the musical shape into which all the 'sounds of sense', syntactical and rhythmical, finally settle. Many poems lack such finality and stay a little unsettled. The formal completeness of a George Herbert is rare indeed. Perhaps reviewers have lost sight of a forlorn hope. Perhaps they forbear to weary their readers with archaic pedantries of metrical analysis. Or perhaps they forget that only the ear can tell us whether a given poem is worth discussing in the first place. Currently, at least three anti-ear orthodoxies influence opinion: prosy high seriousness of *PN Review* and Carcanet writers; the "Martian" stress on metaphor as *visual* transformation; and structuralism, which dissolves form in discourse. Poetry should not be reduced to civics (praise of C.H. Sisson as a 'classical' writer on 'government and polity'[1]), video, or a history workshop; to right-wing polity, left-wing politics, or the floating image. Form, the binding force of poetry's wholeness, is also the last ditch of its aesthetic immunity. Hence Anthony Easthope's eagerness in *Poetry as Discourse* to throw rocks of jargon at one 'hegemonic form':[2]

> Pentameter can be seen as a mechanism by which the poem aims to deny its production as a poem, a mechanism therefore that promotes commodity fetishism.[3]

Easthope leaves himself with an unresolved paradox when he notes: 'Now the pentameter is a dead form and its continued use (e.g. by Philip Larkin) is in the strict sense reactionary.'[4] How strange that Larkin can write living poems in a dead form, or has someone got the march of history wrong?

Derek Mahon's poetry, which also gives sanctuary to expropriated iambics, has sometimes suffered the slings and arrows of a content-fixated period (apart from the 'privileged' arabesques of structuralism, etc) and from consequent deafness, on the part of some critics, to its true stature. There are of course honourable exceptions: for instance, Neil Corcoran's praise of 'the wit, complication and finish of Mahon's best work, its great stylistic zest',[5] Dick Davis's sense of 'a real congruence between the integrity of the writing and the vision the writing conveys'.[6] In contrast, Blake Morrison, reviewing Mahon's *Poems 1962-1978*, wondered why the poems in his first two books 'aroused much interest at all, for though consistently decent and well-made few suggest any very striking talent'.[7] Peter Porter, who recognised Mahon's skills as displayed in the pamphlet *Courtyards in Delft* ('His regular metrical patterns, his use of rhyme and its variants, and elaborate stanzas do not inhibit his emotional response'[8]), reverted to a 'yes, but' attitude when reviewing the subsequent fuller collection, *The Hunt by Night*:

> reading it feels like time-travelling, even if the poetry is full of details from our own age. It is this that separates Irish poets like Mahon and Seamus Heaney from an audacious formalist like Auden, who for all his crustiness and Anglican high jinks is firmly lodged in the twentieth century. The Irishmen seem outside time, to be playing up to some committee preparing a Pantheon. 'Irish poets learn your trade,/ Sing whatever is well made,' wrote Yeats. They have learned it too well . . .[9]

That Irish history does not march with English history, or in certain respects stands still, does not render obsolescent the *poetry* which grows out of it. Once again, what is alive *cannot be* anachronistic. The creative baton changes hands throughout the English-speaking world and the compost of poetry accrues unpredictably. Mahon's 'A Disused Shed in Co. Wexford', on whose stature most commentators agree, may imply this among other things:

> Even now there are places where a thought might grow −

Auden and MacNeice, whose formalism rose from the ashes of *The Waste Land*, were considered reactionary by Modernists (and still are). The history of literary genres does not necessarily correspond to that of literary fashion, nor to social and political history as read by the inevitable near-sightedness of the contemporary. The chief difference in poetry since 1900 is that then most bad poems were sonnets, whereas nowadays most bad poems are chopped prose. Today's reviewers simply encounter a different breed of the poetasters who drove Edward Thomas to humorous despair: 'It had become, thanks to Canon Rawnsley's industry, almost impossible to read a new sonnet without a slight measure of contempt.'[10] There is still of course plenty of bad formal writing around, helping to give the 'well-made' poem a bad name. Occasionally in *The Hunt by Night* Mahon himself goes through the motions rather than re-invents them. But every real poem, nearly all Mahon's poetry, wears form new, is an original life-form in the sense of Keith Douglas's definition:

> Poetry is like a man, whom thinking you know all his movements and appearance you will presently come upon in such a posture that for a moment you can hardly believe it a position of the limbs you know. So thinking you have set bounds to the nature of poetry, you shall as soon discover something outside your bounds which they should evidently contain.[11]

It was outside the bounds of some expectations that the ten-line stanza should be re-animated in 'A Disused Shed', while Morrison remains blind to that poem's genesis in the extraordinary formal achievement of Mahon's earlier collections.

Northern Irish poets come under fire not only for Yeatsian trust in the preservative 'ancient salt' of traditional form – building to last is surely different from seeking membership of a pantheon – but for the perceived incongruity between such trust and their chaotic birth-place. Porter's critique continues: 'they are banishing from their verse whatever parts of experience and necessity pose a problem to the shaping spirit'.[12] Stan Smith from a different standpoint, Marxist-structuralist, uses the 'poetry which has come out of Ulster in recent years' to illustrate 'just how deep this division between poet and history runs in modern poetry'.[13] He uses Mahon's poetry in particular to assail the aesthetic diplomatic status protecting 'the privileged poetic subject':[14]

> In accents familiar from "The Movement" such a poetry performs its civic duties equitably, by reflecting, in an abstracted kind of way, on violence, but its hands are indubitably clean. It speaks, at times, with the tone of a shell-shocked Georgianism that could easily be mistaken for indifference before the ugly realities of life, and death, in Ulster.[15]

Mahon's poem 'Rage for Order' fully acknowledges shock and impotence, although in a spirit of 'enforced humility' rather than inviolate privilege. The poem also implies that the very nature of the poet's activity, a search for form, relegates him to the sidelines:

> Somewhere beyond
> The scorched gable end
> And the burnt-out
> Buses there is a poet indulging his
> Wretched rage for order –
>
> Or not as the
> Case may be, for his
> Is a dying art . . .

History marginalises poetry, not poetry history. Steven Tuohy provides a superb summary: 'At the heart of [Mahon's] poetry, beneath all the brilliance and sophistication, lies a doomed gesture of appeasement of extraordinary pathos'.[16] This covers all the layers of Mahon's apologia, from Ulster Protestant historic guilt, to human guilt, to the poet's guilt that poetry by definition is not enough: 'An eddy of semantic scruple/ In an unstructurable sea.'

My next essay takes as an epigraph Mahon's contention that 'A good poem is a paradigm of good politics':[17] an ideal, at least, to set against its other incarnation as 'the anxiety of a last word// When the drums start'. But, conversely, inaccurate criticism is a paradigm of bad politics, of propaganda: .

> 'Neither here nor there' [Mahon's poetry] approaches reality 'at one remove, a substitute/ For final answers'. Literariness becomes a recurrent technique for putting a distance between the middle-class self and its panic.[18]

It is an oblique tribute to some elusive, non-ideological, non-discursive component in poetry that Stan Smith should pick on Mahon rather than the millions of panicking middle-class who never put pen to poem, or that Easthope's social mission should bypass more flagrant promoters of 'commodity fetishism' than the iambic pentameter. However, my main point is that Smith fakes the evidence. He quotes not from a post-1969 poem about Northern Ireland, as the unwary might be led to think, but from a mid-sixties love poem. And he misrepresents a lyric whose music is central to its meaning:

Preface to a Love Poem

This is a circling of itself and you –
A form of words, compact and compromise,
    Prepared in the false dawn of the half-true
Beyond which the shapes of truth materialise.
    This is a blind with sunlight filtering through.

This is a stirring in the silent hours,
As lovers do with thoughts they cannot frame
    Or leave, but bring to darkness like night-flowers,
Words never choosing but the words choose them –
    Birds crowing, wind whistling off pale stars.

This is a night-cry, neither here nor there –
A spooky echo from the clamorous dead
    Who cried aloud in anger and despair
Outlasting stone and bronze, but took instead
    Their wan smiles underground with them for ever.

> This is at one remove – a substitute
> For final answers. But the wise man knows
> To cleave to the one living absolute
> Beyond paraphrase, and shun a shrewd repose.
> The words are aching in their own pursuit
>
> To say *I love you* out of indolence,
> As one might speak at sea without forethought,
> Drifting inconsequently among islands.
> This is a way of airing my distraught
> Love of your silence. You are the soul of silence.

Besides transferring the poem's attitudes from a sexual to a political context, taking a strategy literally, ignoring ironies and reversals ('shun a shrewd repose'), Smith clearly has little time for Mahon's delicate fusion of emotional and formal 'circling'.

The refrain 'This is a' generates rhythmic movements, in conjunction with verbal repetition, which swing between 'here' and 'there', between strong stresses and weaker clusters:

> Words never choosing but the words choose them . . .

> This is a night-cry, neither here nor there . . .

Although 'distraught/ Love' breaks up mainly end-pausing cadences, the last line restores a swaying suspension:

> Love of your silence. You are the soul of silence.

The internal self-rhyming of 'silence', its assonance with 'soul', and the strong caesura conspire to prevent a smoothly complete transition to the end-rhyme with 'islands'. This effect, however, completes the poem's own formal shape as advance and undertow, as a half-way house of un-utterable feeling.

'Preface to a Love Poem' is also more metaphysically concerned with relations between silence and sound. As a preface to poetry, it circles itself, communicates the labour-pains of all poetry as 'a stirring in the silent hours' when the poet is chosen by words. In the second and third stanzas, various eerie noises – crowing, whistling, cry, echo – impinge upon dark silences between death and birth. But these individual sounds and the whole poem as a 'cry out on life' also seek and find a pattern: 'the shapes of truth'. The ambiguous 'form of words' loses its provisional significance; 'blind' is unmasked as partly bluff, a pretence that a poem is not actually taking shape. 'Preface to a Love Poem' takes us not one step away from reality but into the compulsion towards its articulation, into the crucible of formal making. The 'clamorous dead', bygone poets ('Exegi monumentum'), may have in one sense gone under. But this does not exempt their 'distraught' successor from the responsibility to break silence with his own clamour, 'To cleave to the one living absolute/ Beyond paraphrase'.

Mahon's stanzaic skill serves a poetry of statement pushed to prophetic extremity: not full-throated Yeatsian declamation, but the rhetoric Yeats might have produced had he entered more fully into either the *fin de siècle* or the modern city:

> If it were said, let there be no more light,
> Let rule the wide winds and the long-tailed seas,
> Then she would die in all our hearts tonight . . .
> ('The Death of Marilyn Monroe')

'Canadian Pacific', which interestingly links the poet's visionary quest with Non-conformist emigration to North America, travels more gradually through a similar thematic and rhythmic sweep:

> From famine, pestilence and persecution
> Those gaunt forefathers shipped abroad to find
> Rough stone of heaven beyond the western ocean,
> And staked their claim and pinned their faith.
> Tonight their children whistle through the dark,
> Frost chokes the windows. They will not have heard
> The wild geese flying south over the lakes
> While the lakes harden beyond grief and anger –
> The eyes fanatical, rigid the soft necks,
> The great wings sighing with a nameless hunger.

The lines which convey the symbolic flight of the wild geese (an inspirational *sound*) are equal to the grandeur they celebrate: 'The great wings sighing with a nameless hunger'. Assonance feathers the impetus of a finale almost worthy of Crane's 'The seal's wide spindrift gaze toward paradise'. In a line whose music is inseparable from its meaning, the suggestion of 'sighing' wingbeats interprets 'nameless hunger'.

Like Auden and Larkin, Mahon learned stanzaic aspects of his trade from Yeats. The many differences between Mahon's stanza and Larkin's are attributable in part to the greater centrality of MacNeice than Auden as an intermediate exemplar, as well as to the distinctively Irish cultural factors shaping Mahon's sensibility and intonation. (Nor should the example of Robert Graves – a shellshocked Georgian? – be overlooked.) It is not outrageous to compare the opening stanza of Mahon's 'An Unborn Child' with that of

Yeats's 'A Prayer for my Daughter', two poems in which birth is embryonic of troubled future history:

> I have already come to the verge of
> Departure. A month or so and
> I shall be vacating this familiar room.
> Its fabric fits me almost like a glove
> While leaving latitude for a free hand.
> I begin to put on the manners of the world,
> Sensing the splitting light above
> My head, where in the silence I lie curled.
>
> (Mahon)

> Once more the storm is howling, and half hid
> Under this cradle-hood and coverlid
> My child sleeps on. There is no obstacle
> But Gregory's wood and one bare hill
> Whereby the haystack- and roof-levelling wind,
> Bred on the Atlantic, can be stayed;
> And for an hour I have walked and prayed
> Because of the great gloom that is in my mind.
>
> (Yeats)

Mahon, like Yeats, plays syntax against stanza to stake out a dramatic situation. Both poets begin with their shortest sentence unit, speaking from *in medias res* ('Once more', 'already') and ending in mid-line. The resultant impulsion takes each stanza through a variety of grammatical and emotional twists, without losing the metrical coherence that ultimately shapes Yeats's 'great gloom', Mahon's microcosmic womb. The latter's less regular syllable-count and rhyme-scheme reflect an idiom which has absorbed the demotic revolution of the thirties. Nevertheless, Mahon's methods differ both from Auden's tendency to use the big stanza as a container, and MacNeice's to let the container overflow.

Auden's 'Through the Looking-Glass' (earlier version) begins:

> The earth turns over; our side feels the cold;
> And life sinks choking in the wells of trees:
> The ticking heart comes to a standstill, killed;
> The icing on the pond waits for the boys.
> Among the holly and the gifts I move,
> The carols on the piano, the glowing hearth,
> All our traditional sympathy with birth,
> Put by your challenge to the shifts of Love.

The more homogeneous iambic movement here establishes a beat for the whole poem, even for the individual line. This is possibly the poem of Auden's that comes closest to full Yeatsian self-dramatis-ation, to 'phantasmagoria'. Nevertheless, sound and rhythm play less flexible roles than in the Yeats and Mahon stanzas. Syntax coincides more with line than it counterpoints with stanza. And the dynamic does not refer back and forth unlike, for instance, Mahon's contraction and expansion at the half-way stage:

> Its fabric fits me almost like a glove
> While leaving latitude for a free hand.

In these lines (which might fit the poet inhabiting the stanza as much as the foetus inhabiting the womb) 'latitude', by virtue of length and alliteration, commands appropriate space. 'Free hand' echoes 'fabric fits', but broadens the vowel and ends the rhythmic sequence on two stresses which add to the sense of opening out. Shuttling threads of alliteration and assonance tend to distinguish dramatic zig-zags from more linear progression. Yeats's 'storm – howling – half-hid – cradle-hood – coverlid – child – obstacle', and Mahon's 'come – verge – departure – month – vacating – familiar – room' inscribe a more intricate design than Auden's 'sinks – choking – ticking' and 'feels – wells – standstill' united in 'killed'. Such design is not a two-dimensional matter but deep ordering structure breaking surface. Notions of 'onomatopoeia' sometimes obscure metre's less paraphrasable punctuation by subliminal sound-sequences.

The opening of MacNeice's 'Schizophrene' finally respects the line, but makes little effort to satisfy the stanza:

> Hearing offstage the taps filling the bath
> The set dissolves to childhood – in her cot
> Hearing that ominous relentless noise
> Which the grown-ups have started, who are not,
> She knows, aware of what it means; it means
> The Dark, the Flood, the Malice. It destroys
> All other meanings – dolls or gingerbread;
> It means a Will that wills all children dead.

Here colloquial syntax does not adjust itself to the demands of form: 'who are not,/ She knows, aware of what it means'. At the end of 'An Unborn Child' – which after all inserts the theme of MacNeice's 'Prayer Before Birth' into a stanzaic womb – Mahon integrates the phrasing of casual speech with the formal dynamic:

> Perhaps I need not worry – give
> Or take a day or two, my days are numbered.

Idiom, tone, a final organic pun, springy enjambement, and the movement from shorter to longer line, working in unison, bring to a climax the collision between free will and fate which has been the poem's subject. Mahon has undoubtedly absorbed and refined MacNeice's use of the six-line stanza, a form popular with both poets. MacNeice's 'Autolycus' celebrates the spirit of Shakespearean creation, rather as Mahon's elegy 'In Carrowdore Churchyard' celebrates MacNeice himself:

Such innocence – In his own words it was
Like an old tale, only that where time leaps
Between acts three and four there was something born
Which made the stock-type virgin dance like corn
In a wind that having known foul marshes, barren steeps,
Felt therefore kindly towards Marinas, Perditas . . .

(MacNeice, fourth stanza of six)

This, you implied, is how we ought to live –

The ironical, loving crush of roses against snow,
Each fragile, solving ambiguity. So
From the pneumonia of the ditch, from the ague
Of the blind poet and the bombed-out town you bring
The all-clear to the empty holes of spring,
Rinsing the choked mud, keeping the colours new.

(Mahon, last stanza of four)

Both these stanzas express resurrection, art's powers of renewal and self-renewal, the imagination's hard-won victories over time. But Mahon again enlists the stanza itself more specifically for this purpose. MacNeice as in 'Schizophrene' allows phrases and syntactical links to run almost their prose length: 'In his own words', 'only that where', 'that having known . . . therefore'. Mahon's prefatory 'you implied' carries more weight than 'In his own words' because of its precisely timed position.

Mahon packs a lot of syntax, a lot of drama, into the single word: 'This' and 'So', also metrically emphatic ('So' in the only stanza to begin with a couplet). While extending other lines beyond ten syllables, both poets revert to pentameter for the rhythmically pivotal 'something born/ Which made the stock-type virgin dance like corn' and 'you bring/ The all-clear to the empty holes of spring'. Here MacNeice compresses his language more intensely and exploits the central couplet of a chiastic stanza (abccba) to suggest the leaping of time. However this central climax does not quite equal the rhythm sprung by Mahon's delaying tactics. Like Yeats, Frost and

Thomas he understands the extent to which poetry can claim the licence of an inflected language in ordering clauses, in calculating rhetoric. By placing the main verb 'you bring' where dramatic metre can co-operate with dramatic grammar, Mahon pivots the stanza so that, still more powerfully than MacNeice's, it enacts art's therapeutic transformation.

The poems by Mahon so far discussed belong to *Night-Crossing* (1968). In *Lives* (1972) and *The Snow Party* (1975) the influence of Beckett, as well as other developments, adds diminuendo to his formal repertoire. Whereas some poems in *Night-Crossing* confront even death with a certain metrical verve ('Girls all, be with me now/ And keep me warm/ Before we go plunging into the dark for ever'), 'An Image from Beckett' ends:

> It was good while it lasted;
> And if it only lasted
> The Biblical span
>
> Required to drop six feet
> Through a glitter of wintry light,
> There is No-one to blame.
>
> Still, I am haunted
> By that landscape,
> The soft rush of its winds,
>
> The uprightness of its
> Utilities and schoolchildren –
> To whom in my will,
>
> This, I have left my will.
> I hope they had time, and light
> Enough, to read it.

These triplets collapse the big stanza as the poem collapses history into 'that instant'. Latinate or polysyllabic words, formerly reverberant within a longer line and stanza, now function as rungs of resistance on some inexorable descent. The repeated line-endings 'lasted' and 'will' also convey inevitability staved off only for a second. However the designation of the poem itself as both will and legacy again constitutes a residual faith in form amid circumstances which offer nothing else – more codicil than preface to poetry. In 'Matthew V. 29-30' satirical purpose imparts 'momentum' rather than diminuendo to the triplet (Mahon's medium despite a later change of layout):

> But now, the thing
> Finding its own momentum,
> The more so since
>
> The offence continued,
> I entered upon
> A prolonged course
>
> Of lobotomy and vivisection . . .

'Silence', not the pregnant silence of 'Preface to a Love Poem' but terminal quiet, is the theme and goal of such poems, as for Beckett. 'Silence' is the refrain-word of 'The Antigone Riddle', which essentially regards humanity as noise-pollution:

> Shy minerals contract at the sound of his voice,
> Cod point in silence when his bombers pass,
> And the windfall waits
> In silence for his departure
> Before it drops in
> Silence to the long grass.

Written later, the sequence 'Light Music' represents some kind of formal *reductio*. Its punning title at once disowns mighty metres and suggests an effort to capture in sound qualities that usually travel too fast. 'Revelation' lives up to its name:

> A colour the fish know
> we do not know, so
> long have we been ashore.
>
> When that colour
> shines in the rainbow
> there will be no more sea.

Here Mahon miniaturises all his skills. The hypothetical rapprochement of sea and sky, genesis (or the origin of human species) and revelation, is reflected by the unifying echo 'colour – ashore – colour – more'. The repeated 'know' and the internal rhyme 'know, so' which throws emphasis on the enjambement 'so/ long' makes 'Revelation' the ultimate in yearning for the ultimate. Its brief cadence distils and fuses elements of the *fin de siècle* and the millennial in Mahon's sensibility.

After 'Revelation', it might well seem there could be no more poetry. But apart from his Beckettian interest in silence, Mahon has had the creative courage not to confuse quantity with quality. Unlike Yeats, Frost, Thomas, Larkin, some poets lack the nerve to shrink their forms when they have nothing more to say, or nothing they can say otherwise. And it is rare nowadays to find a critic brooding so lovingly on a single couplet as does Randall Jarrell on Frost's 'An Answer'.[19] Perhaps this courage enabled Mahon, in 'A Disused Shed in Co. Wexford', to snatch crescendo out of diminuendo. He resumes the big stanza (ten lines); but whereas in 'An Unborn Child' the relation of foetus to womb affirmatively parallels the poet's imagination within the stanza, such a parallel now stems from the odder relation of 'a foetor of/ Vegetable sweat' to a derelict construction. Again Mahon negotiates between silence and sound. The first stanza lists fading sounds:

> An echo trapped for ever, and a flutter of
> Wildflowers in the lift-shaft,
> Indian compounds where the wind dances
> And a door bangs with diminished confidence . . .

The mushrooms weirdly preserved in the shed 'since civil war days' 'have learnt patience and silence/ Listening to the crows querulous in the high wood'. This is another image of poetry-in-waiting, of latent articulation on the margin of history. Or is it the discords of history, onomatopoeically symbolised by the crows and 'the gravel-crunching, interminable departure/ Of the expropriated mycologist', that are truly marginal?

The mushrooms eventually acquire an implicit voice: 'Elbow room! Elbow room!', 'groaning/ For their deliverance' (a phrase which subliminally returns to the womb), 'the ghost of a scream'. The last stanza interprets their silence:

> They are begging us, you see, in their wordless way,
> To do something, to speak on their behalf
> Or at least not to close the door again.
> Lost people of Treblinka and Pompeii!
> Save us, save us, they seem to say,
> Let the god not abandon us
> Who have come so far in darkness and in pain.
> We too had our lives to live.
> You with your light meter and relaxed itinerary,
> Let not our naive labours have been in vain!

This plea for someone to speak on behalf of victims of unnatural and natural disaster ('Treblinka and Pompeii') throughout history, seems finally directed towards the poet in particular: 'You with your light meter and relaxed itinerary'. The pun summons poetry, not photojournalism, to order 'darkness' and 'pain'.

181

The metre of 'A Disused Shed' is 'light' only in the sense of flexible delicacy, 'relaxed' only in the sense of easily accommodating sentences to stanza. As compared with 'An Unborn Child', the big stanza has grown further 'beyond nature'. Paul Fussell observes: 'Between the nine lines of the Spenserian stanza and the fourteen of the sonnet, English offers no conventional fixed forms.'[20] The 'Disused Shed' stanza takes more liberties with line-length than that of 'An Unborn Child': fourteen syllables for the interminable departure, six for 'Elbow room! Elbow room!'. The syntax inclines more towards the serial structures of Mahon's triplet poems, than to tautly angled clauses derived from argument. Yet the stanza's own resurrection winds up what elsewhere imitates running-down. The transition from first to second stanza detonates the formal surprises in store:

> Lime crevices behind rippling rainbarrels,
> Dog corners for shit burials;
> And in a disused shed in Co. Wexford,
>
> Deep in the grounds of a burnt-out hotel,
> Among the bathtubs and the washbasins
> A thousand mushrooms crowd to a keyhole.

The rhythms of 'diminished confidence' end in a line whose content, diction and resonance might mark some kind of nadir in English poetry, as in Irish history. At one extreme: 'Is this the face that launched a thousand ships'; at another: 'And in a disused shed in Co. Wexford'. Yet that apparent flatness initiates a powerful counter-movement (partly impelled by the continued rhyme rainbarrels/ burials/hotel/keyhole). Henceforth rhythms expressive of the mush-rooms crowding to the poem's keyhole, of growth and accumul-ation, answer those of diminuendo. Complementary rhythms trace a 'posture' of 'expectancy' and 'desire':

> What should they do there but desire?
> So many days beyond the rhododendrons
> With the world waltzing in its bowl of cloud . . .

This self-parodies the integrative thrust of the embryo's assertion in 'An Unborn Child': 'I know . . . the clouds/ Of goldfish mooning around upon the shelf'. However, the overall movement of 'A Disused Shed' enacts a renewal of faith in the possibility of imaginative action ('They are begging us . . . To do something'), in poetry's ability to redeem the 'wordless'.

182

The penultimate stanza exemplifies many aspects of the poem's formal success:

> A half century, without visitors, in the dark –
> Poor preparation for the cracking lock
> And creak of hinges. Magi, moonmen,
> Powdery prisoners of the old regime,
> Web-throated, stalked like triffids, racked by drouth
> And insomnia, only the ghost of a scream
> At the flash-bulb firing squad we wake them with
> Shows there is life yet in their feverish forms.
> Grown beyond nature now, soft food for worms,
> They lift frail heads in gravity and good faith.

Although orchestrated very differently from the first stanza of 'An Unborn Child', these sentences also order their clauses according to dramatic logic. We are 'prepared' for 'the cracking lock/ And creak of hinges' by the exclamatory first line's suspense. And when the door has been onomatopoeically opened over two lines, the caesura wins space for continued verbless apostrophe: 'Magi, moonmen . . .' which does not find a vestigial grammatical attachment, as appositional object, until the seventh line. After that astonished, astonishing catalogue Mahon delays until the end the first really active verb associated with the mushrooms: 'They lift frail heads . . .' The beginning and end of a ten-line stanza cannot connect as closely as those of an eight-liner. This moves more like a spiral than a foetal 'curl'. However the DNA of assonance and alliteration still unifies. For instance, the emphatic alliteration of the first four lines – 'Poor preparation', 'cracking lock/ And creak', 'Magi, moonmen,/ Powdery prisoners' – develops into more complicated sound-patterns in which the 'f' inaugurated by 'triffids' plays an important role. Particularly associated with the mushrooms' physical state (the previous stanza has 'pale flesh flaking'), 'f' modulates from sounding alarm in 'flash-bulb firing squad', which again presents the world as dangerous noise, to conveying organic 'life': 'feverish forms', 'soft food', 'lift frail', 'faith'. The solider 'gravity' and 'good' also lift the last line towards possibility. Poetry thus finds an alternative voice to that of 'the flash-bulb firing squad' – which partly suggests Ulster and Ireland returning to the violent limelight of history. However, the efforts of both mushrooms and poet still come frighteningly close to 'a last word': 'Let not our naïve labours . . .'

Whether 'feverish', or calmer 'shapes of truth', Derek Mahon's forms imitate the rhythms of life and death in a way 'Beyond paraphrase'. His early poem 'Early Morning' takes on Genesis:

No doubt the creation was like this –
Slower than time, spectacular only in size,
Revealing coldly what there is of chaos.
First there is darkness, then somehow light.
We call this day and the other night
And watch in vain for the second of sunrise.

Suddenly, near at hand, the click of a wooden shoe –
An old woman among the primeval shapes
Abroad in the field of light, sombrely dressed.
She calls good-day, since there are bad days too,
And her eyes go down. She has seen perhaps
Ten thousand dawns like this, and is not impressed.

'Tractatus', one of the best poems in *The Hunt by Night*, also
consists of two six-line stanzas. Like 'Early Morning', it concentrates
the quart of creation into a formal pint-pot. And it moves in a
contrary direction (and manner) to that of 'Revelation'. The first
three lines cosmically cheek Wittgenstein by rising from the lowest
order of defeated nature, in another shed, to the highest order of
triumphant art; while the rhythm simultaneously rises from low-key
to relish a resonant name in a full-rhymed line:

'The world is everything that is the case'
From the fly giving up in the coal-shed
To the Winged Victory of Samothrace.

The second stanza outflanks philosophy by appealing to the ear:

The world, though, is also so much more –
Everything that is the case imaginatively.
Tacitus believed mariners could *hear*
The sun sinking into the western sea;
And who would question that titanic roar,
The steam rising wherever the edge may be?

Mahon's aural imagination also outflanks more prosaic historians,
or perhaps anyone whose definitions limit history as well as philosophy, by conferring validity on Tacitus's poetic error. Stress and
assonance celebrate the limitless horizons of the imagination working in its own terms, by making us 'hear' the sun sinking, the steam
rising. 'Roar' is sometimes pejoratively opposed to 'silence' in a
poetry inclined to see itself as just more noise-pollution. The word
comes into its own at a climax which sings with undiminished
confidence.

Poetry and Politics in Northern Ireland

'*The antagonist of imaginative writing in Ireland is not a habit of scientific observation but our interest in matters of opinion . . . All fine literature is the disinterested contemplation or expression of life, but hardly any Irish writer can liberate his mind sufficiently from questions of practical reform for this contemplation. Art for art's sake, as he understands it, whether it be the art of the* Ode on a Grecian Urn *or of the imaginer of Falstaff, seems to him a neglect of public duty. It is as though the telegraph-boys botanised among the hedges with the undelivered envelopes in their pockets . . .*'
— W.B. Yeats, EXPLORATIONS

'*A good poem is a paradigm of good politics*' — Derek Mahon

1.

Poetry and politics, like church and state, should be separated. And for the same reasons: mysteries distort the rational processes which ideally prevail in social relations; while ideologies confiscate the poet's special passport to *terra incognita*. Its literary streak, indeed, helps to make Irish Nationalism more a theology than an ideology. Conor Cruise O'Brien calls 'the area where literature and politics overlap' an 'unhealthy intersection'; because, 'suffused with romanticism', it breeds bad politics – Fascism and Nationalism.[1] But it also breeds bad literature, particularly, bad poetry, which in a vicious circle breeds – or inbreeds – bad politics. As Yeats says: 'We call certain minds creative because they are among the moulders of their nation and are not made upon its mould, and they resemble one another in this only – they have never been foreknown or fulfilled an expectation.'[2] Ulster poets today are sometimes the victims of improper expectations. Whatever causes they may support as citizens, their imaginations cannot be asked to settle for less than full human truth. And no cause in Ireland (unlike, say, opposition to Adolf Hitler) carries such an *imprimatur*. This does not let the poet off the hook of general or particular 'responsibility' towards political events. The price of imaginative liberty is eternal vigilance.

Yet Yeats's very formulation gives the poet a national if not a Nationalist role. And in the early years of the century creating literature and creating a nation could validly be seen as concentric labours. Even Yeats's later reflections on the transition from cultural to political Nationalism balance profit and loss:

This is not', I say,
'The dead Ireland of my youth, but an Ireland
The poets have imagined, terrible and gay.'

But later still, Louis MacNeice anticipated O'Brien by wondering:

> what is a nation?
> Have with you to the Post Office! Was it a nation
> They gave their lives for, was it rather a gesture
> That as in a poem, a play, a flourish of brushwork,
> Gives meaning to an accident, in passing
> Confirms what was not there? So in their passing
> Did sixteen men impose upon their fellows
> An unsolicited poetry? Which, needless
> To say, as soon as it could relapsed to prose –
> A land of priests and grocers.[3]

'Unsolicited poetry' has also influenced British political life. Newbolt and Brooke manufactured the same kind of rhetorical bullets as did 'the rhymed lesson-book of Davis' and Pearse's prayer-book of blood sacrifice. The Falklands *Sun* was the dustbin of imperial poetry, as is *An Phoblacht* of Republican poetry. Perhaps poetry always coarsens to verse before it really influences action. Thus Wilfred Owen's protest was also a form of literary criticism, correcting a false vocabulary, imagery, and consciousness. Although Yeats disliked Owen's work, and although his politics after 1916 were neither single nor simple, essentially he moved into the same critical mode: 'We, who seven years ago/ Talked of honour and of truth.' Certainly the breaking of nations loomed larger than the making. But if Yeats's vision pivots on construction *versus* destruction, Ulster poetry since 1969 has felt little of the former possibility. Its inevitable ancestor is not *Cathleen ní Houlihán* but 'Meditations in Time of Civil War'. Aidan Carl Mathews argues that the poets 'are engaged upon a profound and responsible quest for community; an idiom of restoration and homecoming pervades their work'.[4] He may overstate the pluses, though such aspiration counts even as a subtextual presence. But beyond imageries of homecoming and healing, poetry as therapy for 'wounds', the very existence of the poetry repeats in new terms Yeats's effort towards 'unity of culture', what F.S.L. Lyons calls 'cultural fusion'.[5] A corollary of this, and of Mathews's argument, is that poetry can be 'political' only on behalf of its own values.

Yeats of course placed the tension between poet and man of action at the centre both of his personal drama and of his aesthetic. His attacks on other 'opinionated minds' (on *women* of action as poems marred by politics) were sharpened by his own suppressions: 'it is a hard law that compels us to cast away our swords when we enter the house of the Muses, as men cast them away at the doors of the banqueting-hall at Tara'.[6] When we glimpse the occasional sword-flash or slash, Yeats's poetry too coarsens and confirms his point. But, on the whole, that lament of 1905 legitimately fathers this retrospect in 1935: 'I have been always a propagandist though I have kept it out of my poems.'[7] Thus, although Yeats, and Abbey Theatre policy, supported the Nationalists during the Anglo-Irish war[8] (1916-1919), critics quarrel over whether the 'rough beast' of 'The Second Coming' (1919) most resembles the IRA, or the Black and Tans, not to mention Bolshevism or Fascism. The rhetorical question at the end of the poem was never meant to be answered in the way Malcolm Brown demands: 'there has probably never been a reader of "The Second Coming" who has not been dissatisfied with its generalities'. And Brown calls Yeats's universal suggestiveness 'forensic masking'.[9]

Earlier, the techniques of Yeats's 1916 poems had marked the limit to which his poetry could swim with a political current. By adopting popular forms he fulfilled (as before in 'September 1913') his youthful ambition 'that the ballad-writers might be the better'.[10] But in writing these last and greatest 'Songs and Ballads of Young Ireland', Yeats rediscovered the rift between 'the obsession of public life'[11] and the private imagination. He delegates reportage and commentary to the impersonal medium ('I write it out in a verse') or to third persons ('"O words are lightly spoken,"/ Said Pearse to Connolly'). Again all three poems – 'Easter, 1916', 'Sixteen Dead Men', 'The Rose Tree' – are concerned with another dichotomy: not simply that between word and deed, but between debate and symbolic act, prose and poetry. The transforming power of Yeats's poetry contemplates an equivalent transformation in the outer world ('changed utterly'). 'Sixteen Dead Men', much quoted during the Hunger Strike, weighs the language of reason, the terminology of argument, in a scale where they cannot win:

> And is their logic to outweigh
> MacDonagh's bony thumb?

This perception parallels Seamus Heaney's 'two languages' in *North* (the definitions of political journalism as compared with those of 'religious intensity')[12] except that Yeats stands outside both. He registers the politico-poetic potency of the bony thumb, the rose tree, the rosary of names which he too helps to weave into legend. But in a sense his own poetry extricates itself from this poetry that has become public property. In 'Easter, 1916' Yeats's bardic voice as spokesman ('Now and in time to be,/ Wherever green is worn'), alternates with the poet as man speaking, 'troubled' by 'Hearts with one purpose alone'. The pronouns of the poem, 'they and I' 'We', approximate to Yeats's shifts between solitariness and solidarity. 'A terrible beauty is born' suggests, among other things, that the Rising and its consequences gave him more poetry than he had 'solicited'.

2.

Seamus Heaney has been under greater pressure than other contemporary Ulster poets to reconcile Yeats's divorce. Mark Patrick Hederman, for instance, looks to him as 'the most potent Orpheus who would lead us through that psychic hinterland which we shall have to chart before we can emerge from the Northern crisis'.[13] I have argued in my discussion of *North* that psychic hinterlands can be imaginative dead ends. But the demands made on Heaney testify to the persistent Irish belief that within one tribe, one nation, the poet's organic bardic function can still be performed – without the fissuring strains of 'Easter, 1916'. John Montague's conviction that 'What's in the poet's blood must speak through him', percolating 'a slow drip-drop of knowledge', contrasts with the Protestant John Hewitt's categorical 'I have no evidence to support the fact that [Northern poetry] has made any difference at all.'[14]

The literary intellectual too assumes (or assumes that he has) more prominence in Irish than in British life. Seamus Deane explains: 'in literature at least Ireland has sometimes overcome the severe limitations of its geography and of the catastrophic burden of its history'.[15] Despite (or because of) Joyce, Faustian overcompensations beckon. Deane makes this claim in a retrospect on *Crane Bag*, a journal which has often hovered over O'Brien's 'unhealthy intersection'. In the first issue Richard Kearney's 'Beyond Art and Politics' begins: 'Politics is far too grave a matter for the politician. Art is far too potent a medium for the artist.'[16] What is already powerful should not be encouraged to covet art's 'potency', and vice versa. In the same issue, Deane's interview with Heaney (see page 168) introduces a key *Crane Bag* word, 'atavism', another intersection of literary and political emotion. With regard to O'Brien's demythologising of Republicanism, he asks: 'is not his humanism . . . being used as an excuse to rid Ireland of the atavisms which gave it life even though the life itself may be in some ways brutal?'[17] Despite the plural, 'atavism' is *never* applied favourably to Ulster Protestant gut-feelings. Try this triad: 'I'm atavistic; you're bigoted; he's a terrorist.' In *Crane Bag*'s New Ireland Forum issue Kearney's study of similar Irish journals approves those that 'refused the polarisation of literature and politics into opposed discourses'.[18] Rebuking Sean O'Faolain's forgivable weariness after six years vain crusade in *The Bell*, he comments: 'he now has recourse to the individualistic model of the romantic, solitary poet nursing his genius far from the madding crowd'.[19] (Note the weasel-word 'individualistic', presumably as used in Chinese self-criticism sessions.) O'Faolain in fact signed off: 'It may be, and one hopes so, that somewhere some young poet, scornful of us and our controversies, has been tending in his secret heart a lamp which will, in the end, light far more than we can ever do.'[20] How many lamps did Yeats light?

The dwindling optimism of *The Bell* may still accurately graph Irish realities. Contrary to Kearney's strange accusation of a 'partitionist' mentality, O'Faolain understood Ireland's truly partitionist gang of 'Little Irelanders, chauvinists, puritans, stuffed-shirts, pietists, Tartuffes, Anglophobes, Celtophiles'.[21] And no editor of a Southern periodical was ever more generous to the *whole* of Northern culture. I doubt whether any reconciliation, as Kearney retrospectively urges, of 'the socio-political debate' with 'the literary debate' would have modified his 'defeatism' – or his defeat, at a time when politics censored literature. In fact *Crane Bag*, sucked back like so much else in the South by the undertow of the North, seems partly anxious to remythologise what O'Faolain, before O'Brien, demythologised. O'Faolain's first editorial asserted:

> All our symbols have to be created afresh, and the only way to create a living symbol is to take a naked thing and clothe it with new life, new association, new meaning, with all the vigour of the life we live in the Here and Now.[22]

And in 'Tradition and Creation', written twenty-five years after the Rising, he insists: 'The process of liberation . . . will go on until we have got rid of that Old Man of the Sea – our Glorious Past; and that equally tyrannical Old Man of the Sea – our Great Future.'[23] Richard Pine in the Forum *Crane Bag* also equates these chimerical tyrants, rejecting 'a mythical past because that leads only to a mythical future'. As he shrewdly observes: 'The dispossessed Gaels of the early eighteenth century looked forward in their aislingí to redemption by a Stuart saviour, unaware that their future, if it existed at all, lay among real rather than illusory alternatives.'[24] However, the editorial, while stating that Ireland stands at a 'cultural crossroads', also offers this sophistication of the backward look:

we might take our cue from Brian Friel when he writes in *Translations* that 'it is not the literal past, the "facts" of history that shape us, but images of the past embodied in language'. A central preoccupation of this *Crane Bag* is the problem of how, if at all, the inherited 'images of the past' may be translated into idioms for a new society.[25]

A cue from *Translations*? Does *Translations* itself renew 'images of the past', or does it recycle a familiar perspective? Is it an aisling? *Translations* has its context in the poetic and political nexus of the Field Day theatre company, whose directors include Seamus Heaney, Seamus Deane and Tom Paulin. The Forum *Crane Bag* juxtaposes Friel's account of translating 'history' (a word which has replaced 'atavism' as flavour of the month, though it means much the same) with the reactions of John Andrews who wrote *A Paper Landscape*, the history of the nineteenth-century Irish Ordnance Survey that gave Friel ideas. Kevin Barry's introduction to their dialogue gilds the backward look with forward-looking terminology:

> It is certain that both history and fiction imagine and structure a past which neither could make known without sharing the images and structures of narrative. Both discourses enable the entry of what has been lost into a society's understanding of its present.[26]

In fact his description of *Translations* assumes more than 'imaginative' accuracy: 'The "hidden Ireland" emerges from Friel's play . . . By imagining an unwritten past Friel translates a defeated community into the narrative of history.'[27] Has it never been so translated before? As O'Brien asks, 'if Ireland were ever to cease to be oppressed, what would happen to "history", how would one get into it?'[28] Andrews the historian gets nearer the mark when he reads *Translations* as 'a play about late twentieth-century Ireland' whose 'real subject . . . is the relation between authority and alienation'.[29] The play does not so much *examine* myths of dispossession and oppression as repeat them.

When Friel's soldier-researchers deploy unhistorical bayonets after Lieutenant Yolland goes missing, his subject is the behaviour of British troops in the Catholic ghettoes of Belfast and Derry during the 1970s. At the end of the play Owen, who has 'collaborated' with the Survey, perceives the middle ground as a premature illusion and reverts to potentially violent tribal loyalty. He rejects the translated names as 'A mistake, my mistake – nothing to do with us.' Owen's final adherence to 'fact' ('if Yolland is not found, we are all going to be evicted') contrasts with the concluding attitudes of Hugh, his drunken hedge-schoolmaster father. Hugh accepts linguistic change, and advises: 'Take care Owen. To remember everything is a form of madness.' In one sense, then, Hugh has taken his other advice: 'we must never cease renewing [the images of the past] because once we do, we fossilise'. But the 'language' here appears theoretic, chosen with *Crane Bag* already in mind. And Owen is the doer, Hugh the dreamer who turned back on the road to '98. Hugh himself embodies the play's pervasive nostalgia for 'what has been lost': for the hedge-school era, for a land of saints and scholars, for Ballybeg as a kind of Eden. In his last speech, Aeneas making good the fall of Troy stands in for another restored civilisation: 'a race was springing from Trojan blood to overthrow some day these Tyrian towers'. Friel, then, translates contemporary Northern Catholic feeling into historical terms. He does this very well. But the play is partly 'fossilised' because he explores the ethos of a particular community exclusively in relation to British dominion over the native Irish. No perspective discriminates between past and present, nineteenth-century Ireland and twentieth-century Northern Ireland. There is simply equation (as in Heaney's *North*). *Translations* refurbishes an old myth. Its imagery, structure of feeling, and cultural vision correspond to John Wilson Foster's account of Montague's *The Rough Field* (if we substitute culture for agriculture), itself perhaps a seminal work behind both *Translations* and Heaney's *Wintering Out*:

> The Ulster Catholic writer has lived so long with the imagery of land-decay and land-loss that he has become addicted to it . . . What he wants is not progress, a forward-looking reversal of decay through agricultural improvement, but rather a return, the recovery of a politico-spiritual impossibility – a mythic landscape of beauty and plenitude that is pre-Partition, pre-Civil War, pre-Famine, pre-Plantation and pre-Tudor.[30]

Field Day, like Hugh, 'dreams of a perfect city' as well as a promised land. Hence Tom Paulin's romantic programme-note to Friel's later play *The Communication Cord*, a farce which comfortably fails in its intention to subvert the pieties of *Translations*:

> anyone who looks at the Hobbesian civic wilderness which is Derry now is likely to nourish a similar dream. Nevertheless, they can also perceive that there is in Derry an effort at civil definition which appears to be absent, or at least less keenly felt, in Belfast and Dublin. Imaginatively, Derry is the most advanced city in Ireland and the Guildhall is a temple which joins the stained, bright images of empire to the idea of a new *res publica*.

The projection on to 'history' of contemporary aspirations accords with the Republican viewpoint from which history stands still: an attitude that refuses to accept the internal Northern vendetta as at least a variation on the old colonial theme, that writes Northern Protestants out of history unless prepared to go back and start again in 1798. Other members of Field Day have adopted such projections both as an artistic and an argumentative strategy. The simplicities of the strategy, if it continues, make Field Day less likely to create, in Kearney's words, 'a "fifth province" of cultural understanding and exchange, where the divisions of the four political provinces might be confronted and resolved'.[31] (Perhaps Ulster readers are better equipped than Southerners to crack the codes that emanate from part of one province.) Paulin's collection of poems *Liberty Tree*, as its title suggests, attacks contemporary Unionism for betraying the French and Irish Republican principles of '98. His ideal unifying symbolism of 'dissenting green', 'the northern starlight', 'the green tide rising/ through Mayo and Antrim' (another pre-lapsarian dream), carries less poetic conviction than his satire, which castigates the Northern state in the light of British colonialism and other master-races:

> Chitchat evaporates at this charred altitude — *wasting time*
> Like letters airmailed to Great Namaland   *— no action.*
> Or Deeko's postcards to his old headmaster
> Who wrote the school would be most pleased to learn
> Of his promotion to the Chair of Social Justice
> At Jan Smuts college in the Orange Free State.
> He thanked him also for his learned article,
> 'Samuel Twaddell: a Co. Down Man at the Cape'.
> Even now, at a bring-and-buy in Cleaver Park,
> His Aunt Mina is telling Lady Lowry,
> 'That boy's gone far, but we've heard nothing yet.'

However, when Paulin comes nearer home, he cannot temper the extremist techniques of satire for purposes of inward dissection:

> This bitter village shows the flag
> In a baked absolute September light.
> Here the Word has withered to a few
> Parched certainties, and the charred stubble
> Tightens like a black belt, a crop of Bibles.
>   ('Desertmartin')

That clichéd, external impression of the Protestant community exposes Paulin's own 'parched certainty'.

At least he notices that community's existence. Seamus Deane's Field Day pamphlet, *Civilians and Barbarians*, resembles *Translations* and *North* in concentrating on the Anglo-Irish axis. He traces current discussion of 'terrorism', dirty protesters and hunger strikers, back to Spenser's (1612) comment on the 'stern and savage nature'[32] of the Irish, Coleridge's (1814) fear of 'a wild and barbarous race',[33] and other English smears. (Spenser's rise to fame as the anathema of the Nationalist literary intellectual deserves a study in itself.) But though he accurately unmasks the rhetoric of centuries, many *Irish* voices, North and South, today join in more complicated debate than civilian putting down barbarian. The pamphlet's subtext is again Catholic grievance in the North, the rightly hurt pride of second-class citizenship, of slighted civilisation, translated into historical terms that purport to complete the whole picture. Deane ends with a wild generalisation: 'Of all the blighting distinctions which govern our responses and limit our imaginations at the moment, none is more potent than this four hundred year-old distinction between barbarians and civilians.'[34] He acknowledges but does not unmask the rhetoric of Republicanism itself, the blighted seed of 'MacDonagh's bony thumb'. Deane's polarised vista of endlessly 'competing discourses'[35] – rival propagandas? – frighteningly rules out any objective language of fact or value. *Civilians and Barbarians* accepts, what Spain portended for Orwell, that 'the very concept of objective truth is disappearing out of the world'.[36] Structuralist relativism supports ideological absolutism. But the 'competing discourses' that really count are still to be found where Louis MacNeice found them – without benefit of structuralism:

> And one read black where the other read white, his hope
>   The other man's damnation:
> Up the Rebels, To Hell with the Pope,
>   And God Save – as you prefer – the King or Ireland.[37]

Deane, Paulin and Friel (in Heaney's wake) are highly conscious of the political role of language. They rebel against name-calling and name-changing. Paulin's pamphlet *A New Look at the Language Question* begins: 'The history of a language is often a story of possession and dispossession, territorial struggle and the establishment or imposition of a culture'.[38] Yet Field Day's resistance to linguistic colonialism (which logically requires the revival of Irish) must remain even more of a rearguard action than the liberation-struggles of Feminist and working-class writers. Meanwhile, their ability to use the English language contradicts their inclination to abuse it. Friel's clever device in *Translations* of making the audience believe that English *is* Irish may imply more irrevocable loss than he intended. At the period of the Irish Literary Revival it seemed at least conceivable that a 'Battle of Two Civilisations' might result in victory for the Gaelic League and the Irish language. But although 'Irish Ireland' won the social and political battle in the Free State/ Republic, it lost the language battle, making literary partition and apartheid forever impossible (surely a source of hope as well as regret). In default of Gaelic, Paulin opts for local English speech as the linguistic arm of his new *Res Publica:*

> Many words which now appear simply gnarled, or which 'make strange' or seem opaque to most readers would be released into the shaped flow of a new public language. Thus in Ireland there would exist three fully-fledged languages – Irish, Ulster Scots and Irish English. Irish and Ulster Scots would be preserved and nourished, while Irish English would be a form of modern English which draws on Irish, the Yola and Fingallian dialects, Ulster Scots, Elizabethan English, Hiberno-English, British English and American English. A confident concept of Irish English would substantially increase the vocabulary and this would invigorate the written language. A language that lives lithely on the tongue ought to be capable of becoming the flexible written instrument of a complete cultural idea.[39]

In fact since Yeats, such an idea, shorn of Paulin's totalitarianism, has informed the practice of the best poets. Nor can Ulster Scots, either for conversational or literary purposes, be cordoned off in some linguistic zoo-park as a backward species whose robust primitivism may one day contribute to the national bloodstock. The natural spectrum of Seamus Heaney's vocabulary shows the way that Paulin would harshly floodlight with academy or dictionary. Moreover, Paulin has invented a new form of poetic diction by sprinkling his poems with dialect, or would-be dialect, words (in Edward Thomas's phrase) 'like the raisins that will get burnt on an ill-made cake':[40] scuffy, choggy, glooby, claggy, biffy, keeks, glup, boke. If that's meant to be Ulster-Scots idiom, the implications are almost racist. A poet's language derives from how he talks and what he hears. As Thomas maintained: 'Only when a word has become necessary to him can a man use it safely; if he try to impress words by force on a sudden occasion, they will either perish of his violence or betray him.'[41] Even Synge went a bit far in the matter of idiomatic vitamin-injections. And prose-writers, particularising character and scene, can perhaps do more than poets to preserve local words. Lallans poetry, in the mouth of Hugh MacDiarmid, was virtually a one-man show. On the political front, Paulin's advocacy of a 'confident concept of Irish English' has met with some amazement among Nationalist Irish-language enthusiasts, who refer scornfully to 'the creole dialects of English'.

Paulin creates division where unities already exist. And his own writing proves that excessive awareness of linguistic difference, of 'competing discourses', the loss of creative innocence once language is comprehended as political, can damage your style. Propaganda breeds antithesis: black-and-white readings, black-and-white writings. Deane structures the past as two 'symbolic' cathedrals, the present as 'the new security barracks, and, confronting them, the new and increasingly violent housing estates'.[42] He sees civilians and barbarians, cops and robbers, wherever he goes, no inbetweeners. The same polarity shapes 'The Longing for Modernity', his editorial in the Winter 1982 issue of *Threshold*. Here 'modernity' replaces 'humanism' as the wolf in sheep's clothing eager to devour that harmless lamb, atavism. Responding to the secular assault on religion (mainly Catholic, since he insults Irish Protestantism as 'essentially a negative religion, more accurately defined as being anti-catholic on principle than anything else'), Deane offers 'an equally polemical account of modernism and its triumph in a century of almost unbroken disasters . . . global war, threat of holocaust, concentration camps, wastelands, alienation, cancer, bureaucracy, mock-religious cults, crime waves, propaganda, the creation of plenty by the starvation of millions – and so on. Rationality, it appears, needs no encouragement to compete with atavism in the production of misery.'[43] Polemical indeed! Did rationality or atavism, in its nationalist guise, set up the concentration camps? Rationalised atavism, perhaps. Deane's own atavised rationalism betrays more clearly than usual the strains of reconciling Derry with Derrida. Even Heaney (in prose) occasionally succumbs to easy and false antithesis:

> far from the elegances of Oscar Wilde and the profundities of Shakespeare, I was acting with the Bellaghy Dramatic Society in plays about 1798, now playing a United Irishman . . . now playing Robert Emmet . . . Far from discussing the Victorian loss of faith, I was driving my mother to evening devotions in the "chapel" . . . Far from the melodies of courtly love, I was acting as *fear a' tigh* at the GAA ceilidh . . .[44]

Since Heaney, Deane and Paulin no longer live in Northern Ireland, it may be inevitable that they should fall into the tropes of stylised retrospect.

All this antithesis yearns for Edenic oneness as opposed to plural-
istic 'fusion', for a monolithic nation. Southerners too may contract
the rhetorical habit. For instance, an unnecessary opposition (to
which Deane has contributed) in current literary-political debate, is
that between Yeats and Joyce. Declan Kiberd's lecture 'Inventing
Irelands' once again exemplifies the desire for a literary signpost with
one arm, for a clear mythic lead. He oddly bolsters his welcome call
for socialist perspectives by aligning Yeats with de Valera, and 'the
mystical, conservative and rural'; Joyce with Connolly and 'the
Protestant, socialist and cosmopolitan'.[45] Neither literary nor historical analysis would support the extraction of such simple ideological
juice from complex oeuvres and circumstances. The mutual creative
awareness between Yeats and Joyce, the extent to which Joyce's own
development was shaped by a form of sibling-differentiation, prove
that we need them both – as writers, as poet and prosewriter. Kiberd
in fact conscripts Yeats and Joyce into an updated version of the
fifties cultural argument that Ireland is European. Perhaps, but not
yet. The false optimism of the fifties rested on the premise that –
whether as modernist or atavist or both – you can write off Ireland's
Anglo-Irish past and Northern Ireland's Protestant present.
Southern poets today – Paul Durcan, and Brendan Kennelly in
Cromwell – understand unresolved cultural trauma better than the
intellectuals, themselves traumatised if unable to celebrate Joyce
without stigmatising England's 'long decline into provincialism'.[46]

Due to an unfortunate error on the part of 'history', Northern
Irish poetry of the sixties (including Heaney's) emerged in close
proximity to English modes. This foresighted appropriation by
perfide Albion may explain the low commitment-count that today
exasperates Deane and Paulin, neither of whom can abide
'botanisers among the hedges'. Deane's 1975 essay 'Irish Poetry and
Irish Nationalism' outlines a position which he has never essentially
altered: 'Northern Ireland is in political crisis and Northern Poets
seem more remote from it than any other group, even when they are
not writing poetry – which in some cases is seldom.'[47] His interview
with Heaney tries to lick him into political shape, and to drive a
polarising wedge (see page 167)   between form and content: 'Do
you think that if some political stance is not adopted by you and the
Northern poets at large, this refusal might lead to a dangerous
strengthening of . . . the autonomy of poetry and corroborate the
recent English notion of the happy limitations of a "well-made
poem"?'[48] Similarly, Paulin's 'A Nation, Yet Again' attacks most
Northern poetry as frivolously irrelevant: 'That kitsch lumber-room

196

is stacked/with a parnassian dialect.' Reviewing *Liberty Tree*, Deane quotes the poem as 'a good epigraph for "northern" poetry of the last twenty years'.[49] Presumably the opposite of 'a kitsch lumber-room' is an earnest seminar:

> Action is solid: this one day in March
> a hijacked saloon smacks a dozen rounds
> > into the Bunch of Grapes
> > and in Desertmartin
> men in lockram masks and dark glasses
> dig down through sandy soil to a bristling dump
> of lumpy kapok, cortex fuse and green jerricans . . .
>
> and the dunchered skip of the *Clyde Valley* slips a short
> to an invisible quartermaster in the Klondike
> > and a van waits, waits at the corner
> > of Atlantic and Baltic avenues
> all to no purpose, yet affecting a cause
> > like a stubbed toe, a cracked axle
> > or a backfiring old banger
> > for these acts must come back
> > as syntax, as grammar
> > and a temporal fiction.

This, from Paulin's 'Martello', obviously prides itself on getting down to the 'solid' nitty-gritty. A prosaic history lesson, underlining Protestant militarism since 1912 as *particularly* ugly and pointless, concludes with a structuralist moral. Academic language – 'parnassian dialect'? – especially literary-critical terminology pervades *Liberty Tree*: epic, autarkic, baroque, 'pure narrative', phonic, classic. Deane's review finds Paulin's counterpoint between 'stage Ulsterism' and 'a kind of academic surrealism' 'ironic'. It seems to me deeply affected and patronising: a talking-down to people whose own talk ('dunchered') he misappropriates in order to despise them. Paulin's version of two-language polarity epitomises how politics abuses poetry: by an intellectual bullying of subject-matter, by exploitation akin to what the poet deplores.

Another bully, the structuralist levelling-word 'discourse' (much favoured by Deane and *Crane Bag*) fits Paulin's approach. 'Discourse' abolishes any boundary between poetry and prose, poetry and politics, in the same spirit as 'comrade' abolishes class-distinctions. The only casualty is imagination. Louis MacNeice in the thirties saw off the All-Poetry-is-Propaganda brigade of that time, when he said:

> The propagandist is consciously and solely concerned with converting people to a cause or creed. If Homer, Virgil, Shakespeare, or Milton meant to do this, they were thoroughly bad propagandists.[50]

Republicanism fuses with structuralism as readily as does Marxism, due to similar faith in an historic destiny. Literature unproductive of that destiny, that neither wills it nor bends to its will, is disregarded as marginal 'botany'. (MacNeice points out the inconsistency between the revolutionary's determinism and his determination, the 'crate-loads of pamphlets and polemics'.[51]) Fiction and drama survive reductiveness and their own messages, better than poetry, which loses everything if it becomes a telegram. In fact Deane's latest collection of poems, *History Lessons*, interprets its title more personally than *Liberty Tree*, although the melancholia of the Derry exile shapes poetic emotion no less than prose thought:

> But for us it was always a street
> Hissing with rain, a ditch running
> Svelte with filth, mouths crabbed
> With rancour and wrong, the smooth
> Almond of speech burnt. And the
> Cropped hair of children with lice . . .

However, Deane's longest poem, 'Christmas at Beaconsfield', is indistinguishable from Paulin's politico-historical discourse (compare the anonymous unanimity of Young Ireland's verse):

> Beaconsfield. The snottish son dead.
> Europe awash. Ireland in her
> Customary decline. Omens.

Poetic telegrams often resort to telegraphese and inert collage. We chiefly learn that Deane dislikes Edmund Burke, who is in any case on the losing side of history. Paulin dislikes him too. His poem 'And Where Do You Stand on the National Question?' assures a member of the Stormont establishment: 'You don't *have* to fall back/ on Burke and the Cruiser,/ on a batty style/ and slack o' whoozy emotion.' This itself hardly achieves the 'classic and secular' form of which Paulin earlier dreams. Perhaps Paulin and Deane are simply flipping Yeats's 'haughtier-headed Burke' coin. Yet when Yeats welcomes Burke to the tower of his poetry, or celebrates-creates 'The people of Burke and of Grattan' in a memorable rhythm, he subjects history to his imagination rather than the other way around. And indeed both references occur in contexts where 'I declare' prefaces an announcement of artistic 'faith' (to which many ingredients contribute) rather than of political attitude: 'Bound neither to Cause nor to State'. In any case Deane and Paulin, for all their scholarly airs, are no less historically selective than Yeats, and for different reasons. In a curious way Field Day itself has enacted the process whereby political fixity shuts off imaginative possibility, the ideo-logical tail wags the creative dog. The originality of Heaney's *Wintering Out* has been cannibalised into increasingly sterile slogans.

3.

After 1939 Louis MacNeice wrote:

> If the war made nonsense of Yeats's poetry and of all works that are called "escapist", it also made nonsense of poetry that professes to be "realist". My friends had been writing for years about guns and frontiers and factories, about the "facts" of psychology, politics, science, economics, but the fact of war made their writing seem as remote as the pleasure dome in Xanadu. For war spares neither the poetry of Xanadu nor the poetry of pylons.[52]

Since 1969 all Northern Irish poetry has shared the same bunker. Thus what Derek Mahon calls 'An eddy of semantic scruple/ In an unstructurable sea'[53] might as well concentrate on 'semantic scruple'. Nevertheless MacNeice, knowing Yeats and Ireland, did not follow Auden into his post-Marxist conviction that 'poetry makes nothing happen': 'The fallacy lies in thinking that it is the *function* of art to make things happen and that the effect of art upon actions is something either direct or calculable.'[54] Yet Auden's own phrase in his Yeats elegy – 'A way of happening' – defines the only social and political role available to poetry *as* poetry. In my view the emergence of something recognised and recognisable as 'Ulster poetry' out of the experience of the North – from 'that once birdless if still benighted province'[55] – marks an irreversible shift of sensibility, if slow as a glacier.

Now the term "Ulster" or "Northern Irish" poetry may itself bring me into conflict with a third Field Day pamphlet, Heaney's *Open Letter*, in which he objects to the ethno-political heading under which his poems appear in *The Penguin Book of Contemporary British Poetry*. Eavan Boland's *Irish Times* review queried the necessity for a statement so mild ('Don't be surprised/ If I demur'), and so unlike the polemics of Deane and Paulin, that it seems to realise its own superfluousness: 'Poetry is defined by its energies and its eloquence, not by the passport of the poet or the editor; or the name of the nationality. That way lie all the categories, the separations, the censorships that poetry exists to dispel.'[56] Nobody doubts Heaney's Irishness. But his or Field Day's exclusive insistence, like the triumphalism which wants Londonderry to obliterate Derry and now vice versa, denies other contexts which his poetry nourishes and which nourish it. Ulster poets have been appearing for years in anthologies of English, Irish and British poetry. The confusion is perhaps more accurate than any attempt to tidy it up. (Frank Ormsby succeeded with the elegant diplomacy of *Poets from the North of Ireland*, itself a history-making anthology.) That notorious Penguin generously represents no less than five Northerners besides Heaney, to the point where *English* poets complain of colonisation. And younger poets in both England and the South of Ireland look North, not only to Heaney. On the other hand, the historian A.T.Q. Stewart tried in a TV talk to familiarise and normalise Belfast for British viewers, by informing them that 'Philip Larkin wrote many of his early poems there'. This does not make Belfast Hull. Larkin's retrospect begins: 'Lonely in Ireland, since it was not home', and refers to 'The salt rebuff of speech,/ Insisting so on difference'.[57] Yet like Mahon, just then starting to write, his voice flavoured by that speech, Larkin owes a profound debt to Yeats. None of the lines of creative energy runs straight.

Nor do they run straight within Ulster itself. Zig-zags of energy are not picked up by receiving apparatus tuned to 'two traditions'. Ulster people hug wonderfully 'fossilised' versions of their own or someone else's Irishness/Britishness, which retards newer definition in the Republic and Britain. Yet one of the junctures where the North may harbour a cultural vanguard as well as a rearguard is the point where traditions meet and fuse in poetry. Early in the 1960s, not for the first time though more intensely than before, political confrontation – as during the Irish Literary Revival – turned into cultural encounter. Contraries no longer found in the South became progressive instead of regressive, and even adumbrated genuine unity. Within that space, for instance, the 'slightly aggravated young Catholic male' in Seamus Heaney was submerged by his urge to express 'the private county Derry childhood part of myself'.[58] Besides the local Muse, Heaney's early influences include Robert Frost, Patrick Kavanagh, Ted Hughes, and the stimulus of his Belfast contemporaries. His poetic landscape receives a particular assent from all kinds of Ulster readers as an authentic common ground; almost, despite subterranean tensions, as a *de facto* imaginative recognition of the whole terrain. Although Heaney saw himself as 'politicising' Mossbawn[59] in *Wintering Out* (1972), the poems respect dialect more than dialectic. 'The Other Side' characterises the distances between Catholic speaker and Protestant farmer in simultaneous terms of land, religion and language:

For days we would rehearse
each patriarchal dictum:
Lazarus, the Pharaoh, Solomon

and David and Goliath rolled
magnificently, like loads of hay
too big for our small lanes,

or faltered on a rut –
'Your side of the house, I believe,
hardly rule by the book at all.'

His brain was a whitewashed kitchen
hung with texts, swept tidy
as the body o' the kirk.

The point of the poem is Heaney's imaginative entry into the mind
and idiom of the other side, into the 'other', beyond psychic hinterlands, across psychic frontiers. 'Rehearse' suggests how childhood
mimicry (an articulation of the peculiar Northern intimacy, com-
moner in rural areas, that knows if not loves its neighbour) has
nurtured the poet's ear and negative capability. Although the poem
does not minimise difference, its cultural vision, much more humanly sedimented than the coy polarity between Wilde and Emmet,
spans two languages to create a third. As throughout his work,
Heaney relishes the whole heritage of Ulster English, graces with
equal humorous affection Graeco-Latin 'patriarchal dictum' and
Scots 'body o' the kirk'. (Contrast Paulin's autarkic boke.) 'The
Other Side' stresses its own language to raise the language question
at another level: not as power-struggle but as a struggle towards
expression. Can there be communication, community, even communion founded on a shared landscape?

Should I slip away, I wonder,
or go up and touch his shoulder
and talk about the weather

or the price of grass-seed?

This is the question on which Ulster, let alone Anglo-Irish, agreement depends. 'The price of grass-seed' symbolises the cost of fundamental growth and change. However, the poem itself symbolises
the cross-fertilisation between poets and traditions in Ulster. Language which crosses rather than takes sides is not merely the poetic
wing of wet Alliance Party liberalism, of middle-class middle
ground. 'The Other Side' stretches Heaney to full emotional and

verbal sensitivity. I have already noted the absence of mediating language, complicating language, in the antithetical word-worlds of Deane and Paulin. *Translations* too may fall short of complete human complexity, as in the rather stereotyped renderings of Irish peasant girl and English soldier, because Friel simplifies the concept of translation itself. Andrews comments on the Ordnance Survey procedures presented in the play: 'the commonest is the one which gives the play its title, the method whereby the Irishman's Cnoc Ban appears on the map as the Englishman's Fair Hill'. But 'this policy was very seldom adopted by the real Ordnance Survey'.[60]

Towards the end of the polarised thirties MacNeice prefaced his *Modern Poetry*:

> The poet is a maker, not a retail trader. The writer today should be not so much the mouthpiece of a community (for then he will only tell it what it knows already) as its conscience, its critical faculty, its generous instinct.

This suggests how empathy with one Ulster community, such as Heaney's in *North*, might constrain rather than release a poet's imagination. You can't purify the language of the tribe if you speak it. In contrast with the seductions of Dark Rosaleen, nobody can accuse Unionism of being an inspiration to poets. Protestant poets usually have no trouble getting *their* 'critical faculty' going. By a curious paradox this means they sometimes sing more in tune with progressive voices in the Republic than do their Northern Catholic contemporaries. The latter may be reluctant to criticise what for them is not yet realised: the Irish nation. Thus Derek Mahon embraces Paul Durcan:

> I can imagine your dismay
> As, cornered in some zinc café,
> You read of another hunger-strike,
> A postman blasted off his bike . . .
> Oh, Hölderlin no fly would hurt,
> Our vagabond and pilgrim spirit,
> Give us a ring on your way back
> And tell us what the nations lack![61]

For Seamus Deane, the enemy without looms larger than the 'lack' within. For Seamus Heaney, the umbilical cord between poet and tribe inhibits discrimination between positive and negative elements. This inhibition paralyses his imagination in 'Punishment'; but a later poem, 'Casualty', resolves any ambivalence towards victims of rough justice. Identifying with one who 'broke/ our tribe's

202

complicity', the poet breaks it too.[62]

John Hewitt, on the other hand, has always been able (or free) now, to affirm the long human tenure of the Planters in 'Ulster clay'; now, to indict their socio-political conduct of that tenure: 'you coasted along . . . And all the time the old lies festered'.[63] Mahon's criticism locates still deeper rottenness in the soul of the state:

> Bury that red
> bandana and stick, that banjo, this is your
>   country, close one eye and be king.
> Your people await you, their heavy washing
>   flaps for you in the housing-estates –
> a credulous people. God, you could do it, God
>   help you, stand on a corner stiff
> with rhetoric, promising nothing under the sun.
>
> ('Ecclesiastes')

Here mock-identification with the tribe operates as a satirical strategy. But although the poet rules out not only personal but literary modes of belonging ('stiff/ with rhetoric'), he characteristically internalises the sins of his fathers. Just as empathy may be a pitfall (Heaney), so may total absence of sympathy (Paulin), since both stances preclude imaginative tension. When Mahon's poetry explicitly returns to roots, his persona acknowledges responsibility towards 'this desperate city', 'a credulous people', 'the stricken souls/ No spring can unperturb'. 'Courtyards in Delft', a recent exploration of his native ethos, links the Protestant housework ethic with the colonialist urge to 'punish nature in the name of God' (a gloss from a rather over-explanatory stanza added later). And South African connections – 'veldt' – become part of a complex picture:

> I lived there as a boy and know the coal
> Glittering in its shed, late-afternoon
> Lambency informing the deal table,
> The ceiling cradled in a radiant spoon.
> I must be lying low in a room there,
> A strange child with a taste for verse,
> While my hard-nosed companions dream of war
> On parched veldt and fields of rain-swept gorse.

This interior, reluctantly appreciated as well as hated, says much more than Paulin's flailing at exteriors. It both defines and exemplifies the subtle posture of Mahon's poetry, not just in relation to Northern Irish Protestantism but to the whole world of political action.

His recurrent phrase, 'through with history', relieves anyone surfeited by the writings of Deane and Paulin. At once an impossible condition and a salutary irony, it asserts the artist's need to be 'The Last of the Fire Kings', to strike

> out over the fields
> Where fireflies glow
> Not knowing a word of the language.

Mahon insists on the poet serving humanity on his own terms. He should feel, but resist, the contrary pressure that would make him in the image of the people: 'Not to release them/ From the ancient curse/ But to die their creature and be thankful.' Since poetry cannot be the 'creature' of politics, Unionist and Republican ideologies are equally off the map. Mahon also sloughs off the liberal-humanist socialism that MacNeice could espouse, without undue artistic compromise, during the thirties: 'What middle-class cunts we are/ To imagine for one second/ That our privileged ideals/ Are divine wisdom . . .' ('Afterlives'). (Deane's dualism ignores inclusive perspectives beyond both humanism and atavism.) Similarly, Mahon intensifies MacNeice's pronouncement of a plague on all Irish houses, by conflating our conflicts within a universally fallen world, where

> they are burning
> Witches and heretics
> In the boiling squares.
>   ('The Snow Party')

This tragic consciousness has an artistic integrity which refuses the consolations of either the elegiac (no poems for individual victims), or the Utopian. 'Matthew V. 29-30' wittily eradicates humanity's collective guilt 'Until, at last, offence// Was not to be found/ In that silence without bound'. 'After Nerval' postulates 'the ideal society' as non-human: 'Already in a lost hub-cap is conceived/ The ideal society which will replace our own.' Those occasions on which Mahon relents thus carry more conviction than Paulin's single-minded solutions ('that sweet/ equal republic'). He creates socially redemptive symbols: 'a sunken city/ Sea-changed at last'; or this, which sets everyone in Ireland an educational exercise, our homework:

> But the hills are still the same
> Grey-blue above Belfast.
> Perhaps if I'd stayed behind
> And lived it bomb by bomb

I might have grown up at last
And learnt what is meant by home.

('Afterlives')

'Learning what is meant by home' might on one level be a prag-
matic definition of Nationalism, *a posteriori* rather than *a priori*.
The poet's humble demeanour as returning exile indicates how
Mahon's strategic anarchism covers the pure politics of the poetry
itself, intervenes between the heat of hatred and the light of art.
While he denies the subservience of poetry to ideology or history, he
also eschews the triumphalism that art itself can assume in Yeats's
vision, on those occasions when the poet answers the world's
arrogance with his own. Less well fortified than Yeats, Mahon's poet
indulges 'his/ Wretched rage for order'.

    far
From his people
And the fitful glare
Of his high window is as
Nothing to our scattered glass.

The pun on 'fitful glare' mocks the irrelevance of *all* fine poetic
frenzies, all 'midnight candles'. Nor would Yeats have characterised
Raftery or himself as a 'grinning disc-jockey between commercials',
as Mahon does in 'I Am Raftery'. This humility, chastened and
chastening, at once demythologises the poet's importance, and highlights the 'people's' plight. However, the most inward qualities of the
imagination (detachment, patience, silence, a 'cold dream/ Of a
place out of time') offer sanctuary. Mahon's many variations on
Arnoldian 'sweetness and light' also fend off the 'barbarians' – not
for him, as for Deane, a propagandist slur, but all antagonists of the
true civilisation his poetry models. 'Patience and silence' are of
course qualities of the mushrooms given a new lease of life in 'A
Disused Shed in Co. Wexford'. More anthropomorphic than his
other animal, vegetable and mineral rebukes to the human, the
mushrooms embody a minimal (good) will to survive: 'They lift frail
heads in gravity and good faith.' This astonishingly inclusive symbol
('Magi, moonmen,/ Powdery prisoners of the old regime . . . Lost
people of Treblinka and Pompeii') develops from nothing, a disused
shed, a detail in an Anglo-Irish novel. Part of the point is the ironic
swivel to molehill rather than mountain. Small is beautiful; 'places
where a thought might grow' – or a poem – need not steam with
orthodox historical or mythic compost. 'A Disused Shed in Co.
Wexford' makes and proves Edward Thomas's point, fundamental

205

to the issue of poetry and politics, as to poetry in general: 'Anything, however small, may make a poem; nothing, however great, is certain to.'[64] Mahon does more than 'translate a defeated community into the narrative of history', or even a 'lost people' into symbolic salvation. (The resonance of Mahon's 'lost' stretches from bewildered, to astray, to damned, to doomed.) He receives a defenceless spirit into the protectorate of poetry.

Since Partition, *Ulster* Protestant poets have erroneously been regarded as less central to the Irish experience than, say, Yeats or Beckett (both influences on Mahon). Maurice Harmon's anthology contains not one.[65] However, they may be infiltrating their sensibilities by way of younger Northern poets who have inextricably pooled the genes of traditions. Paul Muldoon's poetry exhibits all the strengths of the hybrid. Indeed 'Mules', the title-poem of his second book, explores the painful value of cross-bred ambiguity, not only in the fourth green field:

> We had loosed them into one field.
> I watched Sam Parsons and my quick father
> Tense for the punch below their belts,
> For what was neither one thing or the other.

Technically, Muldoon has learned from his Ulster predecessors, as well as from international influences. And heir to alienation as well as roots, he can criticise from both inside and outside the Catholic community. Heaney's richly created early world (a genuinely prelapsarian vision) has a boundless self-confidence which seems no longer possible without running into the barbed-wire of ideology. What is physical in Heaney becomes metaphysically problematic in Muldoon.

Muldoon's latest collection, *Quoof*, responds to the North in a radically different – and differently radical – manner from *Liberty Tree*. In their very titles, disenchanted insider faces zealous convert. Paulin opts for a public Republican symbol, Muldoon for 'our family word/ for the hot water bottle' – actually another defamiliarising place 'where a thought might grow'. This thought grows where Mahon's Fire King goes, into strange territory, a strange 'language':

> An hotel room in New York City
> with a girl who spoke hardly any English,
> my hand on her breast
> like the smouldering one-off spoor of the yeti
> or some other shy beast
> that has yet to enter the language.

Muldoon's 'Gathering Mushrooms' in fact examines the possibility of writing committed poetry (perhaps redeploying Mahon's symbol for the purpose). Unlike Paulin, he does not dismiss alternative perspectives out of hand. The poet moves from his mushroom-cultivating father caught in the attitude of an early Heaney poem: 'He'll glance back from under his peaked cap/ without breaking rhythm'; to what roots, 'fifteen years on', may exact. In a magic-mushroom induced nightmare, metaphor for the transformations of violence, for things 'changed utterly', he finds himself ventriloquising the voice of dirty protester and hunger-striker:

> Come back to us. However cold and raw, your feet
> were always meant
> to negotiate terms with bare cement.
> Beyond this concrete wall is a wall of concrete
> and barbed wire. Your only hope
> is to come back. If sing you must, let your song
> tell of treading your own dung . . .

The poem lets this terrible duty have its say, but a Republican poet is not born. 'Aisling', too, touches on the hunger strike in its allegory of how Dark Rosaleen can damage your moral health:

> Was she Aurora, or the Goddess Flora,
> Artemidora, or Venus Bright,
> or Anorexia, who left
> a lemon stain on my flannel sheet?

Muldoon subverts martyrs and goddesses, fixed ideas and 'concrete' categories, by means of language that undermines its own solidity (Pinter to Mahon's Beckett). As Aidan Carl Mathews says, the poetry itself 'melts under the search-lights'.[66] This suggests a political posture as of escaped prisoner-of-war, secret agent, double agent, saboteur. Muldoon's methods give the lie to the notion that language can operate politically in Irish poetry only by declaring firm allegiances. Thus 'The Right Arm' handles place-names in a different spirit from some of Heaney's poems, perhaps queries that spirit:

> I was three-ish
> when I plunged my arm into the sweet-jar
> for the last bit of clove-rock.

> We kept a shop in Eglish
> that sold bread, milk, butter, cheese,
> bacon, eggs,
> Andrews Liver Salts,
> and, until now, clove-rock.

I would give my right arm to have known then
how Eglish was itself wedged between
ecclesia and *église*.

The Eglish sky was its own stained-glass vault
and my right arm was sleeved in glass
that has yet to shatter.

As with a Pinter-character, we distrust these innocent specifics (warned by '-ish'), including the speaker's undue etymological passion. The ironic disproportion applied to two versions of 'church' and a place that falls short of English, together with the echo of 'Rock of Ages, cleft' and 'stained-glass vault', hints at the claustrophobia of definitions. The poem's own way with language substitutes puns for etymology as a method of uncovering meaning. Linguistic depth-charges expose latent horror in 'stained' and 'vault', in the subliminal presence of a 'shattered' right arm. 'Sleeved in glass' – another difficult midpoint like a mule – implies the precarious balance of the artist amidst potential mutilation. Bernard O'Donoghue comments: 'The tenses are disconcerting: why would I give my right arm (*now*) to have known "then" what is, on the face of it, a fact about language?' The answer may be more than that the poem 'unmistakably, if obscurely, suggests the continuity and discontinuity of experience at the same time: what is known or not, and what is believed or not'.[67] Muldoon's procedures are always epistemological – and *ipso facto* more radical than putting old whines into new bottles. But in this case the shuttles between ignorance and 'knowledge', innocence and experience, once again span fifteen uncertain years.

Quoof ends with a long poem, 'The More a Man Has the More a Man Wants'. This disconcerts on a larger scale as it juggles with tenses and moods, history, literary history, places and names, an anarchic version of sonnet-form, and a cosmopolitan vocabulary. 'Obair' chimes with 'Edward Hopper', 'Derricke' with 'Durex', 'Minneapolis' with 'thrapple'. Wearing many languages lightly, Muldoon follows MacNeice and Mahon into the city, into urban demotic. After the Chandleresque 'Immram' (see the next essay), Red Indian trickster-transformer legend enables him to take new liberties with 'the matter of Ireland', a Joyce to Heaney's Corkery. However, Muldoon emulates Mahon in crushing any occupational or compensatory arrogance on the part of the artist. (Yeats and Joyce were, after all, 'last romantics'.) Like his 'hero' Gallogly, transparently a figment of the imagination, the poet himself may be

Disappearing up his own bum.
Or, running on the spot
with all the minor aplomb
of a trick-cyclist.
So thin, side-on, you could spit
through him.

A string of parodies insinuates that other writers also should not take
themselves too seriously:

Gallogly lies down in the sheugh
to munch
through a Beauty of
Bath. He repeats himself, *Bath*,
under his garlic-breath.
Sheugh, he says. *Sheugh*.
He is finding that first 'sh'
increasingly difficult to manage.
Sh-leeps.

That layered joke at the expense of Heaney-Sweeney refuses and
defuses Ango-Irish linguistic confrontations. Similarly Gallogly,
already compounded of gallowglass and his pursuing alter ego, an
'Oglala Sioux', can change colour in a syllable: 'otherwise known as
Golightly,/ otherwise known as Ingoldsby,/ otherwise known as
English' – 'cultural fusion' indeed! But for all its comic versatility, the
poem never loses sight of Gallogly as a terrorist on the job and on the
run, as guilty party and scapegoat, prisoner of conscience and
unconscious, of an aisling turned nightmare. Muldoon's sensibility
reaches the parts where the hidden Ireland is usually kept hidden,
where it involves suppressions as well as oppressions. Gallogly's trail
is a trail of blood: the spoor of civil war, glimpsed here as a booby-
trapped councillor ('Once they collect his smithereens/ he doesn't
quite add up'), there as:

Such is the integrity
of their quarrel
that she immediately took down
the legally held shotgun
and let him have both barrels.
She had wanted only to clear the air.

This passage combines two kinds of cliché: Churchill's 'the integrity
of their quarrel', the media's 'legally held shotgun'. Whereas Heaney
exchanges such rationalisations for the language of myth, Muldoon
blows the whistle on the conspiracy between myth and cliché. Here

disproportion minimises historical cliché in order to maximise its human damage, to telescope neurosis. And Muldoon's own revitalisation of cliché ('add up', 'clear the air'), like that of the later MacNeice, finds the booby-traps in phrases. This is how poetry remakes language, wears it new, acts as midwife to a future not predicated on the past – unlike Paulin's ideal Republican dictionary or a Stuart saviour.

Thus the poem's political message remains, above all, its medium. And its medium is metamorphic – in metre, syntax, diction, and cultural co-ordinates. Muldoon truly discriminates between history and fiction, politics and poetry. 'The More a Man Has' could not, on the one hand, be more open about its fictional artifice; or, on the other, more coldly faithful to irreducible cruelties. Literary theorisers of 'history' either substitute one politicised version for another; or dangerously devalue both intellect and imagination by claiming that all historians and poets are propagandists anyway. Muldoon's metamorphoses melt or expand rigid understandings of history; make us experience history as an arbitrary kaleidoscope, a form of mental illness; ironically insist that *plus ça change*. The poetry of Mahon and Muldoon signposts neither Kiltartan nor Europe, atavistic boreen nor humanistic motorway, but the path Yeats outlined as: 'every country passing out of automatism passes through demoralisation, and . . . has no choice but to go on into intelligence'.[68] They have absorbed, too, Keith Douglas's demanding advice to a fellow-poet during the Second World War (see page 100):

> To be sentimental or emotional now is dangerous to oneself and to others. To trust anyone or to admit any hope of a better world is criminally foolish, as foolish as it is to stop working for it. It sounds silly to say work without hope, but it can be done; it's only a form of insurance; it doesn't mean work hopelessly.[69]

A detumescent recommendation for those who crave poetry in their politics and politics in their poetry. But good poems are exciting enough in themselves, while bad politics should remain unexciting. However, poets make their long-term contribution by refusing to betray 'semantic scruple' in a country of unscrupulous rhetoricians, where names break bones, where careless talk costs lives.

'Varieties of Parable': Louis MacNeice and Paul Muldoon

1.

Several of the preceding essays refer to poetic journeys or quests: Frost's and Thomas's roads, MacNeice's autumnal odyssey through time and space, Muldoon's hallucinatory trips. Despite many divergences, the paths of all four poets cross at certain points. But the two latter, like the two former, share some specific means and ends in their imaginative travels. Paul Muldoon's poetry has affinities with the MacNeice of *Solstices* (1961) and *The Burning Perch* (1963), with the syntax of 'dream logic' these collections develop. The relation between MacNeice and Muldoon as practitioners of 'double-level writing . . . sleight-of-hand'[1] is clarified by MacNeice's analysis of this mode in *Varieties of Parable* (his Clark Lectures published posthumously in 1965), and by their common interest in the *immram*.

Immram literally means 'rowing around' – an appropriate term for Muldoon's poetry in general – hence an Irish tale of 'otherworld' voyages to fantastic islands. The most celebrated of these is the ninth-century *Navigatio* of St Brendan, written in Latin, which 'exercised the imagination of medieval Christendom and helped to arouse the spirit of adventure which prompted the great voyages of the fifteenth and sixteenth centuries'.[2] *Immram Mael Duin*, also dating from the ninth century, is a Gaelic narrative which draws on the same stock of Celtic legendary matter. Muldoon's thirty-stanza poem 'Immram' (published in *Why Brownlee Left*, 1980), perhaps deliberately just short of the number of islands visited by Mael Duin, links his ancestral name to a reading of Whitley Stokes's translation of *Immram Mael Duin*.[3] For MacNeice, 'Round the corner was always the sea' with its promise of 'union in solitude' and 'anarchic democracy' ('Round the Corner', 1961). Seeking a dimension where social and spiritual isolation born of Ulster might be dissolved, he found a poetic role-model in Brendan:

> O Brandan, spindrift hermit, who
> Hankering roaming un-homing up-anchoring
> From this rock wall looked seawards to
> Knot the horizon round your waist,
> Distil that distance and undo
> Time in quintessential West . . .
>
> ('Western Landscape')

211

Muldoon's 'Lives of the Saints' also seems to approve Brendan's act of faith:

Drifting along wherever God liked
And the people living by bread alone
Shouting after Good Luck, Good Luck.
All the Chronicles agreed. The boat was stone.

MacNeice's radio-play *The Mad Islands* (1962) is a variation on the Mael Duin theme, with a hero called Muldoon. Written during the period of the *Burning Perch* lyrics, which proved to be MacNeice's last collection, *The Mad Islands* throws light on their more concentrated expeditions; as do the potholing journeys in *Persons from Porlock*, broadcast four days before his death on 3 September 1963. The *immram*-imagery of 'Thalassa', MacNeice's last poem, strangely sums up not only the voyage of life, but the late intensification of his whole poetic career:

Run out the boat, my broken comrades;
Let the old seaweed crack, the surge
Burgeon oblivious of the last
Embarkation of feckless men,
Let every adverse force converge –
Here we must needs embark again . . .

Varieties of Parable is, up to a point, a recantation. Since these lectures interpret MacNeice's poetic practice in the late fifties and early sixties, as *Modern Poetry* (1938) interprets his practice during the thirties, the two *credos* accordingly contrast. *Modern Poetry*, while never losing sight of formal necessities, announces a swing back 'to the Greek preference for information or statement'.[4] *Varieties of Parable*, on the other hand, contains several obituaries for realism, 'slices or chunks of life'.[5] However, even in the forties MacNeice had set himself an aesthetic agenda different from the one that reached its apotheosis in *Autumn Journal*. *The Dark Tower* (1946), which he like others considered his best radio-play, and which left its imprint on his later poetry, was subtitled 'a radio parable play'. MacNeice's introductory note anticipates *Varieties of Parable* in declaring that 'pure "realism" is in our time almost played out'.[6] His important essay 'Experiences with Images' (1949) sums up a change of direction: 'After *The Earth Compels* I tired of tourism and after *Autumn Journal* I tired of journalism'; and tabulates 'a stricter kind of drama which largely depends upon structure':

(1) the selection of – or perhaps the being selected by a single theme which itself is a strong symbol, (2) a rhythmical pattern which holds that theme together, (3) syntax (a more careful ordering of sentences, especially in relation to the verse pattern), and (4) a more structural use of imagery.[7]

Before *Solstices* and *The Burning Perch* (and the transitional *Visitations*) MacNeice was to write *Autumn Sequel* (1954), a sprawling negation of these principles. But artistic evolutions often occur in fits and starts: *Autumn Journal* itself is by no means all journalism. MacNeice's childhood 'black dreams' and their adult successors inspired a few structures, as well as much imagery, from the outset:

> The candle in his white grave-clothes, always turning his cowled head,
> Stood in his own shadow at the foot of my grave-bed;
> Ho, said the candle with his rich dark beard,
> How they howl like the dead!
> And wagging his cowled head,
> Ho, said the candle, they would make a body afeard.

('Candles', 1927)

In 'Experiences with Images' he cites later poems, 'The Springboard', 'The Dowser' and 'Order to View' (1940) as blending 'rational allegory' and 'dream logic':[8]

Order to View

> It was a big house, bleak;
> Grass on the drive;
> We had been there before
> But memory, weak in front of
> A blistered door, could find
> Nothing alive now;
> The shrubbery dripped, a crypt
> Of leafmould dreams; a tarnished
> Arrow over an empty stable
> Shifted a little in the tenuous wind,
>
> And wishes were unable
> To rise; on the garden wall
> The pear trees had come loose
> From rotten loops; one wish,
> A rainbow bubble, rose,
> Faltered, broke in the dull
> Air – What was the use?
> The bell-pull would not pull
> And the whole place, one might
> Have supposed, was deadly ill:
> The world was closed,

And remained closed until
A sudden angry tree
Shook itself like a setter
Flouncing out of a pond
And beyond the sombre line
Of limes a cavalcade
Of clouds rose like a shout of
Defiance. Near at hand
Somewhere in a loose-box
A horse neighed
And all the curtains flew out of
The windows; the world was open.

Whereas most of MacNeice's lyrics before 1940 were principally compounded of imagery and statement, 'Order to View' explores in a new way his obsession with the 'grave-bed', with a deathly stasis. The poem's materials and syntactical and metrical oddities all feed into the 'strong symbol' of the house. But 'Order to View' also draws on archetypal folk-tale elements: ominously deserted mansion, wary travellers with an inexplicable sense of *déjà vu*, creepy signs such as the 'tarnished/ Arrow' and the bell-pull not pulling, 'wishes', and the whole atmosphere of spellbound sleeping beauty or horror. Defying paraphrase, as MacNeice insisted parable should, 'Order to View' simultaneously communicates nightmare and neurosis. The finale synthesises waking-up, therapeutic release and fairy-tale happy ending: 'the world was open'.

'Order to View' is a parable or 'dark conceit' according to the description elaborated in *Varieties of Parable* with reference to such writers as Spenser, Bunyan, Herbert, Lewis Carroll, George MacDonald, Kafka, Beckett, Pinter and Golding. Muldoon's poetry too satisfies many of the criteria among MacNeice's 'tentative conclusions'[9] as to the constituents of parable writing, e.g. 'the creation of a special world',[10] allegorical or emblematic elements, dream logic, Everyman protagonists, a concern with questions of identity ('Gallogly, or Gollogly'), Muldoon's own admitted interest 'in the narrative, the story',[11] and various other formal qualities such as his being, in MacNeice's phrase for Carroll, 'a parodist and a punster'.[12] Less obviously relevant to Muldoon is MacNeice's comment that its 'preoccupation with an inner reality naturally means that parable writing has often a strong spiritual, or indeed a mystical, element'.[13] However, in addition to his poems' atmospheric strangeness, one could apply to Muldoon MacNeice's special-category status for Beckett as a religious writer: 'the absence of God implies the need of God'.[14] Muldoon's early poem 'Hedgehog', virtually a parable in the biblical sense, suggests how this might be so:

214

The hedgehog gives nothing
Away, keeping itself to itself.
We wonder what a hedgehog
Has to hide, why it so distrusts.

We forget the god
Under this crown of thorns.
We forget that never again
Will a god trust in the world.

Perhaps God and a poet's imagination hide in parable for similar reasons.

A number of poems in *New Weather* (1973), like some of MacNeice's parables, follow the aesthetic suggested by MacNeice's praise of Herbert's 'Redemption': 'an out-and-out allegorical sonnet in everyday diction and with images drawn from something so prosaic as real estate'.[15] MacNeice allegorises taxi-rides and traffic jams, makes emblems of 'a watched clock' or 'a box of truisms'. Muldoon (also interested in the Metaphysicals and the conceit) produces subtle moralities from 'Blowing Eggs', 'The organised crime/ Of the kissing seat', 'The Radio Horse', 'Blemish':

Were it indeed an accident of birth
That she looks on the gentle earth
And the seemingly gentle sky
Through one brown, and one blue eye.

Muldoon himself associates his poetry with the Morality/ Humours tradition to which MacNeice traces parable: 'I use names perhaps far too often in a Jonsonian, emblematic way.'[16] Hence appearances by Will and Faith ('So Will had finally broken off with Faith!'), 'Our Protestant neighbour, Billy Wetherall', Ireland as 'Anorexia', or the first mention of 'Golightly' – who might personify Muldoon's sleight-of-hand – in the emblematic 'Boundary Commission':

You remember that village where the border ran
Down the middle of the street,
With the butcher and baker in different states?
Today he remarked how a shower of rain

Had stopped so cleanly across Golightly's lane
It might have been a wall of glass
That had toppled over. He stood there, for ages,
To wonder which side, if any, he should be on.

On the whole, Muldoon's most recent poetry goes more and more lightly, sews a point invisibly to its embodiment. 'Beaver', like 'Order to View' and Frost's 'Directive', combines fairy-tale mystery, dream logic, and psychic depths. A characteristically circular journey enacts the diminishing returns of sexual adventure, endlessly renewed despite past destructiveness:

> Let yourself in by the leaf-yellow door.
> Go right up the stairs.
>
> Along the way you may stumble upon
> one girl in a dress
>
> of flour-bag white, the turkey-red
> of another's apron.
>
> Give it no more thought
> than you would a tree felled across a stream
>
> in the Ozarks or the Adirondacks.
> Step over her as you would across
>
> a beaver dam.
> And try to follow that stream back
>
> to the top of the stairs,
> to your new room with its leaf-yellow floor.

From the outset Muldoon's poetry created a more homogeneous special world than MacNeice's: almost a murkier Celtic Twilight. But he has also created such worlds more specifically: 'I look on each poem as being a little world in itself'.[17] 'The Electric Orchard', the first poem in *New Weather*, invents a whole anthropology:

> The early electric people had domesticated the wild ass.
> They knew all about falling off.
> Occasionally, they would have fallen out of the trees.
> Climbing again, they had something to prove
> To their neighbours. And they did have neighbours.
> The electric people lived in villages
> Out of their need of security and their constant hunger.
> Together they would divert their energies
>
> To neutral places. Anger to the banging door,
> Passion to the kiss.
> And electricity to earth.

At one level the ritualised danger of this bizarre society may reflect the 'electric poles' of an ironically pre-lapsarian, pre-1969 Ulster:

216

For their own good, they threw a fence
Of barbed wire round the electric poles. None could describe
Electrocution, falling, the age of innocence.

However, as MacNeice always emphasises: 'The [parabolist's]
mythopoeic faculty transcends both his personal background and his
so-called message'.[18] This applies to Muldoon's extended special
world, the Moy: a metaphysical region derived from his actual
background in county Armagh. The Moy at once parodies the parish
and uses the parish as parody. Here familiar features of rural Ulster,
perhaps of rural Ulster poetry, enter another dimension:

> Once Duffy's Circus had shaken out its tent
> In the big field near the Moy
> God may as well have left Ireland
> And gone up a tree. My father had said so.
>
> There was no such thing as the five-legged calf,
> The God of Creation
> Was the God of Love.
> My father chose to share such Nuts of Wisdom.

In fact, throughout the poem stranger things occur than the father's
theology admits. They add up not merely to loss of innocence ('From
under a freighter/ I watched a man sawing a woman in half') but to
the perception of experience as a surreally disturbing circus. The
Moy expands, like the parishes of Edward Thomas and Patrick
Kavanagh, from the fine line of 'The Boundary Commission'
(MacNeice notes the mystique of boundaries in parable) to the
county, the country, the universe. Muldoon, echoing Kavanagh's
views on 'The Parish and the Universe', has said: 'I'm very interested
in the way in which a small place, a parish, can come to stand for the
world.'[19] However, the Moy's adventures through the looking-glass
are foreign to the symbolic landscapes of Thomas and Kavanagh.

These adventures, as in Lewis Carroll, involve close encounters
with weird characters – Faith, Anorexia, Golightly, Billy Wetherall
and Co. – diverse incarnations of a diversified metaphysic. For
instance if Faith is a moral abstraction, Brownlee in the title-poem of
Muldoon's third book, criticises and condenses a community.
Muldoon comments: 'Brownlee suggests a brown meadow, a
ploughed field, and so – in a strange sort of way – his end is in his
name; he's fulfilled his purpose even before he begins.'[20] In reaction
against predestination, Muldoon's hall of metamorphic mirrors
shatters fixed identities (not only Irish ones) by reflecting multiple
and ambiguous human faces. Although he enlarges Mutabilitie's

sphere, and tests all ethical systems, his poetry reaches back to Spenser's allegorical gallery. MacNeice quotes Graham Hough on Spenser's 'collective and composite personages', and continues:

> As Mr Hough points out, Spenser also illustrates another Freudian dream-process which is the converse of condensation: 'an individual dream-thought may be represented by several different elements in the dream-content'. Hough gives as example the figures of Amoret, Belphoebe and Florimell where an original bud or cell has broken, so to speak, into three.[21]

'The More a Man Has the More a Man Wants' operates a continual shuttle between cell-division and cell-coalescence. Thus Gallogly's alternating ego has its counterpart in a shifting female scapegoat and Muse, here doubly metamorphosed:

> Her lovely head has been chopped
> and changed.
> For Beatrice, whose fathers
> knew Louis Quinze,
> to have come to this, her perruque
> of tar and feathers.

Yet the seeming fragmentation of the poem's personnel establishes powerful archetypes, serves an infinitely delicate moral unity.

Muldoon's earlier version of sonnet-sequence, 'Armageddon, Armageddon' in *Mules* (1977), is not yet the psychedelic pageant of 'The More a Man Has'. Nevertheless it rings the changes on 'Larry Durrell', Jeanne Duval, Macha (legendary foundress of Armagh), Swift, 'Grace' from a divided family ('Some violence had been done to Grace,/ She had left for our next-of-kin'), and a fully allegorical Oisin returning to Ireland:

> There and then he began to stoop,
> His hair, and all his teeth, fell out,
> A mildewed belt, a rusted buckle.
> The clays were heavy, black or yellow,
> Those were the colours of his boots.
> And I know something of how he felt.

In 'Armageddon, Armageddon' the microcosmic Moy includes within its frontiers both the county and the constellations, although not in the manner of Kavanagh's 'Cassiopeia was over/ Cassidy's hanging hill'. In keeping with the disproportionate apocalypse implied by the title's pun on the county name, local details assume a mock-heroic aspect. Sonnet V co-opts the Armagh Planetarium:

Why should those women be carrying water
If all the wells were poisoned, as they said,
And the fish littering the river?
Had the sheep been divided from the goats,
Were Twin and Twin at each other's throats?

But this zodiac is mythic as well as mock-heroic and allegorical. Despite the poem's irony at the expense of inflated parochial wars, and perhaps at the expense of poetic afflatus on the subject, Muldoon's mythopoeic faculty yet transmits an ominous special world.

2.

Syntax reinforces the 'spine of allegory' which MacNeice considers essential to parable. Although narrative elements may also be present, syntax stands to the lyric poem as plot to fiction, in that it articulates the logic – or dream logic – of the action. MacNeice was attracted to Rosalind Tuve's contention that 'metaphysical wit and concord of unlikes in an image is precisely the operation, much condensed, of the old (and maligned) allegorical mode of writing'.[22] Similarly, a parable-poem's syntax can constitute the condensed operation of allegory's metaphysical direction. In 'Order to View' MacNeice's 'careful ordering of sentences' makes asyndeton fundamental to the poem's orchestration, heard over the metre, or transforming it, so that 'rose,/ Faltered, broke' defines the movement of the first two stanzas. (Contrast the conjunctions of *Autumn Journal*.) MacNeice's more complete creative breakthrough in the fifties was largely a formal breakthrough, and the formal breakthrough largely a syntactical breakthrough. This throws retrospective light on his lack of final concentration as a stanzaic artist (see page 177). The early poem 'River in Spate' points the way by combining internal rhyme with unusual syntax in a long line:

The river falls and over the walls the coffins of cold funerals
Slide deep and sleep there in the close tomb of the pool,
And yellow waters lave the grave and pebbles pave its mortuary . . .

However 'Déjà Vu' (1962) goes much further in that sentence-sound and sentence-structure not only interact with metre but shape it:

It does not come round in hundreds of thousands of years,
It comes round in the split of a wink, you will be sitting exactly
Where you are now and scratching your elbow, the train

Will be passing exactly as now and saying It does not come round,
It does not come round, It does not come round . . .

So that, whatever the rules we might be supposed to obey,
Our love must extend beyond time because time is itself in arrears
So this double vision must pass and past and future unite
And where we were told to kowtow we can snap our fingers and laugh
And now, as you watch, I will take this selfsame pencil and write:
It does not come round in hundreds of thousands of years.

This parable love poetry unites a paranormal experience with a metaphysical point about love and time. In communicating his point primarily through syntax, MacNeice explodes the old notion that syntax, unlike other linguistic phenomena, is inherently unpoetical. Although the prolonged sentence (seventeen lines in all), which elongates the metre too, dramatises the breaking of time's 'rules', it does so by breaking not rules but norms of grammar. 'Déjà Vu' exploits, as no prose sentence could, a sentence's full licence to stack up tenses and moods around a 'split of a wink'. A master of perodic structure, partly due to his classical training, MacNeice in his later poetry exaggerates specific features for specific purposes instead of holding a balance. Subverting the golden means of humanism may be an overall purpose. Nevertheless the exaggerations of 'Déjà Vu' and 'All Over Again' – a series of 'as if' clauses – exploit legitimate syntactical possibilities to assert what seems humanly impossible: 'as if/ This one Between were All and we in love for years'. Just as these poems give definitive syntactical expression to MacNeice's recurrent ideal that love suspends ordinary relations between past and future, so 'Variation on Heraclitus' celebrates another positive, flux, in a mimetically fluid syntax surpassing that of 'River in Spate':

Nor can this now be the chair – the chairoplane of a chair –
That I sat in the day that I thought I had made up my mind
And as for that standard lamp it too keeps waltzing away
Down an unbridgeable Ganges where nothing is standard . . .

Non-standard syntax plays another role in MacNeice's more typically *dark* conceits. Here too it is a matter of perennial themes entering a new parabolic dimension under the aegis of syntax. 'Reflections', a starker look at relativity than 'Variation on Heraclitus', develops MacNeice's recurrent image of mirrored loneliness by deploying mirror-image phrases: 'The fire in the mirror lies two rooms away through the window,/ The fire in the window lies one room away down the terrace'. MacNeice also develops new syntactical means of articulating the concern with mortality he shares with Hardy and Larkin. In contrast to syntax which transcends or outruns time, other kinds of syntax represent humanity as its pawn, out of step with its pace. 'Another Cold May' endows a suspended moment with the stasis of death rather than the shimmer of permanence:

> With heads like chessmen, bishop or queen,
> The tulips tug at their roots and mourn
> In inaudible frequencies, the move
> Is the wind's, not theirs; fender to fender
> The cars will never emerge, not even
> Should their owners emerge to claim them, the move
> Is time's, not theirs; elbow to elbow
> Inside the roadhouse drinks are raised
> And downed, and downed, the pawns and drains
> Are blocked, are choked, the move is nil,
> The lounge is, like the carpark, full,
> The tulips also feel the chill
> And tilting leeward do no more
> Then mimic a bishop's move, the square
> Ahead remains ahead, their petals
> Will merely fall and choke the drains
> Which will be all; this month remains
> False animation of failed levitation,
> The move is time's, the loss is ours.

This partly parallels Larkin's 'Spring' (and Thomas's 'October') except that 'The tulips also feel the chill'. MacNeice translates into a parable-microcosm Hardy's insistence that Time governs all phenomena, with no exemption for seasonal rhythms. Thus all the images compose a surreal scenario on a Carroll-like chessboard, while asyndeton again calls the tune. In addition, the repeated words and syntactical patterns (parison) convey 'False animation of failed levitation' by seeming to mark time, by failing to move towards any rhythmic resolution. A typical blocking structure is 'fender to fender', 'Are blocked, are choked', 'the square/ Ahead remains ahead'. This stop-go syntax also shapes 'Hold-up' and 'Sunday in the Park' ('the walkers-out forget/ Why they are out'). Not every poem in *Solstices* and *The Burning Perch* manifests such a primarily syntactical inspiration as those I have mentioned. But the strategies which they pursue to the limit, together with many related devices, are crucial to MacNeice's later aesthetic. Thus in 'Charon', another poem in which movement goes awry, slower than life, parison as a species of dispersed zeugma provides a chilling refrain: 'black with money . . . black with suspicion . . . black with obols'. And 'The Introduction', a poem about mis-timed love, combines the surreal refrain 'Crawly crawly' with one based on cruelly over-logical syntax: 'she frightened him because she was young/ And thus too late . . . he frightened her because he was old/ And thus too early'. This foreclosed sentence is at the opposite pole from the endlessly open 'Déjà Vu' and 'All Over Again'.

Muldoon's interest in syntax attaches less to its temporal and logical aspects, sequence and consequence, than to its capacity for playing the angles. His syntax is the first cause of a multi-dimensional geometry: 'structures that can be fixed like mirrors at angles to each other – it relates to narrative form – so that new images can emerge from the setting up of the poems in relation to each other: further ironies are possible, further mischief is possible'.[23] If MacNeice's poetry sometimes perceives life as a prism, Muldoon's poetry perceives life through one. Whereas MacNeice's mirror-reflections are an imagery, relevant to his theme of man-in-time, and dramatised in 'Reflections' by syntactical mimicry, Muldoon's whole aesthetic is founded on the placing of clauses and sentences as facets of a metaphysical issue. He exploits and investigates the structure of grammar rather than grammatical constructions. MacNeice's odd syntactical shapes might be termed in one sense 'post-sentence' in their reaction against the poetry of statement. (He significantly found Movement poetry short of a level.) Muldoon's syntax, on the other hand, might be termed pre-sentence in its postponement rather than subversion of the indicative, its distrust of the definitive. He goes further than Frost in asking how we know what we think we know. Thus the speaker of 'Lunch with Pancho Villa' ponders: 'there's no such book, so far as I know/ As *How It Happened Here,*/ Though there may be. There may'. Muldoon's imagination works within an ironic 'eternal interim' ('Lull'), very different from MacNeice's 'split of a wink', which has something to do with differing slants on history. MacNeice the disenchanted progressive and Muldoon, never-enchanted chronicler of the Ulster standstill, seize on syntax as a crucial agency of their special perspectives on the relation between past and future. Or perhaps the two syntactical endeavours ultimately meet if Muldoon's poetry is the labour-pains of progress, MacNeice's, like Mahon's, a deathbed repentance on the part of Whig history. 'As In Their Time', MacNeice's satirical sequence of riddling five-liners, uses syntactical circles to mock progress, his own thirties idealism:

> For what it was worth he had to
> Make a recurring protest:
> Which was at least a gesture

Which was a vindication
Or excuse for what it was worth.

The indicative mood has a low count in Muldoon's poetry, as compared with subjunctive, conditional, optative, interrogative and imperative forms of the verb. The latter, as 'Beaver' shows, is self-subverting, not the Yeatsian or even Frostian directive. 'Beaver' also contains the characteristic Muldoon 'would'. Muldoon's brand of the present habitual – a tense in the Irish language and geared to eternal interims – occupies an area between the indicative and the conditional, where it shades into 'might'. 'The Bishop', for instance, uses the construction to hold alternative lives in historical suspension:

> The night before he was to be ordained
> He packed a shirt and a safety razor
> And started out for the middle of nowhere,
> Back to the back of beyond,
>
> Where all was forgiven and forgotten,
> Or forgotten for a time. He would court
> A childhood sweetheart . . .
>
> His neighbours might give him a day
> In the potatoes or barley . . .
>
>   His favourite grand-daughter
> Would look out, one morning in January,
> To find him in his armchair, in the yard.
>
> It had snowed all night. There was a drift
> As far as his chin, like an alb.
> 'Come in, my child. Come in, and bolt
> The door behind you, for there's an awful draught.'

This eerie 'double vision', very unlike that of 'Déjà Vu', drives ordination in tandem with family, secular, communal life. The poem's arrested development, rather than arrested moment, comments on what is pre-ordained in Ireland, though a universal draught also blows through it. *Oratio obliqua* is another way of avoiding statement, or implying the difficulty of statement. 'The Boundary Commission' sits on a syntactical fence too: '*You remember* . . . he remarked how . . . It might have been . . . To wonder which'. The rhetorical question, or a series of them as in the Planetarium sonnet, is also a pervasive strategy. However just as Muldoon's imperatives actually sabotage authority, so his questions mystify more than demystify. Retaining a narrative aspect as well, they frustrate the argumentative thrust with which Frost's questions address mysteries. Although Frostian in the matter of knowing, seeing, and saying, Muldoon's quietist understatment (pre-statement) is sometimes closer in spirit to Edward Thomas.

Frost is another point where MacNeice and Muldoon meet. I quoted above (page 43) MacNeice's marvellous image for poetic syntax, called forth in 1963 by a critical book on Frost: 'A sentence in prose is struck forward like a golf ball; a sentence in verse can be treated like a ball in a squash-court.'[24] However, it is Muldoon who follows Frost as, in MacNeice's phrase, 'a master of angles'[25] and a mischief-maker: 'I think the writer who excited me most at university was Robert Frost: an apparently simple, almost naive, tone of voice and use of language, underneath which all kinds of complex things are happening.'[26] (It is proof of Frost's variety that Seamus Heaney should admire and absorb such very different qualities: the instinctive force of 'The Most of It', 'that surrender, the entranced thing, in "After Apple-Picking".'[27]) Frost and Thomas wrote occasional parables: 'Design', 'Directive', 'The Gallows', 'The Other'. However, their less heavily masked dramatic lyrics do not suppress and displace the 'I' persona as commonly as does parable. MacNeice, who wrote an Everyman play, *One for the Grave* (1958-9), frequently resorts to a third-person Everyman. Muldoon refers to 'a number of poems [coming] out of a single, if dislocated, personality'.[28] Yet Thomas's 'The Other', although its first-person narrator is closer to the poet than Muldoon's in 'Immram', constitutes a model for all modern parable-quests. It converts into symbolic terrain an archetypal folk-tale road between dangerous forest and 'the sum/ Of what's not forest' – an uncertain computation like Frosts's spiritual accountancy. 'The Other' penetrates both the inner and outer unknown; traverses mystical borders; presents the 'dislocated personality' searching for locus and focus. And it enlists syntax to enact self-pursuit through all the mazes:

> What to do
> When caught, I planned not. I pursued
> To prove the likeness, and, if true,
> To watch until myself I knew.

This confuses ego and alter ego as does 'The More a Man Has'. Interestingly, the quest for the self – rendered as pursuit and flight – is currently a growth-point in Irish literature North and South. But the theme involves painful psychic probing, not external questions of national identity. Indeed one question asked is whether identity *can* be national. Contributions to this mode of personal and communal introspection include Brendan Kennelly's *Cromwell* and portrayals of Sweeney, mad fugitive king of Ulster, by Seamus Heaney[29] and Tom MacIntyre.[30] 'The More a Man Has' also alludes to Sweeney.

Muldoon's debt to Frost, as his acknowledgements suggest, is a matter of tone as well as syntax: 'But all the fun's in how you say a thing'. This, together with other lines from Frost's 'The Mountain', forms the basis of Muldoon's 'The Country Club':

> 'But what would interest you about the brook,
> It's always cold in summer, warm in winter.'
> 'Warm in December, cold in June, you say?'
> Doc Pinkerton was a great one for chapter and verse.
>
> 'I don't suppose the water's changed at all.
> You and I know enough to know it's warm
> Compared with cold, and cold compared with warm,
> But all the fun's in how you say a thing.'
>
> 'Well, it shouldn't seem true when it's not.'

Muldoon has described the poem as 'about being implicated in a society, and more specifically in a violent event in a society – implicated simply by being on the sidelines.'[31] The poem's 'implication' turns on 'how you say a thing', the ambiguous 'far gone':

> Just after three. The bar was shutting down.
> Ella Stafford was high as a kite . . .
>
> She was right side of thirty, husband out of town,
> It seemed I might have fallen on my feet.
>
> Neither of them was so far gone, as it turned out . . .
>
> I was coming back down onto the highway
> When I met Lee Pinkerton's Chevrolet.
> We drew up close. He rolled down his window.
>
> 'There's been some trouble over Stafford's way.
> Took a shot at his wife.' He gave me a knowing look.
> 'She'd been seeing a lot of some other fella,
> Or so it seems. I can't make head nor tail of it.'

When Lee Pinkerton, compounded of the detective agency and Robert Lee Frost, gives 'a knowing look' – two words central to Frost's epistemology – he assumes what he cannot know. The contrast with his bafflement over the riddle or parable of the brook suggests that poetry, unlike rumour, never lies. Muldoon quotes from Frost in a number of other poems, but 'The More a Man Has' follows 'The Country Club' in making such quotation vital to the entire structure. In the second stanza the vengeful Indian goes through customs at Belfast airport:

> 'Anything to declare?'
> He opens the powder-blue attaché-
> case. 'A pebble of quartz'.

This allusion to the last line of 'For Once, Then, Something ('Truth? A pebble of quartz? For once, then, something') warns that the poem's own contents, or 'declaration', may be highly provisional. Later 'A weekend trip to the mountains/ North of Boston' registers Muldoon's imaginative latitude. He also twice double-quotes Frost, because he uses phrases which 'Directive' itself quotes from earlier poems. Thus Gallogly being strip-searched 'perches . . . till both his instep arches/ fall' – the instep arch from 'After Apple-Picking' and the one from 'Directive'. The poem ends by fusing 'The Mountain' again, 'Directive' and 'For Once, Then, Something':

> 'They foun' this hairy
> han' wi' a drowneded man's grip
> on a lunimous stone no bigger than a . . .'

> 'Huh.'

'The Mountain' comes to a similar non-conclusion:

> 'You've lived here all your life?'
>   'Ever since Hor
> Was no bigger than a –' What, I did not hear.
> He drew the oxen toward him with light touches
> Of his slim goad on nose and offside flank,
> Gave them their marching orders and was moving.

'Directive' echoes this with its field 'no bigger than a harness gall'. The disintegrated body (an image at the heart of 'The More a Man Has') retains a problematic grasp on 'truth'. 'No bigger than a . . .', another Frostian computation, unites enormity with futility.

Muldoon resembles Frost rather than MacNeice in his preference for counterpointing syntax with 'spaces of the footed line'. His equivalent of MacNeice's syntactical elasticity is the shape-changing sonnet-form which yet (despite 'Huh') retains its cadence. However, he resembles MacNeice rather than Frost in his structural reliance on idiom, the revitalised cliché. This marries tone of voice to a punning

226

wit. MacNeice in the thirties pioneered slang and cliché as a shot-in-the-arm for poetic diction:

> the popular imagination, as shown, for example, in the American wisecrack, is something with which the poet should stay in communion. Poetry can become too niggling. Synge was right when he said 'in countries where the imagination of the people, and the language they use, is rich and living, it is possible for a writer to be rich and copious in his words, and at the same time to give the reality, which is the root of all poetry, in a comprehensive and natural form,' but he was wrong in implying that such language is nowadays found only among peasants. Witness the English music-halls or the newspaper articles of many of the sporting journalists, the slang talk of New York or the stories of Ring W. Lardner.[32]

That in 'Homage to Clichés' MacNeice could use the 'whole delightful world of cliché and refrain' as a part ironic, part life-affirming metaphor, emphasises its significance as technique. As for refrains, *The Poetry of W.B. Yeats* devotes four pages to defending them against the twentieth-century suspicion of 'poetic repetition-devices on the ground that repetition saves thinking or excuses the lack of thought, that by sheer hypnotic force it can persuade the reader to buy his twopence coloured when he would certainly reject the penny plain'.[33] MacNeice's analysis of Yeats's refrains in *Words for Music Perhaps* implies the increasing complexity of his own practice: 'First the music of his refrain is often less obvious or smooth than that of the verses themselves . . . Secondly, his refrains tend to have either an intellectual meaning which is subtle and concentrated, or a symbolist or nonsense meaning which hits the reader below the belt.'[34] '*Come back early or never come*' in 'Autobiography' (1940) joins the forces of Yeats's two kinds of refrain. MacNeice's developed structural use of syntactical refrain, or parison, sometimes interacts with the 'symbolist or nonsense' variety ('tra-la', 'Crawly crawly') pushed to even more sinister extremes.

Cliché and refrain, since the former so often doubles as the latter, are inseparable in MacNeice's poetry. Although on balance all this 'twopence coloured' progressively takes darker turns, once again earlier poems, such as 'Glass Falling' (1926), point forward:

> The rain is coming down, the frown
> Is coming down of heaven showing
> A wet night coming, the glass is going
> Down, the sun is going down.

Later, the cliché-refrain of 'Bagpipe Music' (1937) – words for music perhaps – 'It's no go' anticipates 'In Lieu' (1961), which also detects

227

the bottom line in an idiom: 'in lieu of a flag/ The orator hangs himself from the flagpost'. 'The Slow Starter' makes a new parable by taking apart the proverbial 'watched clock':

> Who said a watched clock never moves?
> Look at it now. Your chance was I.
> He turned and saw the accusing clock
> Race like a torrent round a rock.

'Birthright', which allegorises life as a 'rearing beast', also ends with a cliché turning the tables on the assumption that man controls language and life: 'My gifthorse looked me in the mouth.' (This reverses MacNeice's earlier celebration of an empirical 'given glory' in 'The Cromlech' and 'London Rain'.) 'For what it was worth', by different means, is dishearteningly devalued second time round. 'Idle Talk' still affirms a creative dynamic linking word and world:

>   the rotten compost of hackneyed phrase
>   Reprieves the captive, feeds the future . . .
>
>   Shop-talk, club-talk, cliché, slang –
>   The wind that makes the dead leaf fall
>   Can also make the live leaf dance . . .

And the poem ends by renewing the cliché 'I love you'. But paradoxically most of MacNeice's revitalised clichés, his verbal leaf-dances, express devitalisation. 'Sports Page' enjoys the language of sporting journalists, but in order to conclude: 'The lines of print are always sidelines/ And all our games funeral games'. In 'Children's Games', too, word-games turn into funeral games: 'Keep your fingers crossed when Tom Tiddler's ground is over you.' Cliché, like syntax, influences the structure and texture of MacNeice's later poetry. Its potential for his kind of parable lies partly in its ability to expose society's own cliché. Various poems present artifical environments whose inhabitants, like the grotesque blooms of 'Flower Show', no longer 'speak a living language'. 'The Suicide' abandons cliché as a way of life ('the ash in the ashtray, the grey memoranda stacked/ Against him'), in a manner which suggests MacNeice's elusive aesthetic: 'By catdrop sleight of foot or simple vanishing act'. Ultimately, however, the social dimension of cliché blends into its larger gnomic fatality: the 'manhole under the hollyhocks' on which the suicide stumbles. 'Charon' ends with a particularly deadly cliché, a Parthian shot from the ferryman: 'If you want to die you will have to pay for it'.

If MacNeice's clichés harbour omens, obituaries and moral

lessons, often in terms of discrepancies between depth and surface, Muldoon's more tongue-in-cheek irony achieves similar results: 'She had wanted only to clear the air.' His poetry brings to light an alarming collective unconscious in everyday speech-habits. As MacNeice's 'Birthright' and 'The Slow Starter' make metaphysical points by realising cliché's physical shape, so Muldoon's punning idioms constantly visualise their own implications: the hedgehog 'keeping itself to itself', the 'man sawing a woman in half', the not 'so far gone' wife and husband, the 'sheep . . . divided from the goats', the female scapegoat's head 'chopped/ and changed'. Muldoon does not so much employ "imagery", as allow language to yield its latent metaphor. He also restores full significance to more abstract phrases. In 'The Bishop' the easy 'forgiven and forgotten' acquires a renewed sense of its own difficulty. Here and elsewhere Muldoon uses cliché to question the specific clichés of Irish experience as well as of humanity in general. 'Come into my Parlour' features a cliché-ridden gravedigger, as disconcertingly 'knowing' as Charon ('He knew exactly which was which/ And what was what'). Coulter, his own life like Brownlee's pre-empted by his name (= Spade), sees Ulster or earth only as a predestined grave: 'family plots'. 'October 1950' starts at the other end:

> Whatever it is, it all comes down to this;
> My father's cock
> Between my mother's thighs.
> Might he have forgotten to wind the clock?
>
> Cookers and eaters, Fuck the Pope,
> Wow and flutter, a one-legged howl,
> My sly quadroon, the way home from the pub –
> Anything wild or wonderful –
>
> Whatever it is, it goes back to this night,
> To a chance remark
> In a room at the top of the stairs;
> To an open field, as like as not,
> Under the little stars.
> Whatever it is, it leaves me in the dark.

The list in the second quatrain of this sonnet combines different kinds of verbal and experiential cliché. 'Cookers and eaters', colloquial for the apples of Muldoon's Armagh orchard-country, additionally invokes a polarised cannibalism, as does 'Fuck the Pope'. In the next two lines hybridised diction emphasises the actual strangeness of all the clichés conception sets in motion. Thus 'chance', as much as predestination, seems to govern a less or more than dualistic universe ('quadroon', 'one-legged') summed up by 'Anything wild or wonderful'. The latter, an Ulster greeting which requests news, is once again an abstraction made concrete, or restored to its full meaning and beyond. Thus cliché of birth/place/ culture, as rendered for instance by the expression 'born an Ulster Catholic', becomes 'a chance remark . . . Whatever it is, it leaves me in the dark'. However, the speaker's uncertainty is no more comforting than Coulter's certainty. Widening cliché's franchise need not mean loosening its grip.

3.

In equating the variousness of language and of life, whether apparent or real, Muldoon continues down the path opened up by MacNeice's 'Snow' and the later 'Autolycus' which celebrates Shakespeare's romances as 'conjuring/ With rainbow names and handfuls of sea-spray'. But 'Autolycus' might denote the mythic as well as linguistic 'eclecticism' that the two poets share with the 'master pedlar's' parables:

> Eclectic always, now extravagant,
> Sighting his matter through a timeless prism
> He ranged his classical bric-à-brac in grottos
> Where knights of Ancient Greece had Latin mottoes
> And fishermen their flapjacks – none should want
> Colour for lack of an anachronism.

Between them 'Immram' and 'The More a Man Has' follow this recipe up to the hilt: American-Indian and Irish legend; legendary literary sources which include Byron, Chandler, Frost, Gertrude Stein, Robert Louis Stevenson, Lewis Carroll, Dante, and parodied Irish poets; not to mention countless other pockets of the myth-kitty. For instance, Muldoon's arrangement of 'classical bric-à-brac' has all MacNeice's slangy irreverence:

> In Ovid's conspicuously tongue-in-cheek
> account of an eyeball
> to eyeball
> between the goddess Leto
> and a shower of Lycian reed-cutters . . .

('Shower' is one of the terms of insult unusually abundant in Ulster speech.) As well as the classics – and the *Odyssey* underlies all quests including *immrama* – MacNeice musters such resources as the Bible, Scandinavian and Irish legend, and a range of English lore and literature in which Arthurian legend predominates. Muldoon's several allusions to the latter include a bomb-disposal expert in 'The More a Man Has', who wears 'a green helmet of aspect terrible' and 'goes in search of some Gawain'.

The Strings Are False testifies to the formative influence of Malory on MacNeice:

> Inspired by Mr Charles [at Sherborne preparatory school] I had read Malory's *Morte d'Arthur*, sitting in a windowseat and reading with such concentration that my hair stuck to the paint of the woodwork. The book was very long but by no means too long for me; I revelled in the reiteration of incident; to go from joust to joust and count how many knights Sir Tristram or Sir Pelleas unseated was as exciting as reading the County Cricket batting averages.[35]

MacNeice and his schoolfriends 'became the knights ourselves . . . my last open make-believe before my adolescence, after which time, like everyone else, I lived half the time in fantasy, but craftily, deceiving both others and myself'.[36] This reminiscence, written in 1940,conflates *Morte d'Arthur* with MacNeice's new wartime awareness of a place for make-believe and parable. He continues:

> This adult make-believe is something we have foolishly ignored . . . in the epoch of Hitler – Siegfried Redivivus – it is not only a mistake but a disaster to ignore those underground motives which cause both art and war . . . [Man] cannot live by bread or Marx alone; he must always be after the Grail.[37]

Hence perhaps 'The Trolls' and 'Troll's Courtship', fantastic personifications of the forces let loose in the London Blitz:

> I am a lonely Troll after my gala night;
> I have knocked down houses and stamped my feet on the people's heart . . .

Parable may afford strategies whereby archetypes can be detached from interior drama – the technical dimension absent from Seamus Heaney's *North*. 'Woods' (1946) also registers Malory's impact on MacNeice's mythic and moral imagination. For his father on the other hand, coming late to English landscape and legend: 'Malory's knights . . . Could never arras the room, where he spelled out True and Good/ With their interleaving of half-truths and not-quites'. Ten years earlier MacNeice had contributed a provocative essay on Malory to Derek Verschoyle's *The English Novelists*. It too anticipates later developments in praising the non-realist "reality" of Malory's characters and the 'delicate virility' of his narrative style.[38] Most importantly, MacNeice begins by drawing an analogy with dream:

> Sometimes in dreams the dream becomes palpably more substantial. The process is like scrambling eggs. From an indefinite froth comes, seemingly instantaneously, something with a recognisable texture, something one can put in one's mouth. When a dream behaves in this way, it is becoming a work of art. The effect is often one of healthy bathos. From a sickly-sweet twilight of indefinite sensations there emerges perhaps the exceedingly familiar, exceedingly detailed, figure of someone one knows, and this at once makes the dialectic of the dream concrete. So it is with Malory.[39]

MacNeice's radio-plays, like his autobiography and criticism, often pioneered material and methods subsequently perfected in poetry. (*The Strings Are False* contains images and parables which resurface in the later poems.) The plays were a workshop for parable and for redirected legend long before MacNeice's full poetic capitalisation on these assets. *The Dark Tower*, steeped in Malory and the Quest, marks both a culmination and the potential for further concentration. MacNeice's Opening Announcement runs:

> The theme is the ancient but ever-green theme of the Quest – the dedicated adventure; the manner of presentation is that of a dream – but a dream that is full of meaning. Browning's poem ends with a challenge blown on a trumpet:
>
>
>
> 'And yet
> Dauntless the slughorn to my lips I set
> And blew. "Childe Roland to the Dark Tower came".'
>
>
>
> Note well the words 'And yet'. Roland did not have to – he did not wish to – and yet in the end he came to: The Dark Tower.[40]

The Dark Tower endorses the Quest as dedication, purpose, more emphatically than does *The Mad Islands*. The temptations which assail Roland's oath include love and domesticity (people 'Who keep themselves to themselves or rather to each other'). Nevertheless, the play cheers him on to fulfil his destiny as 'one of the dedicated/ Whose life is a quest, whose death is a victory'. This insistence (in contrast with 'As In Their Time') recalls MacNeice's self-dedication in the thirties: 'Minute your gesture but it must be made'. The Dragon, whom all Roland's family must confront, fuses the political evils of the thirties and early forties with the source

Of evil through the world. It is immortal
But men must try to kill it – and keep on trying
So long as we would be human.

In *The Mad Islands*, on the other hand, Muldoon's quest to
avenge his allegedly murdered father comes more and more into
question. To his comment 'My quest makes no more sense', Skerrie
the seal-woman, his supernatural mentor, replies 'It never did'. In the
original *Immram Mael Duin* Mael Duin's father Ailill has innocently
fallen victim to 'marauders of Leix'. This makes his avenging mission
honourable though finally unfulfilled, since he takes an old hermit's
Christian advice: 'forgive him, because God hath saved *you* from
manifold great perils, and ye, too, are men deserving of death'.
MacNeice's Muldoon sets out on a fool's errand, because the mother
who urges him to kill the Lord of the Eskers in fact seeks vengeance
on a faithless lover: Muldoon's real father, and murderer of his
supposed father at her behest. Mother Ireland plays a part in darkening this figure and the quest: 'of advanced years but . . . well-
preserved in hatred'. It is part of Muldoon's ill-fate that all his
companions ultimately slay each other. This seems to echo
Tennyson's 'The Voyage of Maeldune' whose refrain carries a stern
moral for Irish feuding: 'But I knew we should fall on each other, and
hastily sailed away.' Tennyson's hermit admonishes politically as
well as religiously:

> His fathers have slain thy fathers in war or in single strife,
> Thy fathers have slain his fathers, each taken a life for a life,
> Thy father had slain his father, how long shall the murder last?
> Go back to the Isle of Finn and suffer the Past to be Past.

However, MacNeice's imaginative mood of the sixties counts most.
He invents such subsidiary parables as the befogged Island of
Progress, and reinvents the Miller of Hell (an 'original motif which
Tennyson ignored and I jumped at')[41] who in *Immram Mael Duin*
grinds everything 'which is begrudged'. MacNeice's Miller offers to
grind away 'your shiploads of folly. All your bad debts and your
crooked contracts, your election speeches and your changing maps,
your mergers and treaties and dud manifestoes, your flashy red
herring, your brand-new obsolescent weapons.'

Paul Muldoon's 'Immram' seems darkened by the mood of the
late 1970s in Ireland and elsewhere. No clear purpose, no clearcut
innocence or guilt can be discerned, as we follow an obviously less
reliable narrator than Tennyson's: 'I am telling this exactly as it
happened.' Wanting 'to know more about my father' after being told

'"Your old man was an ass-hole./ That makes an ass-hole out of you"', the narrator-hero embarks on a circular journey. His mother, who like Anorexia may represent Ireland in a terminal state, cannot expound her son's mission in the traditional manner:

> Now she'd taken an overdose
> Of alcohol and barbiturates,
> And this, I learned, was her third.
> I was told then by a male nurse
> That if I came back at the end of the week
> She might be able to bring herself to speak.

The son's own plight certainly refers at one level to post-1969 Ulster, in that he has been jerked back from a promising future:

> I was fairly and squarely behind the eight
> That morning in Foster's pool-hall . . .

by atavistic forces, by his share in an inheritance at once threatened and dubious. He too encounters self-cancelling violence:

> They came bearing down on me out of nowhere.
> A Buick and a Chevrolet.
> They were heading towards a grand slam.
> Salami on rye. I was the salami.

But Golightly 'side-steps' again. Muldoon comments on his overall design:

> The quest is the powerful and important centre of the poem. Both the protagonist and his father are led through a maze. The protagonist is a cipher, the world envelops him, everything happens to him; he directs very little, and I'm very sceptical about how much we direct anything that happens to us. And the end of it is this whimsical – I would tend to use the world 'whimful', which doesn't exist – this whimsical dismissal by the bane of both their lives. 'I forgive you . . . and I forget'.[42]

Muldoon's hermit is naked and hairy like the original, but 'huddled on an old orthopaedic mattress' and modelled on Howard Hughes reclusive in his 'exclusive penthouse suite'. He certainly jams all the moral signals of earlier *immrama* in presuming to give an absolution he might be receiving. This 'whimfulness' may again introduce chance into predestination. More resolvingly, after his multi-faceted ordeal the protagonist follows precedent in that he appears liberated from the past. He returns to 'Foster's pool-room' (a pun on *mixed* inheritance and the fostering of Mael Duin), fresh from 'a steady stream of people/ That flowed in one direction,/

Faster and deeper,/ That I would go along with, happily'. Although pushed around by the world and the poem the cipher/quester survives. His rejoining the flow of life to Main Street parallels MacNeice's Muldoon's final condition, which itself anticipates 'Thalassa'. Hardly 'dauntless', he yet resumes his journey:

> So here I am at the end alone in a small boat and it has all been for what? I thought that vengeance was mine but the fates took it away from me and what was I avenging anyway? . . . Well, let's try once more. She said it should work now.
>
> [*He makes two vain attempts at cranking; at the third the engine starts and the motorboat carries him away.*]

If MacNeice's thrust in his later work is to pursue the quest but question it, Muldoon's may be the other way round. MacNeice's parables proceed in a straight line complicated by hold-ups, diversions and time-warps; Muldoon's in loops and parabolas, occasionally straightened out. Muldoon's 'I Remember Sir Alfred' contrasts the straight line, as a means of questing, with 'singleminded swervings'. However, the latter image applies to both poets' quests as opposed to undeviating purposes:

> The spirit of Sir Alfred McAlpine
> Paces the meadow, and fixes his theodolite
> On something beyond the horizon,
> Love, or fidelity.
>
> Charles Stewart Parnell, the I.R.A. . . .
>
> Now Sir Alfred has dislodged a hare
> That goes by leaps and bounds
> Across the grazing,
> Here and there,
> This way and that, by singleminded swervings.

Compare Edward Thomas's dove that 'slants unswerving'.

MacNeice's later poetry, taken as a whole, constitutes a much richer *immram* than *The Mad Islands*. Many poems of course are self-contained miniature quests, which allegorise life's journey as a dream-like train-ride, car-ride, taxi-ride, bus-ride, horse-ride. Like MacNeice's syntax these poems sometimes speed life up or slow it down. In 'Birthright' life goes so fast the rider never mounts; while in 'Charon' 'we just jogged on', time runs down and out:

> We could see the pigeons through the glass but failed
> To hear their rumours of wars . . .

Too fast or too slow denies purpose, as do the world's charges on the individual in 'The Taxis':

> In the second taxi he was alone tra-la
> But the clock showed sixpence extra . . .

This casts into very different terms Larkin's 'Something is pushing them/ To the side of their own lives'. Nevertheless certain poems – 'Thalassa', 'The Wiper'– renew 'the dedicated adventure':

> While we, dazzled by darkness,
> Haul the black future towards us
> Peeling the skin from our hands;
> And yet we hold the road.

MacNeice's quest resembles in spirit, if not in form, Thomas's sticking to the road ('The next turn may reveal/ Heaven'), Larkin keeping the ideal option just open. However MacNeice's agnosticism, shaped by his Ulster background, is more immediately post-religious. It thus retains not only Thomas's sense of mystery but a sense of sin, of the tension between belief and disbelief, of man 'born/ For either the heights or the depths'. Hence his – and Muldoon's – sixteenth- and seventeenth-century affinities. 'The Blasphemies' traces a child's frightened question till it again becomes urgent to the fifty-year-old man: 'The sin/ Against the Holy Ghost – What is it?' The poem also implies the need for a profounder 'myth', or aesthetic of parable, than 'my childhood symbols/ Divorced from their context'. If imaginative agnosticism works through complementary poems, the addition of parable makes it more like an *immram*, a voyage among variegated islands. MacNeice's happy isles are 'green improbable fields' of love; his nightmare landfalls the abode of denatured freaks, like 'Flower Show': 'Squidlike, phallic or vulvar, hypnotic, idiotic, oleaginous,/ Fanged or whaleboned'. 'Flower Show' illustrates how some poems not only take shape as ideal or surreal scenarios, or independent time-zones, but may perform the function of the Island of Progress in *The Mad Islands*. The sequence 'As In Their Time' features a series of grotesques who point a more direct social moral:

> Citizen of an ever-expanding
> Universe, burning smokeless fuel,
> He had lived among plastic gear so long
> When they decided to fingerprint him
> He left no fingerprints at all.

Sometimes the quester lands in impossible circumstances. 'After the Crash', an aftermath of holocaust, recalls the desert Roland has to cross to reach the tower (and a dream-parable recounted in *The Strings Are False*[43]), but terminates the quest without fulfilment:

Then he looked up and marked
The gigantic scales in the sky,
The pan on the left dead empty
And the pan on the right dead empty,
And knew in the dead, dead calm
It was too late to die.

The ferry-terminus of 'Charon' is another dead end, yet both these poems at least preserve a cosmic awe, a grasp of the infinite. The house, a frequent focus for MacNeice's themes of exile, provides a setting for less ultimate stages in the quest, especially intersections between past and future. The protagonist of 'Soap Suds' undergoes dream transitions which, together with the game of croquet, recall *Alice in Wonderland:*

This brand of soap has the same smell as once in the big
House he visited when he was eight: the walls of the bathroom open
To reveal a lawn where a great yellow ball rolls back through a hoop
To rest at the head of a mallet held in the hands of a child.

Also cosmic, the poem transforms life, originally a sunlike ball at one's feet, 'Two great faded globes, one of the earth, one of the stars', into a compulsory and funeral game: 'And the grass has grown head-high and an angry voice cries Play!/ But the ball is lost . . .' Once again MacNeice explores a theme he shares with Larkin – the long perspectives of diminishing choice – but by wholly different means. In contrast, 'Selva Oscura', which features a wanderer 'Lost in the maze/ That means yourself and never out of the wood', ends by conceiving a house which unites past, future and something more: 'The door swings open and a hand/ Beckons to all the life my days allow.' 'The Truisms' too might denote the *immram*'s hero returning from his voyage, absolved or absolving. Arrival 'at a house/ He could not remember seeing before', and a communion between son and father (MacNeice's father was a Church of Ireland bishop), suggest the finding of a grail:

And he walked straight in; it was where he had come from
And something told him the way to behave.
He raised his hand and blessed his home;
The truisms flew and perched on his shoulders
And a tall tree sprouted from his father's grave.

No absolute line can be drawn between the quest as search and the quest as self-pursuit. However, 'Immram' epitomises the role of the former in Paul Muldoon's poetry, as 'The More a Man Has' does that of the latter. Comic and parodic in method, 'Immram' unites the milieu and idiom of Raymond Chandler with the spirit of Byronic picaresque. 'Immram' might be termed, as Byron terms the 'wandering' *Don Juan*, a 'half-serious rhyme': thus toned and tuned because 'if I laugh at any mortal thing, 'Tis that I may not weep'. Muldoon too on close inspection might be accused 'of a strange design/ Against the creed and morals of the land'. More practically, his ten-line stanzas close in couplets like Byron's eight-liners. The poem also nods to several previous composers of *immrama*: the protagonist finds himself 'behind a nervous couple/ Who registered as Mr and Mrs Alfred Tennyson'; he consults Irish-American Lieutenant Brendan O'Leary, whose name joins the saint to LSD guru Timothy O'Leary; *The Tempest* provides a hierarchy for drug-dealing ('over every Caliban/ There's Ariel, and behind him, Prospero'); and mention of the father's getting 'caught in the works/ Of a saw-mill near Ithaca, New York' conjures up the *Odyssey* or even *Ulysses*. It is possible also that the 'little silver knick-knack', which gives the quester as private eye his first lead, evokes the 'five half-ounces' of silver laid by Diuran the Rhymer on the altar at Armagh when the original voyagers return. In this poem about ancestry Muldoon may salute a local bardic ancestor. Another way of keeping poetic faith is the ingenious punning thread which preserves the voyage-motif on Californian dry land: 'Foster's pool-hall', 'Which brought me round to the Atlantic Club' (possibly a poetic school of *immram*-writers by analogy with 'The Country Club'), 'the wild, blue yonder', 'that old Deep Water Baptist mission', or the more elaborate:

> I was met, not by the face behind the voice,
> But by yet another aide-de-camp
> Who would have passed for a Barbary pirate
> With a line in small-talk like a parrot
> And who ferried me past an outer office
> To a not ungracious inner sanctum.
> I did a breast-stroke through the carpet,
> Went under once, only to surface
> Alongside the raft of a banquet-table –
> A whole roast pig, its mouth fixed on an apple.

The poem also refers to visionary lands sought in other voyages or quests: Hy Brasil, which haunts MacNeice, in 'So I drove west to

Paradise'; a 'land of milk and honey'; 'the land of cocaine'. The last reference puns on the medieval Irish poem *The Land of Cockaygne* and suggests the tone in which Muldoon usually renders the visionary: 'How you must get all of wisdom/ As you pass through a wind-shield'. As for intermediate ports of call, these not only take the form of allegorical locations (pool-hall, hospital, Club, mission, morgue, etc); but are symbolised overall by the skyscraper Park Hotel whose various appearances recall the columnar cliffed islands in *Immram Mael Duin*.

'Immram' alludes to its model in numerous other details. Some ingenuities may be virtually an end in themselves:

> My poem takes the episodes and motifs of the original and twists them around, sometimes out of all recognition. At one stage, for instance, a confrontation with a white cat becomes a confrontation with a black cat . . .[44]

The 'black cat' is a negro 'honking to Blind Lemon's blues guitar'. Similar instances are the island with a revolving rampart which becomes a mile-long Cadillac 'wrapping/ Itself round the Park Hotel', stray animal-references which echo the original's copious bestiary (the 'black cat' sports 'A full-length coat of alligator,/ An ermine stole'), and the derivation of the roast pig from fiery animals 'like swine' feeding on great golden apples. (Muldoon relishes what is sheerly wild and wonderful in Irish legend, whereas MacNeice found some of its extravagances artistically unamenable.) Other allusions contribute more centrally to the moral pattern. High waves and a bridge and sea of glass are woven into an ironic Californian version of the grail and Brendan's goal: 'a wholly new religion', a religious high:

> He called it *The Way Of The One Wave.*
> This one wave was sky-high, like a wall of glass,
> And had come to him in a vision.
> You could ride it forever, effortlessly.
> The Lieutenant was squatting before his new guru.

Again, Mael Duin and his crew constantly encounter strange food, drink, women; often falling into enchanted stupors as a result. In 'Immram' this becomes the stench of corruption: cocaine and heroin, girls 'Bronzed, bleached, bare-breasted,/ Bare-assed to a man'. After the banquet-table:

Beyond the wall-length, two-way mirror
There was still more to feast your eyes upon
As Susan, or Susannah, danced
Before what looked like an invited audience,
A select band of admirers
To whom she would lay herself open.
I was staring into the middle distance
Where two men and a dog were mowing her meadow
When I was hit by a hypodermic syringe.
And I entered a world equally rich and strange.

This part of the poem in fact closely parallels a sequence in *Immram Mael Duin* during which the voyagers are drugged by a woman who tantalises Mael Duin sexually, but 'When they awoke, they were in their boat on a crag'. Then: 'As they went from that place they heard in the north-east a great cry and chant as it were a singing of psalms.' The protagonist of 'Immram' experiences hallucinatory sex and violence in a morgue before 'I came to, under a steaming pile of trash/ In the narrow alley-way/ Behind that old Deep Water Baptist mission'. Shortly afterwards, the 'black cat' snorting 'angel dust' alludes to a pilgrim fed 'by the ministry of angels'. Some of Muldoon's ironic transformations perhaps exploit inconsistency between the pagan and Christian layers of his source to satirise the contemporary social equivalent.

In 'Immram' all Muldoon's parable-devices achieve larger architectonic coherence than before. The cipher as narrator resembles Fitzgerald's Nick Carraway in heightening the interest of an exotic cast. Redpath, the tycoon/hermit who lures like Gatsby, may owe his name to a bloodstained island; as well as to behaviour which might concern the Miller: 'She told me how his empire/ Ran a little more than half-way to Hell.' (This balances the reference to Paradise.) Fitzgerald is in fact cited: 'this refugee from F. Scott Fitzgerald/ Who looked as if he might indeed own the world./ His name was James Earl Caulfield III.' Besides echoing the Gatsby guest-list, where G. Earl Muldoon appears, the name is one of Muldoon's far cries from the Moy (built by James Caulfield, Earl of Charlemont). If the poem's *dramatis personae* have not yet assumed the final psychedelic inconsequence 'The More a Man Has', neither has the narrative. Dream-logic, crucial to the whole structure, retains a recognisable connection with MacNeice's account of a neglected Spenserian voyage 'which is allegorical, though not obtrusively so, and at the same time has the haunting quality of a dream; this means that its physical weight is at least equal to its mental weight'. He continues:

Here the Knight of Temperance, attended by his indefatigable Palmer and one professional boatman, is sailing over allegorical seas which are also seas of dream. We may remember, without making too much of it, the importance psychologists attach to dreams of water; we may also remember De Quincey's alarming dreams of endless oceans where innumerable human faces are superimposed upon the waves . . .

Having passed between [the Gulf of Greediness and the Rock of Vile Reproach] they come to another archetypal image, the insidious Wandering Islands where, true to dream behaviour . . . a character left behind six cantos earlier reappears to pursue them in a little skippet.[45]

Similarly that Cadillac 'Came sweeping out of the distant past/ Like a wayward Bay mist' conveying 'Susannah, as you guessed', as well as Caulfield. MacNeice also comments on the 'brothel or harem dream' of walking through a row of rooms, exemplified by the house of the enchanter Busirane.[46] In 'Immram' the preliminary to the Atlantic Club's 'outer office', 'inner sanctum' (holy pun?) and biblical Susannah is:

You remember how, in a half-remembered dream,
You found yourself in a long corridor,
How behind the first door there was nothing,
Nothing behind the second,
Then how you swayed from room to empty room . . .

Other dream-transitions are negotiated by the structural roles of cliché and syntax. The poem and quest effectively begin with 'it came to me out of the blue'. The 'world equally rich and strange' (another *Tempest* reference) triggered by the hypodermic lives up to its billing:

There was one who can only have been asleep
Among row upon row of sheeted cadavers
In what might have been the Morgue
Of all the cities of America,
Who beckoned me towards her slab
And silently drew back the covers
On the vermilion omega
Where she had been repeatedly stabbed,
Whom I would carry over the threshold of pain
That she might come and come and come again.

Conversely, the sequence about the drug-mafia moves *towards* a cliché: 'Everyone getting right up everybody else's nose.' Dream logic fuses with the twists and turns of private investigation and with the narrator's unreliability: 'I was just about getting things in perspective/ When . . .' The syntax, as in the stanzas quoted above, casts further doubt. It abounds in 'might' – truly a land of might-have-been – and to a lesser extent 'would'. These conditional conditions, amid geometrically progressive *oratio obliqua*, are aggravated by phrases like 'This must be', 'It seemed', 'You can imagine how', 'what looked like', 'Who looked as if', 'You remember how'. Subsidiary narrators such as Brendan O'Leary prove equally unreliable, not to mention *their* informants:

> 'My father, God rest him, he held this theory
> That the Irish, the American Irish,
> Were really the thirteenth tribe,
> The Israelites of Europe.
> All along, my father believed in fairies
> But he might as well have been Jewish.'
> His laugh was a slight hiccup.
> I guessed that Lieutenant Brendan O'Leary's
> Grand-mother's pee was green,
> And that was why she had to leave old Skibbereen.

The syntactical contrast between this and the previous stanza quoted illustrates the skill with which Muldoon varies his narrative deployment of the ten-line stanza (as opposed to Mahon's lyrical version). In the first two of these four sentences conversational idiom follows a drunken rather than dream logic, which complements the syntax of the narrator's logical detection, appropriately reserved for the last couplet. A Spenserian alexandrine – found elsewhere in the poem – rounds off a rare deductive triumph. The one-sentence necrophiliac stanza does its narrative and symbolic business differently: through a cunning series of relatives as well as subjunctives, all dependent on 'There was one who'. As regards the father, both case and quest end with an infinite vista of syntactical forks and mazes, future discoveries, further *immrama:*

> He would flee, to La Paz, then to Buenos Aires,
> From alias to alias.
> I imagined him sitting outside a hacienda
> Somewhere in the Argentine.
> He would peer for hours
> Into the vastness of the pampas.
> Or he might be pointing out the constellations
> Of the Southern hemisphere
> To the open-mouthed child at his elbow . . .

In technique as well as content 'Immram' consummates all the possibilities of its genre. Every structural particle joins in the rowing around, the mazed quest.

The social and political strata of MacNeice's and Muldoon's multi-level writing prove that parables are not merely fairy tales, any more than they are merely realist. Parable heightens a poetic dimension in order to deepen a moral one. Here are some of the poets' own comments: 'Parable writing [is] imbued with the true inner feel of its period' (MacNeice).[47] 'I like to think that a whole society is informing the lines of a poem, that every detail is accurate' (Muldoon).[48] 'The fact that there is method in madness and the fact that there is fact in fantasy (and equally fantasy in "fact") have been brought home to us not only by Freud and other psychologists but by events themselves' (MacNeice).[49]

Notes

Abbreviations used in Notes:

Davie   Donald Davie, *Thomas Hardy and British Poetry* (Routledge & Kegan Paul, 1973).

Haffenden   John Haffenden, *Viewpoints: Poets in Conversation* (Faber, 1981).

Heaney   Seamus Heaney, *Preoccupations: Selected Prose 1968-1978* (Faber, 1980).

Longley   *A Language Not to be Betrayed: Selected Prose of Edward Thomas*, edited by Edna Longley (Carcanet, 1981).

MacNeice   Louis MacNeice, *The Poetry of W.B. Yeats* (OUP, 1941; repr. Faber, 1967).

Thompson   *Selected Letters of Robert Frost*, edited by Lawrance Thompson (Cape, 1965).

Yeats   W.B. Yeats, *Essays and Introductions* (Macmillan, 1961).

CB   *The Crane Bag* (Dublin).

HU   *The Honest Ulsterman* (Belfast).

Introduction (pp.9-21)

1.   Michael H. Levenson, *A Genealogy of Modernism* (Cambridge University Press, 1984), pp.153-4.
2.   *The Uncivil Wars* is the title of a book on Northern Ireland by Padraig O'Malley (Blackstaff Press, 1983).
3.   Stan Smith, *Inviolable Voice: History and Twentieth-Century Poetry* (Gill and Macmillan, 1982), p.9.
4.   MacNeice, p.15.
5.   Interview in Haffenden, p.130.
6.   *Inviolable Voice*, p.56.
7.   Review of J.M. Cohen, *The Poetry of This Age*, *Spectator*, 12 February 1960.
8.   'An Alphabet of Literary Prejudices', *Windmill*, 9 (1948), p.40.
9.   *Inviolable Voice*, p.189.
10. A criticism of Mallarmé and others: Louis MacNeice, *Modern Poetry* (OUP, 1938; repr. 1968), p.18.
11. Charles Tomlinson (quoting Kenner), *Poetry and Metamorphosis* (Cambridge University Press, 1983), p.96.
12. Edward Thomas, *Maurice Maeterlinck* (Methuen, 1911), p.28; Longley, p.55
13. Interview in *Gown* (Queen's University Belfast student newspaper), 30 no.7 (May 1984), Literary Supplement, p.5.
14. *A Genealogy of Modernism*, p.168.
15. Edward Thomas, review of W.C. Brownell, *Victorian Prose Masters*, *Daily Chronicle*, 9 May 1902; Longley, p.6.

16. ibid.
17. *Poetry and Metamorphosis,* pp.69-70.
18. Geoffrey Thurley, *Counter-Modernism in Current Critical Theory* (Macmillan, 1983), p.36.
19. *The Sphere Book of Modern Irish Poetry,* edited by Derek Mahon (Sphere Books, 1972), introduction, p.14.
20. Interview, *Poetry Ireland Review,* no.14 (Autumn 1985), p.18.
21. 'A General Introduction for my Work', Yeats, p.522.
22. MacNeice, p.191.
23. *Windmill, 9* (1948), p.39.
24. Randall Jarrell, 'The Obscurity of the Poet', *Poetry and the Age* (Faber edition, 1973), p.23.
25. 'A General Introduction for my Work', Yeats, p.522.
26. Yeats, pp.521-2.
27. *Maurice Maeterlinck,* p.28; Longley, p.55.
28. 'A General Introduction for my Work', Yeats, p.509.
29. 'Experiences With Images', *Orpheus,* 2 (1949); *HU* no.73 (September 1983), p.13.
30. ibid.
31. Thompson, p.427.
32. 'Modern Poetry', Yeats, p.494.
33. Review of new verse, *Daily Chronicle,* 27 August 1901; Longley, pp.62-3.
34. W.B. Yeats, *Autobiographies* (Macmillan, 1955), p.192.
35. *The Letters of W.B. Yeats,* edited by Allan Wade (Hart-Davis, 1954), p.668.

Edward Thomas and Robert Frost (pp.22-46)

1. Thompson, p.220.
2. Stephen Spender, *Love-Hate Relations: A Study of Anglo-American Sensibilities* (Hamish Hamilton, 1974), pp.135-6.
3. See p.250, note 72; and the discussion of Frost's influence on Paul Muldoon, pp.224-6.
4. *Letters from Edward Thomas to Gordon Bottomley,* edited by R. George Thomas (OUP, 1968), p.203.
5. See Longley for a selection of Thomas's reviews.
6. Longley, p.66.
7. Longley, p.256.
8. Eleanor Farjeon, *Edward Thomas: The Last Four Years* (OUP, 1958), p.51. Thomas is commenting on the writing of his autobiography, *The Childhood of Edward Thomas.*
9. Longley, pp.125-31.
10. Thompson, p.263.
11. 'You really should start doing a book on speech & literature, or you will find me mistaking your ideas for mine & doing it myself'. Letter from Thomas to Frost, 19 May 1914.
12. Letter to Grace Walcott Conkling, 28 June 1921, *Poetry Wales,* 13 no.4 (Spring 1978), p.22.

13. 'The Road Not Taken'. See Thompson, introduction, pp. xiv-xv.
14. Thompson, p.216.
15. Letter to Edward Garnett, Thompson, p.217.
16. Thompson, p.192.
17. 'A General Introduction for my Work', Yeats, p.521.
18. Introduction to *Rural Rides* (1912); Longley, p.168.
19. Yeats, p.266.
20. Richard Poirier, *Robert Frost: The Work of Knowing* (OUP, 1977), p.39.
21. John A. Meixner, 'Frost Four Years After', *Southern Review* (Autumn 1966), p.866.
22. Thompson, p.234.
23. Quoted by Donald J. Greiner, *Robert Frost: The Poet and his Critics* (Chicago, American Library Association, 1974), p.274.
24. *Robert Frost: The Work of Knowing*, p.240.
25. Yvor Winters, *The Function of Criticism* (Routledge & Kegan Paul, 1962), p.167.
26. ibid, p.167.
27. ibid, p.163.
28. ibid, p.162.
29. ibid, p.161.
30. *Maurice Maeterlinck* (Methuen, 1911), p.28; Longley, p.55.
31. Denis Donoghue, *Connoisseurs of Chaos* (Macmillan, 1965), p.167.
32. ibid, p.165.
33. ibid, p.164.
34. ibid, p.165.
35. Randall Jarrell, *Poetry and the Age* (Faber edition, 1973), p.49.
36. 'Lessons in Honesty', *Times Literary Supplement*, 23 November 1979.
37. Longley, p.78.
38. Longley, p.79.
39. Robert Frost, *The Letters of Robert Frost to Louis Untermeyer* (Cape, 1964), p.277.
40. Thompson, p.146.
41. Longley, pp.6-7.
42. Longley, p.8.
43. *Poetry and the Age*, p.73.
44. ibid, p.91.
45. E.g. H. Coombes, *Edward Thomas* (Chatto & Windus, 1956); William Cooke, *Edward Thomas: A Critical Biography* (Faber, 1970); Andrew Motion, *The Poetry of Edward Thomas* (Routledge & Kegan Paul, 1980).
46. *English Poetry in 1912* (Open University, 1975), p.55.
47. *Times Literary Supplement*, 23 November 1979.
48. ibid.
49. *Letters to Gordon Bottomley*, p.233.
50. *The Oxford Book of Contemporary Verse*, edited by D.J. Enright (OUP, 1980), introduction, p.xxviii.
51. ibid.
52. Thompson, p.70.

53. Thompson, p.96.
54. Longley, p.117.
55. *Letters to Gordon Bottomley*, p.187.
56. Longley, p.117.
57. Longley, pp.122-3.
58. Longley, pp.122-3.
59. Longley, p.120.
60. Longley, p.121.
61. Longley, p.126.
62. *Walter Pater* (Martin Secker, 1913), p.220; Longley, p.161.
63. *Algernon Charles Swinburne* (Martin Secker, 1912), p.171; Longley, p.47.
64. Thompson, p.192.
65. *Walter Pater*, p.215; Longley, p.160.
66. *Maurice Maeterlinck*, pp.27-8; Longley, p.55.
67. *Maurice Maeterlinck*, p.29; Longley, p.56.
68. 'How to Read', *Literary Essays of Ezra Pound* (Faber, 1960), p.35.
69. Lecture delivered at U.S. embassy in London, early 1970s.
70. For reviews etc, see Longley, pp.66-75.
71. 'Poetry and Tradition', Yeats, p.248.
72. Quoted by Poirier, *Robert Frost: The Work of Knowing*, p.45.
73. Review of *Rio Grande's Last Race, and Other Verses* by Australian poet A.B. 'Banjo' Paterson, *Daily Chronicle*, 8 February 1904.
74. Thompson, p.228.
75. *Raritan*, 3 no.1 (Summer 1983), p.101.
76. '[Jessie B. Rittenhouse] has no right to imply of course that I desired or sought a British-made reputation', letter 1915; Thompson, p.174.
77. *Poetry Wales*, 13 no.4 (Spring 1978), p.22.
78. ibid.
79. *Robert Frost: The Poet and his Critics*, p.80.
80. Quoted by William Cooke, *Edward Thomas: A Critical Biography*, pp.183-4.
81. ibid, p.186.
82. 15 December 1915.
83. Letter to John Freeman, 8 March 1915, in John Moore, *The Life and Letters of Edward Thomas* (Heinemann, 1939), p.326.
84. Thompson, p.217.
85. *Walter Pater*, p.118.
86. *Walter Pater*, p.215; Longley, p.160.
87. *Walter Pater*, p.101; Longley, p.152.
88. Longley, p.125.
89. Quoted in Garnett's introduction to Thomas's *Selected Poems* (Gregynog Press, 1927), p.xi.
90. Thompson, p.159.
91. Letter, 19 May 1914, in which Thomas also says: 'I wonder whether you can imagine me taking to verse. If you can I might get over the feeling that it is impossible – which at once obliges your good nature to say "I can".'
92. *Walter Pater*, p.210; Longley, p.159.
93. F.R. Leavis on Thomas, *New Bearings in English Poetry* (Pelican edition, 1972), p.55. Leavis says: 'the outward scene is accessory to an inner theatre'.

94. *Letters to Gordon Bottomley*, p.251.
95. Letter, 5 March 1916.
96. *Poetry and the Age*, pp.44-5.
97. *Robert Frost: The Work of Knowing*, p.165.
98. ibid.
99. Yeats, p.156.
100. *Southern Review* (Autumn 1966), p.868.
101. 'The Figure a Poem Makes'.
102. Yeats, p.530.
103. *New Statesman*, 12 July 1963.
104. Letter to Edward Garnett, 29 April 1917; Thompson, p.217.
105. *Robert Frost: The Work of Knowing*, p.100.
106. *Poetry and the Age*, p.54.
107. Helen Bacon, quoted by Poirier in *Robert Frost: The Work of Knowing*, p.294.

'Worn New': Edward Thomas and English Tradition (pp.47-77)

1. *The South Country* (J.M. Dent, 1909), p.7; Longley, p.209.
2. *The Country and the City* (Chatto & Windus, 1973), pp.257-8.
3. See Thomas on George Bourne: Longley, pp.181-4.
4. *The Country and the City*, p.257.
5. ibid, p.256.
6. Note to *This England* (OUP, 1915); Longley, p.222.
7. 'England', *The Last Sheaf* (Cape, 1928), p.109; Longley, p.230.
8. *The Country and the City*, p.258.
9. *Autobiographies* (Macmillan, 1955), p.191.
10. *Richard Jefferies* (Hutchinson, 1909; Faber, 1978), p.1.
11. Introduction to *Rural Rides*; see Longley, p.166.
12. *Richard Jefferies*, p.38.
13. ibid, p.34.
14. ibid, p.20.
15. *The Country* (B.T. Batsford, 1913), p.9; Longley, p.200.
16. *The South Country*, p.9; Longley, p.210.
17. 'At Stratford-on-Avon', Yeats, p.109.
18. *The Happy-Go-Lucky Morgans* (Duckworth, 1913), p.221; Longley pp.219-20.
19. *The Longest Journey* (Penguin edition, 1960), p.132.
20. ibid.
21. *The Country*, p.6; Longley, p.198.
22. *The Longest Journey*, p.288.
23. 'Tipperary', *The Last Sheaf*, p.113; Longley, p.231.
24. 'England', *The Last Sheaf*, p.111; Longley, p.231.
25. *Collected Pruse* (MacGibbon & Kee, 1967), p.282.
26. Eleanor Farjeon, *Edward Thomas: The Last Four Years* (OUP, 1958), p.154.
27. Review of 'War Poetry', *Poetry and Drama*, 2 no.8 (December 1914); Longley, p.131.
28. Review of *The Dublin Book of Irish Verse*, edited by John Cooke, *Morning Post*, 6 January 1910.

29. Opening of review of 'Anthologies and Reprints', *Poetry and Drama*, 2 no.8 (December 1914).
30. *The South Country*, pp.147-50; Longley, pp.210-12.
31. *The Oxford Book of Modern Verse*, edited by W.B. Yeats (1937), introduction, p.xiii.
32. *The South Country*, p.4; Longley, p.207.
33. *The Heart of England* (J.M. Dent, 1906), p.226; Longley, p.217.
34. *The South Country*, p.241.
35. Letter, 21 December 1888; *Letters of W.B. Yeats*, edited by Allan Wade (Hart-Davis, 1954), p.98.
36. *Edward Thomas: The Last Four Years*, p.110.
37. Longley, p.63.
38. Letter, 13 June 1915.
39. Review of Robert Frost, *North of Boston*; Longley, p.128.
40. Longley, p.168.
41. Preface to Thomas's autobiography *The Childhood of Edward Thomas* (Faber, 1938), p.8.
42. *George Borrow* (Chapman and Hall, 1912), p.40.
43. Thompson, p.164.
44. Review of Mark H. Liddell, *An Introduction to the Scientific Study of English Poetry*; Longley, p.12.
45. Longley, p.63.
46. *Algernon Charles Swinburne* (Secker, 1912), p.152; Longley, p.45.
47. *Swinburne*, p.153; Longley, pp.45-6.
48. *Swinburne*, p.158; Longley, p.46.
49. *Swinburne*, p.171; Longley, p.47.
50. *Swinburne*, p.15; Longley, p.41.
51. Review of Arthur Symons, *The Romantic Movement in English Literature*, *Morning Post*, 20 January 1910; Longley, pp.18-19.
52. Quoted by Thomas; Longley, p.18.
53. Longley, p.18.
54. *Modernism and Its Origins* (Open University, 1975), pp.30-1.
55. ibid, p.31.
56. *Keats* (T.C. & E.C. Jack, 1916), p.57; Longley, p.33.
57. *Keats*, p.56; Longley, p.32.
58. *Modernism and Its Origins*, p.31.
59. ibid, p.30.
60. *Love-Hate Relations* (Hamish Hamilton, 1974), pp.22-3.
61. Review of 'War Poetry', Longley, p.135.
62. Thompson, p.217.
63. Review of 'War Poetry', Longley, p.132.
64. Letter, 30 March 1917, John Moore, *The Life and Letters of Edward Thomas* (Heinemann, 1939), p.261.
65. Letter to Frost, 22 July 1915.
66. In *The Great War and Modern Memory* (OUP, 1975).
67. William Cooke, *Edward Thomas: A Critical Biography* (Faber, 1970), p.141, p.237.
68. Paper on John Masefield read at Marlborough, 3 November 1912, *The Letters of Charles Sorley* (Cambridge University Press, 1919), pp.37-8.

69. ibid, p.263.
70. Letter to Frost, 19 October 1916.
71. ibid.
72. Those who pay various forms of tribute include W.H. Auden, Alun Lewis and Derek Walcott. An unusual number of poems have been written to or about him.
73. Letter, 2 December 1914.
74. Thompson, p.216.

Louis MacNeice: *Autumn Journal* (pp.78-93)

1. *The Auden Generation* (Bodley Head, 1976), p.373.
2. ibid, p.368.
3. ibid, p.369.
4. ibid, p.369.
5. ibid, p.334.
6. Louis MacNeice, *Modern Poetry* (OUP, 1938; repr. 1968), p.16.
7. ibid, p.15.
8. *New Verse*, nos.31-32 (Autumn 1938), p.2.
9. *New Verse*, nos.31-32 (Autumn 1938), p.17.
10. *The Auden Generation*, p.295.
11. MacNeice, p.18.
12. MacNeice, p.191.
13. MacNeice, p.191.
14. MacNeice, p.203.
15. Yeats, p.506.
16. *Modern Poetry*, p.3.
17. *The Auden Generation*, p.341.
18. Quoted in *The Auden Generation*, p.372.
19. E.M. Forster's 'Post-Munich', in *Two Cheers for Democracy*, has many points of contact with *Autumn Journal*.
20. Orwell, 'Why I Write'.
21. Note to Argo record of MacNeice reading his poetry.
22. 'Northern Ireland and her People', talk (?); typescript.
23. 'Speaking of Poets', talk (?), 15 July 1953; typescript.
24. *The Auden Generation*, p.372.
25. 'Broken Windows or Thinking Aloud', wartime article; manuscript.

'Shit or Bust': The Importance of Keith Douglas (pp.94-112)

General Note: Quotations are taken from Keith Douglas, *Complete Poems*, edited by Desmond Graham (OUP, 1979); except where the *Collected Poems*, edited by John Waller, G.S. Fraser and J.C. Hall (Faber, 1966) seems to me textually more persuasive.

1. *Poetry Review*, 74 no.1 (April 1984), pp.42-5.
2. '"I in Another Place": Homage to Keith Douglas', review of Keith Douglas, *Selected Poems*, in *Stand*, 6 no.4 (1964), p.6.

250

3.   Introduction to Keith Douglas, *Selected.Poems* (Faber, 1964), p.14.
4.   *The Truth of Poetry* (Weidenfeld and Nicolson, 1969), p.175.
5.   *Poetry Nation*, no.4 (1975), p.107.
6.   'The Forties', *A Poetry Chronicle* (Faber, 1973), p.62.
7.   Introduction to *Selected Poems*, p.13.
8.   See for instance *The Achievement of Ted Hughes*, edited by Keith Sagar (Manchester University Press, 1983).
9.   Peter Porter, review of Paul Muldoon's *Quoof* in the *Observer*.
10. *Poetry Nation*, no.4 (1975), p.111.
11. Desmond Graham, *Keith Douglas* (OUP, 1974), p.82.
12. *Alamein to Zem Zem* (Faber, 1966), p.16.
13. ibid, p.17.
14. Keith Douglas, *Collected Poems* (Faber, 1966), Notes, p.150.
15. 'March'.
16. Desmond Graham, *Keith Douglas*, pp.90-1.
17. *Alamein to Zem Zem*, p.18.
18. Letter to Herbert Grierson, 21 February 1926; *The Letters of W.B. Yeats*, edited by Allan Wade (Hart-Davis, 1954), p.711.
19. *Alamein to Zem Zem*, pp.15-16.
20. Introduction to *Selected Poems*, p.13.
21. *Stand*, 6 no.4 (1964), p.8.
22. ibid, p.10.
23. *Alamein to Zem Zem*, p.17.
24. Introduction to *Selected Poems*, p.13.
25. 'Hughes and his Landscape', *The Achievement of Ted Hughes*, p.3.
26. 'The Poet in England Today', *The New Republic*, 25 March 1940, pp.412-3; cf. MacNeice, pp.17-18.
27. *Collected Poems*, Notes, pp.149-50.
28. 'Poets in this war', unpublished essay, *Times Literary Supplement*, 23 April 1971.
29. ibid.
30. *The Truth of Poetry*, p.178.
31. Desmond Graham, *Keith Douglas*, p.79.
32. Graham in the *Complete Poems* prints them as 'Landscape with Figures' 1, 2 and 3.
33. *Stand*, 6 no.4 (1964), p.9.
34. ibid, p.13.
35. *Alamein to Zem Zem*, p.25.
36. ibid, p.26.
37. ibid, p.28.
38. ibid, p.15.
39. In his *Walter Pater* (Martin Secker, 1913). See Longley p.151.
40. *Alamein to Zem Zem*, p.28.
41. ibid, p.50. The passage relates to 'Vergissmeinnicht'.
42. *Poetry Nation*, no.4 (1975), p.107.
43. *Stand*, 6 no.4 (1964), p.10.
44. *Collected Poems*, Notes, pp.149-50.
45. ibid, p.48.
46. Thomas on John Clare who 'reminds us that words are alive'; Longley, pp.29-30.
47. Introduction to *Selected Poems*, p.13.

'Any-angled Light': Philip Larkin and Edward Thomas
(pp.113-139)

1.   Davie, p.12.
2.   Davie, p.40.
3.   Davie, p.82.
4.   Davie, p.71.
5.   Davie, p.64.
6.   Review of *Time's Laughingstocks, Morning Post,* 9 December 1909; Longley, p.71.
7.   Longley, p.70.
8.   Philip Larkin, 'Wanted: Good Hardy Critic', *Required Writing* (Faber, 1983), p.172.
9.   *In Pursuit of Spring* (Nelson, 1914), p.194.
10. Review of *Time's Laughingstocks, Daily Chronicle,* 7 December 1909; Longley, p.67.
11. Longley, p.70.
12. *The Great War and Modern Memory,* (OUP, 1975), pp.3-7.
13. Longley, pp.66-7.
14. 'An Interview with the *Observer', Required Writing,* p.49.
15. *Letters from Edward Thomas to Gordon Bottomley* (OUP, 1968), p.80.
16. Letter to John Freeman, John Moore, *The Life and Letters of Edward Thomas* (Heinemann, 1939), p.326.
17. 'The Booker Prize 1977', *Required Writing,* p.95.
18. *Required Writing,* pp.189-90.
19. Letter to Siegfried Sassoon, 1913, quoted in Christopher Hassall, *Edward Marsh* (Longmans, 1959), p.210.
20. Introduction, *New Lines* (Macmillan, 1957), p.xv.
21. Laura Riding and Robert Graves, *A Survey of Modernist Poetry* (Heinemann, 1927), p.119.
22. Introduction, *New Lines,* p.xv.
23. Davie, p.64.
24. *Required Writing,* p.297.
25. Review, *Daily Chronicle,* 19 November 1902.
26. Louis MacNeice, *The Strings Are False* (Faber, 1965), p.95.
27. *Required Writing,* pp.206, 214.
28. Davie, p.66.
29. Davie, p.66.
30. Davie, p.65.
31. Colin Falck, 'Philip Larkin', in *The Modern Poet: Essays from the Review,* edited by Ian Hamilton (Macdonald, 1968), p.109.
32. Davie, p.65.
33. Davie, p.81.
34. Davie, p.81.
35. Davie, p.81.
36. Review of 'War Poetry', *Poetry and Drama,* II no.8 (December 1914); Longley, p.132.
37. *The South Country* (J.M. Dent, 1909), p.7; Longley, p.209.
38. Davie, p.65.

39. Blake Morrison, *The Movement* (OUP, 1980), pp.82-3.
40. *The Country* (B.T. Batsford, 1913), p.6; Longley, p.198.
41. *The Modern Poet: Essays from The Review*, p.109.
42. H. Coombes, *Edward Thomas* (Chatto & Windus, 1956), p.209.
43. D.W. Harding, 'A Note on Nostalgia', *Scrutiny*, I (1932), p.19.
44. *Keats* (T.C. & E.C. Jack, 1916), pp.55-6; Longley, p.32.
45. 'The Pleasure Principle', *Required Writing*, p.82.
46. 'Writing Poems', *Required Writing*, pp.83-4.
47. Anthony Thwaite, 'The Poetry of Philip Larkin, *Phoenix* 11/12 (Autumn & Winter 1973/4), p.49.
48. Davie, p.73.
49. *Required Writing*, p.190.
50. *Phoenix* 11/12 (Autumn & Winter 1973/4), p.56.
51. 'An Interview with *Paris Review*', *Required Writing*, p.67.
52. Davie, p.75.
53. 'An Interview with *Paris Review*', *Required Writing*, p.74.
54. 'Englands of the Mind', Heaney, p.166.
55. *The South Country*, p.4; Longley, p.207.

'Inner Emigré' or 'Artful Voyeur'? Seamus Heaney's *North* (pp.140-69)

1. Haffenden, p.64.
2. *Times Literary Supplement*, 1 August 1975.
3. 'Speech and Reticence: Seamus Heaney's *North*', *British Poetry since 1970: A Critical Survey*, edited by Peter Jones and Michael Schmidt (Carcanet, 1980), p.103.
4. *The Listener*, 25 September 1975.
5. ibid.
6. 'Feeling into Words', Heaney, p.59.
7. James Randall, 'An Interview with Seamus Heaney', *Ploughshares*, 5 no.3 (1979), p.18.
8. Haffenden, p.71.
9. 'The Poetry of Seamus Heaney', *Critical Quarterly*, 16 (1974), p.40.
10. Seamus Deane, '"Unhappy and at Home"', Interview with Seamus Heaney', *CB*, 1 no.1 (Spring 1977), p.61.
11. '"From Monaghan to the Grand Canal"', the Poetry of Patrick Kavanagh', Heaney, p.115.
12. 'The Sense of Place', Heaney, p.142.
13. 'Feeling into Words', Heaney, p.56.
14. Heaney, p.55.
15. Randall, *Ploughshares*, p.17.
16. ibid, p.20.
17. *CB*, 1 no.1 (Spring 1977), p.62.
18. *The New Review*, 2 no.17 (August 1975), p.61.
19. Heaney, pp.56-7.
20. Randall, *Ploughshares*, p.18.
21. Heaney, pp.57-8

22. 'Escaped from the Massacre?', review of *North*, *HU* no.50 (Winter 1975), pp.184-5.
23. *British Poetry since 1970*, pp.109-10.
24. Haffenden, p.61.
25. P.V. Glob, *The Bog People*, pp.77-8. The body, probably of a Danish Viking, was found in 1781 on Lord Moira's estate in Co. Down.
26. Haffenden, pp.61, 66 .
27. *Critical Quarterly*, 16 (1974), p.45.
28. *HU* no.50, p.184.
29. *British Poetry since 1970*, p.110.
30. *HU* no. 50, p.185.
31. Haffenden asks: *'The word "assuaging" seems a favourite with you; can you say why?'* Heaney replies: 'It's possible to exacerbate . . . I believe that what poetry does to me is comforting . . . I think that art does appease, assuage' (p.68).
32. Haffenden, pp.60-1.
33. Haffenden, p.64.
34. Heaney, p.160.
35. Heaney, p.154.
36. 'Seamus Heaney, the Reluctant Poet', *CB*, 3 no.2 (1979), p.66.
37. Randall, *Ploughshares*, p.16.
38. ibid.
39. Heaney, p.151.
40. *HU* no.50, pp.185-6.
41. 'Irish Poetry and Irish Nationalism', in *Two Decades of Irish Writing*, edited by Douglas Dunn (Carcanet, 1975), p.16.
42. *CB*, 1 no.1 (Spring 1977), pp.62-3.
43. ibid.
44. ibid, pp.63-4.
45. ibid.
46. Hederman, '"The Crane Bag" and The North of Ireland', *CB*, 4 no.2 (1980), pp.98-9. Quotation from a letter of his to Conor Cruise O'Brien, which continues: 'Your desire to demythicise us is, perhaps, an impossibility, and one which can only serve to drive the "reality" even more deeply and dangerously underground.'
47. 'An Unhealthy Intersection', *Irish Times*, 21 August 1975; quoted by Richard Kearney in 'Beyond Art and Politics', *CB*, 1 no.1 (Spring 1977), p.9.
48. *The Snow Party* (OUP, 1975), p.10.

The Singing Line: Form in Derek Mahon's Poetry (pp.170-84)

1. John Pilling, 'The Strict Temperature of Classicism', in *British Poetry since 1970*, edited by Peter Jones and Michael Schmidt (Carcanet, 1980), p.20.
2. Anthony Easthope, *Poetry as Discourse* (Methuen, 1983), p.65.
3. ibid, p.67.
4. ibid, p.76.
5. Review of *The Hunt by Night*, *Times Literary Supplement*, 18 February 1983.
6. Review of *The Hunt by Night*, *Listener*, 5 May 1983.
7. *Times Literary Supplement*, 15 February 1980.
8. *Observer*, 28 June 1981.
9. *Observer*, 19 December 1982.
10. *Morning Post*, 9 August 1909.
11. Keith Douglas, *Collected Poems*, edited by John Waller, G.S. Fraser and J.C. Hall (Faber, 1966), Notes, p.148.
12. *Observer*, 19 December 1982.
13. Stan Smith, *Inviolable Voice* (Gill and Macmillan, 1982), p.188.
14. ibid, p.192.
15. ibid, p.189.
16. Review of *The Hunt by Night*, *PN Review*, 10 no.1, p.73.
17. 'Poetry in Northern Ireland', *20th Century Studies*, no.4 (November 1970), p.93.
18. Smith, *Inviolable Voice*, p.189.
19. Randall Jarrell, *Poetry and the Age* (Faber, 1973), p.66.
20. Paul Fussell, *Poetic Meter and Poetic Form* (Random House, 1979), p.149.

Poetry and Politics in Northern Ireland (pp.185-210)

1. 'An Unhealthy Intersection', *Irish Times*, 21 August 1975. See also 'An Unhealthy Intersection', *New Review*, 2 no.16 (July 1975), pp.3-8.
2. *Explorations* (Macmillan, 1962), pp.158-9.
3. 'Prologue' to *The Character of Ireland* (never published), in *Time Was Away*, edited by Terence Brown and Alec Reid (Dolmen Press, 1974), p.2.
4. Unpublished thesis, 'Affirmations: Motives and Motifs in the Work of Six Contemporary Northern Poets', Trinity College Dublin, 1983.
5. *Culture and Anarchy in Ireland* (OUP, 1979), p.57.
6. *Explorations*, p.200.
7. *The Letters of W.B. Yeats*, edited by Allan Wade (Hart-Davis, 1954), p.831.
8. See Bernard G. Krimm, *W.B. Yeats and the Emergence of the Irish Free State* (New York, Whitston Publishing Co., 1981).
9. *The Politics of Irish Literature* (Allen & Unwin, 1972), p.171, note. Brown's argument that Yeats exclusively attacks the IRA is in line with

a general determination to prove him a Brit-lover: 'One might suppose that the word "England" would be indispensable to speech in a great corpus of verse whose governing theme was modern Ireland. Yet for the first thirty years of his career Yeats succeeded in banning it from his poetry absolutely' (p.321). That's what Yeats *meant* by 'the de-Davisisation of Irish literature'.

10. 'What is "Popular Poetry"?', Yeats, p.4.
11. *Davis, Mangan, Ferguson? Writings by W.B. Yeats etc,* edited by Roger McHugh, (Dolmen Press, 1970), p.20.
12. 'Feeling into Words', Heaney, p.57.
13. '"The Crane Bag" and the North of Ireland', *CB,* 4 no.2 (1980-1), p.102.
14. 'Beyond the Planter and the Gael', Interview with John Hewitt and John Montague, *CB,* 4 no.2 (1980-1), pp.85-92.
15. 'Postscript', *CB,* 3 no.2 (1979), p.93.
16. *CB,* 1 no.1 (1977), p.8.
17. *CB,* 1 no.1 (1977), p.64.
18. *CB,* 7 no.2 (1983), p.160.
19. *CB,* 7 no.2 (1983), p.169.
20. *The Bell,* 12 no.1 (April 1946), p.2.
21. *The Bell,* 12 no.1 (April 1946), p.1.
22. *The Bell,* 1 no.1 (October 1940).
23. *The Bell,* 2 no.1 (April 1941), p.11.
24. *CB,* 7 no.2 (1983), p.131.
25. *CB,* 7 no. 2 (1983), p.3.
26. *CB,* 7 no.2 (1983), p.119.
27. ibid.
28. 'An Unhealthy Intersection', *The New Review,* 2 no.16 (July 1975), p.7.
29. *CB,* 7 no.2 (1983), pp.120-1.
30. 'The Landscape of the Planter and the Gael in the Poetry of John Hewitt and John Montague', *Canadian Journal of Irish Studies,* 1 no. 2 (November 1975). Quoted by Mathews, see note 4.
31. *CB,* 7 no.2 (1983), p.3.
32. Seamus Deane, *Civilians and Barbarians,* Field Day Pamphlet no.3 (1983), p.6.
33. ibid, p.7.
34. ibid, p.14.
35. ibid, p.11.
36. *Homage to Catalonia* (Penguin edition, 1966), p.235.
37. *Autumn Journal,* XVI: *Collected Poems* (Faber, 1966), p.132.
38. *A New Look at the Language Question,* Field Day Pamphlet no.1 (1983), p.5, reprinted in *Ireland & the English Crisis* (Bloodaxe Books, 1984), p.178.
39. *A New Look,* p.17; *Ireland & the English Crisis,* p.191.
40. Edward Thomas on the 'self-conscious' diction of Walter Pater; Longley, p.159.
41. Longley, p.160.
42. 'Another Ulster', *Fortnight,* no.198 (October 1983), pp.18-19.
43. *Threshold,* no.32 (Winter 1982), p.4.

44. 'Forked Tongues, Ceilis and Incubators', *Fortnight*, no.197 (September 1983), p.18.
45. *Ireland: Dependence & Independence: RTE/UCD Lectures*, CB, 8 no.1 (1984), p.13.
46. ibid, p.14.
47. *Two Decades of Irish Writing*, edited by Douglas Dunn (Carcanet, 1975), p.14.
48. *CB*, 1 no.1 (1977), p.62.
49. *HU* no.74 (Winter 1983), p.201.
50. *Modern Poetry* (OUP, 1938; repr. 1968), p.201.
51. MacNeice, p.185.
52. MacNeice, pp.17-18.
53. 'Rage for Order', *Lives* (OUP, 1972), p.22.
54. MacNeice, p.192.
55. Derek Mahon, Introduction to *The Sphere Book of Modern Irish Poetry* (Sphere, 1972), p.14.
56. *Irish Times*, 1 October 1983.
57. 'The Importance of Elsewhere', *The Whitsun Weddings* (Faber, 1964), p.34.
58. *CB*, 1 no.1 (1977), p.61.
59. Interview with James Randall, *Ploughshares*, 5 no. 3 (1979), p.18.
60. *CB*, 7 no.2 (1983), p.122.
61. 'A Postcard from Berlin', *The Hunt by Night* (OUP, 1982), p.49.
62. *Field Work* (Faber, 1979), p.23.
63. 'The Coasters', *The Selected John Hewitt*, edited by Alan Warner (Blackstaff Press, 1981), p.42.
64. Longley, p.55.
65. *Irish Poetry After Yeats* (Wolfhound Press, 1979).
66. Review of *Quoof*, *Irish Times*, 24 March 1984.
67. Review of *Quoof*, *Poetry Review*, 73 no.4 (January 1984), p.54.
68. *Uncollected Prose*, II (Macmillan, 1975), p.484.
69. Keith Douglas, *Collected Poems*, edited by John Waller, G.S. Fraser and J.C. Hall (Faber, 1966), Notes, p.150.

Varieties of Parable: Louis MacNeice and Paul Muldoon (pp.211-43)

1. Louis MacNeice, *Varieties of Parable* (Cambridge University Press, 1965), p.3.
2. Alwyn Rees and Brinley Rees, *Celtic Heritage* (Thames and Hudson, 1961), p.314. MacNeice reviewed the book with enthusiasm and drew on it for *The Mad Islands*.
3. *Revue Celtique*, IX-X (1888-9).
4. *Modern Poetry* (OUP, 1938; repr. 1968), p.21.
5. E.g. *Varieties of Parable*, pp.102-3, pp.129-30.
6. *The Dark Tower* (Faber, 1947), p.21.
7. 'Experiences with Images', *Orpheus*, vol.2 (1949); repr. *HU* no.73 (September 1983), p.20.

8.   ibid, p.21.
9.   *Varieties of Parable*, p.76.
10. ibid.
11. Interview in Haffenden, p.133.
12. *Varieties of Parable*, p.90.
13. ibid, p.77.
14. ibid, p.142.
15. ibid, p.50.
16. Haffenden, p.140.
17. Haffenden, p.133.
18. *Varieties of Parable*, p.78.
19. Haffenden, pp.130-1.
20. Haffenden, p.140.
21. *Varieties of Parable*, p.34.
22. ibid, p.50.
23. Haffenden, p.136.
24. Review of Reuben Brower, *The Poetry of Robert Frost; New Statesman*, 12 July 1963.
25. ibid.
26. Haffenden, p.133.
27. Interview with Seamus Heaney; Haffenden, p.70.
28. Haffenden, p.136.
29. *Sweeney Astray* (Faber, 1984) and the last section of *Station Island* (Faber, 1984).
30. The play *Rise up Lovely Sweeney*, 1985.
31. Haffenden, pp.133-4.
32. *Modern Poetry*, pp.102-3.
33. MacNeice, p.145.
34. MacNeice, p.147.
35. *The Strings Are False* (Faber, 1965), p.77.
36. ibid.
37. ibid, pp.77-8.
38. *The English Novelists*, edited by Derek Verschoyle (Chatto & Windus, 1936), pp.26-7.
39. ibid, p.19.
40. *The Dark Tower*, p.23.
41. *The Mad Islands* and *The Administrator* (Faber, 1964), introduction, p.8.
42. Haffenden, p.140.
43. *The Strings Are False*, pp.204-6. However, the parable ends happily like 'The Truisms': 'he was back in his father's house where everything had always been the same. But now everything was different.'
44. Haffenden, p.139.
45. *Varieties of Parable*, pp.37-8.
46. ibid, p.39.
47. ibid, p.22.
48. Haffenden, p.133.
49. *The Dark Tower*, Introductory Note, p.21.

Acknowledgements

An earlier version of '"Worn New": Edward Thomas and English Tradition' appeared in *The New Review*, 1 no. 11 (February 1975). 'Louis MacNeice: *Autumn Journal*' first appeared in *The Honest Ulsterman*, no. 73 (September 1983). '"Shit or Bust": The Importance of Keith Douglas' first appeared in *The Honest Ulsterman*, no. 76 (Autumn 1984). An earlier version of '"Any-angled Light": Philip Larkin and Edward Thomas' appeared in *Phoenix* 11/12 (Autumn & Winter 1973/4). '"Inner Emigré" or "Artful Voyeur"? Seamus Heaney's *North*' first appeared in *The Art of Seamus Heaney*, edited by Tony Curtis (Poetry Wales Press, 1982; repr. 1985, © Poetry Wales Press, 1982): I have added some material to the text. 'Poetry and Politics in Northern Ireland' first appeared in *The Crane Bag*, 9 no. 1 (1985).

The author and publisher are grateful for permission to reprint the following copyright material:

W.H. Auden: extract from 'Through the Looking-Glass' from *The Collected Poetry of W.H. Auden* (1945), reprinted by permission of Random House, Inc.

Seamus Deane: extracts from *History Lessons* (1983), reprinted by permission of the Gallery Press.

Keith Douglas: extracts from *Complete Poems* (1979), reprinted by permission of Oxford University Press.

Brian Friel: extracts from *Translations* reprinted by permission of Faber and Faber Ltd and Curtis Brown Ltd.

Robert Frost: 'The Most of It', 'Desert Places' and other extracts from *The Poetry of Robert Frost*, edited by Edward Connery Lathem (Copyright 1916, 1923, 1928, 1930, 1934, 1939, 1947, © 1969 by Holt, Rinehart and Winston, Inc. Copyright 1936, 1942, 1944, 1951, © 1956, 1958, 1961, 1962 by Robert Frost. Copyright © 1964, 1967, 1970, 1975 by Lesley Frost Ballantine), reprinted by permission of Holt, Rinehart and Winston, Inc., and Jonathan Cape Ltd; extracts from *Selected Letters of Robert Frost*, edited by Lawrance Thompson (Copyright © 1964 by Lawrance Thompson and Holt, Rinehart and Winston, Inc.), reprinted by permission of the Estate of Robert Frost, Holt, Rinehart and Winston, Inc., and Jonathan Cape Ltd.

Seamus Heaney: extracts from *Death of a Naturalist* (1966), *Door into the Dark* (1969), *Wintering Out* (1972), *North* (1975) and *Preoccupations* (1980), reprinted by permission of Faber and Faber Ltd, and Farrar, Straus and Giroux, Inc.

John Hewitt: extracts from *The Selected John Hewitt*, edited by Alan Warner (1981), reprinted by permission of Blackstaff Press Ltd.

Philip Larkin: extracts from *The Less Deceived* (1955), reprinted by permission of the Marvell Press; extracts from *The Whitsun Weddings* (1964), reprinted by permission of Faber and Faber Ltd; extracts from *High Windows* (1974) reprinted by permission of Faber and Faber Ltd, and Farrar, Straus and Giroux, Inc.

Louis MacNeice: extracts from *Collected Poems* (1966), reprinted by permission of Faber and Faber Ltd; unpublished material printed by permission of Hedli MacNeice and Dan Davin.

Derek Mahon: extracts from *Poems 1962-1978* (1979) and *The Hunt by Night* (1982), reprinted by permission of Oxford University Press.

Paul Muldoon: extracts from *New Weather* (1973), *Mules* (1977), *Why Brownlee Left* (1980) and *Quoof* (1983), reprinted by permission of Faber and Faber Ltd and Wake Forest University Press.

Tom Paulin: extracts from *Liberty Tree* (1983), reprinted by permission of Faber and Faber Ltd.

Edward Thomas: extracts from unpublished letters of Edward Thomas, printed by permission of Myfanwy Thomas; extracts from *Letters from Edward Thomas to Gordon Bottomley*, edited by R. George Thomas (1968), reprinted by permission of Oxford University Press.

W.B. Yeats: extracts from 'Nineteen Hundred and Nineteen' and from other poems in *The Poems of W.B. Yeats*, edited by Richard J. Finneran (1983), extracts from *Essays and Introductions* (1961), and extracts from *Explorations* (1962), reprinted by permission of Anne Yeats, Michael Yeats, Macmillan London Ltd and Macmillan Publishing Company, Inc; extracts from *The Letters of W.B. Yeats*, edited by Allan Wade (1954), reprinted by permission of Anne Yeats.

The author and publisher are grateful to Joseph Brodsky for permission to reprint as an epigraph part of his discussion of poetry and politics with Seamus Heaney, in *Magill*, 9 no.2 (November 1985).

The cover shows a detail from a photograph by Gilles Perres ('During a riot at the bottom of Williams Street, Derry, a clumsy soldier shoots a smoke grenade inside a Saladin', 1972), reproduced by kind permission of Gilles Perres (Side Gallery collection), and part of the manuscript draft of 'How to Kill' by Keith Douglas, reproduced by kind permission of the British Library and J.C. Hall.

Index

IRISH WRITERS

EILÉAN NÍ CHUILLEANÁIN
The Second Voyage*

This *Selected Poems* by one of Ireland's most distinguished writers contains work from several award-winning books, including *Acts and Monuments* and *Site of Ambush*, as well as a number of new poems. 'Eiléan Ní Chuilleanáin's dreamlike world is haunting, alien, full of awe' – EIRE-IRELAND.

(Published in Ireland by the Gallery Press)

BRENDAN KENNELLY
Cromwell

Buffún is wracked by the nightmare of Irish history. He has awful rows with Oliver Cromwell about the killings in Ireland. All Cromwell wants is to retire to his little estate in Kerry, where he can manage a decent football team. Also on hand to torment Buffún (pronounced *Buffoon*) are the Belly, a troublesome giant, Edmund Spenser, Billy of the Boyne and various terrorists.

(Published in Ireland by Kerrymount)

TOM PAULIN
Ireland & the English Crisis

Outspoken essays on Irish and English literature and culture. This controversial book includes Paulin's famous polemic against Conor Cruise O'Brien, attacks on structuralists, and important accounts of Joyce, Lawrence, Paisley, and dictionary English.

TOM PAULIN
The Book of Juniper

'The poems seem coded for Ireland and her perennial troubles. Juniper is both green and gin-coloured, and the poems are riddling evocations of ruin and the gothic extravagance of decrepit colonialism . . . Noel Connor's drawings lend power to the poems' – Peter Porter, OBSERVER

JAMES SIMMONS
Poems 1956-1986*
Poetry Book Society Recommendation

Irish poet and singer James Simmons has been much praised for his 'atrocious honesty' (*Irish Times*), for being 'a dangerous truth-teller' (*Guardian*), 'humane, entertaining, honest' (*TLS*) and 'tender, sensual, totally unromantic and totally honest' (Adrian Henri). This new, large selection includes poems from nine previous books, including *Judy Garland and the Cold War, Constantly Singing,* and *From the Irish.*

(Published in Ireland by the Gallery Press)

BLODAXE BOOKS

POETRY IN THE WARS

ANDREW GREIG & KATHLEEN JAMIE
A Flame in Your Heart

Set in the almost mythical summer of 1940, the story of the all-too-brief love of a Spitfire pilot and his girl, by two young Scottish poets born after the War. 'A most beautiful and musically constructed gaze at life and death over the ripening fields and above the strawberries' – SCOTSMAN

TONY HARRISON
v.*

Thomas Gray composed his Elegy in a quiet country churchyard. Two centuries later, Tony Harrison writes v. in a vandalised cemetery in Leeds during the Miners' Strike. Harrison's v. stands for *versus*. These *verses* capture the angry, desolate mood of Britain in the mid-1980s.

SEAN O'BRIEN
The Frighteners

Sean O'Brien won a Somerset Maugham Award for his first book of poems, *The Indoor Park*. This is his second book: a more biting, aggressive onslaught written to put *The Frighteners* on everyone. 'One of our brightest poetic hopes for the Eighties' – Peter Porter, OBSERVER

IRINA RATUSHINSKAYA
No, I'm Not Afraid
Translated by David McDuff

In March 1983 Irina Ratushinskaya was sentenced to seven years' hard labour and five years' internal exile, accused of anti-Soviet agitation and propaganda. Her crime: writing poetry. In a 'strict regime' women's labour camp, she has suffered beatings, force-feeding and solitary confinement in brutal, freezing conditions. Now aged 32, Ratushinskaya is the most important Russian poet of her generation. 'She is a remarkably genuine poet, a poet with faultless pitch . . . natural, with a voice of her own, piercing but devoid of hysteria' – JOSEPH BRODSKY

KEN SMITH
Terra
Poetry Book Society Recommendation

The latest collection from Ken Smith, writer-in-residence at Wormwood Scrubs prison, his first since his major Selected Poems *The Poet Reclining*. It includes his new *London Poems*, the cryptic *Ignore Previous Telegram*, and *Hawkwood*, the secret journal of a 14th century mercenary.

JENI COUZYN (editor)
Bloodaxe Book of Contemporary Women Poets
Large selections – with essays on their work – by eleven leading British poets: Sylvia Plath, Stevie Smith, Kathleen Raine, Fleur Adcock, Anne Stevenson, Elaine Feinstein, Elizabeth Jennings, Jenny Joseph, Denise Levertov, Ruth Fainlight and Jeni Couzyn.
Illustrated with photographs of the writers.

HART CRANE
Complete Poems
One of America's most important poets. Lowell called Crane 'the Shelley of my age' and 'the great poet of that generation'. This new *Complete Poems*, based on Brom Weber's definitive 1966 edition, has 22 additional poems. *Sunday Times* Paperback of the Year.

DENISE LEVERTOV
Selected Poems
'She is the most subtly skilful poet of her generation, the most profound, the most modest, the most moving' – NEW YORK TIMES
This new *Selected Poems* covers all Denise Levertov's collections up to *Candles in Babylon*.

DENISE LEVERTOV
Oblique Prayers
In America this new book was seen as marking a new phase in Levertov's work – more meditative yet still firmly rooted in everyday experience. It includes her translations of 14 poems by the contemporary French poet Jean Joubert.

MIROSLAV HOLUB
On the Contrary and Other Poems*
Translated by Ewald Osers
Miroslav Holub is Czechoslovakia's most important poet, and also one of her leading scientists. He was first introduced to English readers with a Penguin *Selected Poems* in 1967. This book presents a decade of new work. 'One of the half dozen most important poets writing anywhere' – TED HUGHES. 'One of the sanest voices of our time' – A. ALVAREZ

R.S. THOMAS
Selected Poems 1946-1968
R.S. Thomas is one of the most important poets of our time. This is his own selection from six of the finest books of poetry published since the war. 'One of the half-dozen best poets now writing in English . . . His example reduces most modern verse to footling whimsy' – KINGSLEY AMIS

POETRY WITH AN EDGE

JOHN CASSIDY
Night Cries
Poetry Book Society Recommendation
'John Cassidy has produced a strong, delicate volume of nature poetry in *Night Cries*, sensitively alert to the mysterious unpredictability of natural things, lucid and tenaciously detailed . . . A kind of *Lyrical Ballads* of our time' – TERRY EAGLETON

DAVID CONSTANTINE
Watching for Dolphins
Constantine's second book won him the Alice Hunt Bartlett Prize in 1984, and with it the judges praise for 'a generous, self-aware sensuality which he can express in a dazzling variety of tones on a wide range of themes'. 'His imagination moves gracefully within the classical precincts of the pure lyric . . . There are some very beautiful poems in this collection' – George Szirtes, LITERARY REVIEW

PETER DIDSBURY
The Butchers of Hull
'Peter Didsbury is a clever and original poet . . . He can be simultaneously knowing and naive, wittily deflationary yet alive to every leap of the post-Romantic eye . . . a soaring, playful imagination . . . I suspect that he is the best new poet that the excellent Bloodaxe Books have yet published' – William Scammell, TIMES LITERARY SUPPLEMENT

LAURIS EDMOND
Seasons and Creatures
Lauris Edmond won the 1985 Commonwealth Poetry Prize with her *Selected Poems*. 'She deals with topics people care about – love of all kinds, family relationships, loss, aging, the fragility of happiness – and writes of them with courage, candour, and a maturity of perception which amounts to wisdom' – FLEUR ADCOCK

FRANCES HOROVITZ
Collected Poems*
'She has perfect rhythm, great delicacy and a rather Chinese yet very locally British sense of landscape . . . her poetry does seem to me to approach greatness' – PETER LEVI

PAUL HYLAND
The Stubborn Forest
'Paul Hyland has never written much like anyone else' *(The Cut)*. 'His is a rugged, hewn, earthbound poetry' *(Encounter)*. 'Hyland's work has the character of primitive sculpture . . . an impressive, memorable and powerful talent' *(North)*. 'This is work of power and subtlety . . . *The Stubborn Forest* is a strikingly impressive achievement' *(Anglo-Welsh Review)*. Winner of the 1985 Alice Hunt Bartlett Prize.

INTERNATIONAL WRITING

EDITH SÖDERGRAN
Complete Poems*
Translated by David McDuff

When she died in poverty at 31, Edith Södergran had been dismissed as a mad, megalomaniac aristocrat by most of her Finnish contemporaries. Today she is regarded as Finland's greatest modern poet. The driving force of her visionary poetry (written in Swedish) was her struggle against TB, from which she eventually died in 1923.

MARIN SORESCU
Selected Poems
Translated by Michael Hamburger

'Sorescu is already being tipped as a future Nobel prizewinner. His poems, however, have crowned him with the only distinction that matters. If you don't read any other new book of poetry this year, read this one' – William Scammell, SUNDAY TIMES

LEOPOLD STAFF
An Empty Room
Translated by Adam Czerniawski

'Staff's poetry, which is widely admired in Poland, is mischievously and amiably laconic . . . It is a delightful book, the sort you put down wishing there was more, full of teasing wit, sly humour, clear observation and simplicity of style' – DOUGLAS DUNN

TOMAS TRANSTRÖMER
Collected Poems*
Translated by Robin Fulton

Tranströmer is Sweden's most important poet. This new edition contains all the poems he has written during the past 30 years, including those published in the Penguin *Selected Poems* of 1974. It covers all his collections up to *The Wild Market-Square* (1983), and also includes some recent poems.

MARINA TSVETAYEVA
Selected Poems*
Translated by David McDuff

This important new translation makes available complete versions of Tsvetayeva's major long poems and poem cycles: *Poem of the End, An Attempt at a Room, Poems to Czechia* and *New Year Letter*. David McDuff's edition is based on the new definitive Russica text of Tsvetayeva's poetry.

CHALLENGING FICTION

DAVID CONSTANTINE
Davies

Davies was famous for a moment in 1911 when Home Secretary Winston Churchill raised his case in the House of Commons. But who was Davies? In this fictionalised account of a lifelong petty criminal, Constantine unravels the mystery of a shadowy loner caught in a vicious circle of self-perpetuating crime. (Hardback only)

EVA FIGES
Days

'*Days* has a kind of violent stillness, great turbulence beneath a surface calm . . . It's extraordinary how much this gifted writer manages to pack into her austere frame' – GUARDIAN. 'A very exciting book. I think Eva Figes is probably the most neglected unsung writer in Britain' – SALLY VINCENT

B.S. JOHNSON
House Mother Normal

Anthony Burgess called Johnson 'the only British author with the guts to reassess the novel form, extend its scope and still work in a recognisable fictional tradition. Samuel Beckett described him as 'a most gifted writer and deserving of far more attention than he has received up to now'.

JENNY JOSEPH
Persephone*

'*Persephone* reminds me of nothing else. It is itself . . . Joseph takes the myth of Persephone and makes a litany of it . . . *Persephone* is a deeply serious work and it deserves and will reward the attention of any reader who turns to literature for truths not immediately enjoyable elsewhere' – Robert Nye, THE TIMES

SHENA MACKAY
An Advent Calendar

'Shena Mackay's talent is to put the ruth back into ruthless rhymes. Her novels are visions of universal anguish composed in short, sharp reels of Firbankian action . . . Funny, terrifying and written by an angel' – BRIGID BROPHY

KEN SMITH
A Book of Chinese Whispers

Extraordinary fictions, fables, ill-tempered jokes and 'existential romances' by poet Ken Smith, writer-in-residence at Wormwood Scrubs. Smith writes in the radical European/American (and most unEnglish) tradition of Borges, Brautigan, Burroughs and Buster Keaton. This stunning book is illustrated with mysterious pictures of sub-reality.

DRAMA & PHOTOGRAPHY

ANGELA CARTER
Come unto these Yellow Sands*

Four radio plays, one to pictures by the mad painter Richard Dadd. People and animals (or *both*) are never what they seem: the lady is a vampire, the bridegroom a werewolf, and Puss in Boots is out on the tiles. Includes *The Company of Wolves*.

TONY HARRISON
Dramatic Verse 1973-1985

Tony Harrison is both a major social poet and an innovative dramatist. In his work for theatre, opera and television he has extended the Brechtian tradition of music theatre. This massive volume contains eight plays and operas, including his *Oresteia*, 'the best acting translation of Aeschylus ever written' (*TLS*).
'We have a great poet back in the theatre' – PETER HALL, *Guardian* Books of the Year. (Hardback only)

JIMMY FORSYTH
Scotswood Road

For thirty years Jimmy Forsyth travelled down Newcastle's Scotswood Road, battered Kodak in hand. A chronicle of post-war Britain, a mirror of human life, Jimmy's journey along that road has been described as a work of near genius. His book begins in the early fifties. It is one of the most important records of working-class society that anyone has produced.

SIRKKA-LIISA KONTTINEN
Byker

The words and pictures of *Byker* chronicle much more than the tragedy of a single community in one northern town: they evoke an entire culture.
'A wisdom of the eye and the heart that makes this collection unforgettable'
– NEW SOCIETY.
'Her photos are masterpieces' – NEW STATESMAN

*Asterisked titles are available in hardback and paperback. Other books are in paperback only.

For a complete list of Bloodaxe publications write to:
**Bloodaxe Books Ltd, P.O. Box 1SN,
Newcastle upon Tyne NE99 1SN.**